Endorsements

"This autobiography deals with a subject affecting all of us — directly or indirectly. It's a story told with honesty and humor that's both entertaining and enlightening. I know Vinny Marino personally, I've visited his Habilitat, and I'm aware of the problems our young people are facing today. I found his book fascinating reading."
    — Bob Newhart

"...an intimate glimpse at the drive and sensitivity that the young Vincent Marino possessed, which ultimately resulted in his founding one of the most innovative substance abuse rehabilitative programs in the nation. This thought-provoking autobiography should be read especially by those who have loved ones addicted to drugs. Although the life of an addict is not a pleasant one, Vincent Marino's story provides us with a beginning insight into how complex drug addiction can be and how important every member of the addict's family is to his or her ultimate well-being."
    — Daniel K. Inouye, United States Senator

"This is a time when the word 'rehabilitation' is in wide disrepute, consigned by the tough-minded to the vocabulary of obsolete sentimentalities. But those who have refused to concede the debate is over should find substance in the story of Vincent Marino's remarkable journey from the depths. By every current standard of rage, he might have been easily branded socially incurable. Now he is rescuing and rehabilitating others. Mission impossible?"
    — James A. Wechsler, *New York Post*

"Vinny Marino is an authentic hero. He has turned his drug addiction into an asset for himself, becoming the nation's Number One ex-addict. He's done even more: He has turned his personal success into sucess for his wonderful treatment program. Many Americans do not know that following hard on the heels of the world's most awful drug abuse epidemic, now nearly 40 years old in the United States, we are seeing a remarkable counter-reaction — the culture of recovery. The national focus of this culture is the grassroots Twelve-Step programs, which originated more than a half century ago with Alcoholics Anonymous.... A key part of this culture is the Therapeutic Community movement, which began with Synanon and has now spread to a national network of second-generation programs. Habilitat is one of the best of this new breed."
    — Robert L. DuPont, M.D., Former Director
    National Institute of Drug Abuse

"Life is about people. People overcome their own human problems to live extraordinary lives. Vinny is such a person. His personal power and energy have enabled many to find their own path."
    — Linda Gray

"Vinny Marino's dream has become a reality. Habilitat exists despite innumerable setbacks, thanks to Vinny's patience, love, and unending efforts to reach out to those in need."
    — Dom DeLuise

Journey from Hell

Vinny Marino

Habilitat, Inc
Kaneohe, Hawaii

THIS BOOK IS DEDICATED

To my wonderful mother Gemma:
    You are gone but you will never be forgotten.

To my best friend, Frank M. Cockett, Jr. ("Boysan")
    Who helped me build Habilitat
    And was there whenever he was needed:
    We are where we are because of you.

To my father, Joe, who taught me many things
    And who also became a real close friend:
    I'm sorry I didn't listen sooner.

To my brother Frank:
    Words will never express how much I miss you.
    I'm sorry we didn't have more time together.

SPECIAL THANKS

To my wife Vickie and my daughters, Lila and Victoria,
for all the love, understanding, and patience
that allowed me to continue my work.

To my brother Joe, who has always been there for me:
I love you very much. "Press it."

To my granddaughter, Alicia Marie,
who gives me constant joy.

To my secretary, B. J. Swingle,
whose perseverance, fantastic personality, and talent
helped me weather the storm to finish this book.

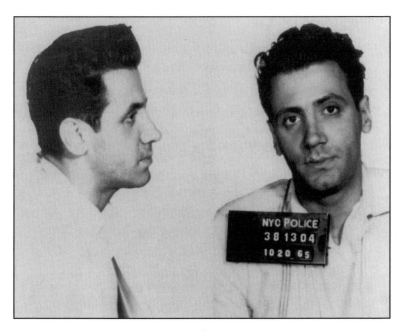

Vinny Marino in 1965

Contents

Prologue 1

Little Italy 5

By Hook or by Crookedness 19

A Junkie with No Relief 29

Making Doctors and Cracking Churches 49

Crazed Addict 59

If You Can't Do the Time 67

A Cornered Rat 75

Synanon 84

Reno Clean 97

The Revolving Door 111

Daytop Rehab Center 122

A Handshake Back to Hell 138

What Goes Around, Comes Around 147

Vocational Training 158

...Who Lived in a Shoe 167

Sitting on the Fence 177

Name That Baby! 184

Encounter Games   190

Making a House into a Home   200

The Infamous Throne Room Episode   209

Life in the Goldfish Bowl   214

Ban or Bust   222

Staying Alive   228

Leader of the Pack   251

Our War of Independence   262

Tomorrow, Today Will Be Yesterday   274

Appendix: Habilitat's Solution   283

Prologue

I'M TALKING TO YOU. Here's this book between us — why do you have it in your hands? Are you a drug addict? Is your life out of control? Are you desperate? Is someone you know at the bottom of the pit? Or are you simply curious? Those are all good reasons to read this book. Reading this book could be your first step toward a better life.

This book is the story of how I made that first step out of my life as a first-degree junkie, shooting up all the time, stealing New York blind to buy heroin and cocaine, fooling myself and everyone else, running every scam my fertile brain could hatch, running to stay ahead of the heat, the cops, the stool pigeons and rats, the law, the deadly prisons, and death itself. When I could no longer crack jokes about my life, I knew it had become a living death. I had to get out.

You, too, can start the process of getting out — from right where you are standing now, with what you have now, with what and who you are. You may be a survivor, someone who wants things to change. That desire to live and to have something interesting in life is often what drives people like us a bit crazy. That is also why people sometimes try to commit suicide — somehow, desperately, trying to change the way life feels. That's the same impulse that can take us beyond the mistake of trying to commit suicide, into real change — recovery. It's also the impulse that leads us, that first time, to take drugs, to risk something bad in the search for something good, to find a new way to feel about the world. To fill up empty places and find comfort in sadness.

But those impulses may drive you to make terrible choices. Suicide just ends life — you never get to change again, not on this earth. And life can be wonderful. Drugs take longer to kill than suicide, but they wreck your life just as thoroughly. If you don't overdose, you end up skinny as a rail, with AIDS, convulsing in withdrawal, scraped up off a highway, or shot dead in a stupid robbery trying to get money for your drugs. This is no way to change your life. To really change, you need help.

So what's new, my friend, besides what you've read? You think, you know you need help. But who's going to help you? You may have run through your friends pretty well by now. Teachers, lawyers — maybe all that's left is someone in your family, someone who remembers you from way back and feels some obligation. And the family is pretty disgusted, too.

Besides, who has enough on the ball to help you? You've never seen a friend or lawyer or teacher or family member you couldn't fool. You're smart. How can you get help from someone you can make a fool of so easily?

Okay. All this is true. You need someone who understands where you're coming from, and who doesn't fool so easily. You need former addicts — people who have been where you are, who have gotten out and stayed out, and who really like life outside the pit. Only smart people can show you how to be happy without drugs. You need a drug rehabilitation program like Habilitat (which I direct) — packed with staff who have all had drug problems but who have gotten out. The staff and the residents together can hold you up when you start going down, keep you moving, and help you manage your life until you learn how to do it yourself.

Let me tell you something. Life on the streets for me, as a junkie, was like being stuck in a revolving door. I got into heroin when I was 14 years old. Then I was in and out of patrol cars, burglaries, muggings, dark alleys, shooting galleries (where addicts use dirty needles for a quick fix), prison, parole, prison again, parole, and in between, my mother's kitchen. When the courts forced me to choose between treatment and prison, I did the same revolving door routine — in and out of Synanon, Daytop, Phoenix House, what have you, the same way. I was a runner. I needed to stop running, to go through a door and stay long enough to learn how to live.

So I know where you're coming from. And I'm telling you, if I can make it, so can you. You come through this door with me, and I'll tell you my story. Both the down part and then the up part — because it's not all down. This is the story of a guy who nearly checked out of life over and over before he got hold of the right decisions. Down at the bottom, you are never alone, and helping others get up is a good way to get yourself up. That's the process — beginning to help others — that brings me here where I am today, director of (no lie, even the experts say so) the best drug treatment center in the United States today.

And I did it being the same person I was as a drug addict. Only, I learned how not to take drugs, and how to make that decision stick. You see? The same person you are right now, that's good enough to start making the right decisions to succeed and be happy in a good life. You need the skills to learn how to build that life — you need help, sure — friends, time, teachers, support, connections. But you already have strengths to work with. Maybe a sense of humor? Quick wit? A taste for luxury? A sense of pleasure? Good storyteller? Money counter? Maybe just an inkling of the person you would like to become, a person valuable to be. It's a start.

Read this book. It shows where your life can go. Me, I'm pretty happy now. I'm married, and Vickie and I have two daughters and a family of hundreds — maybe thousands — in the Hawaiian tradition of 'ohana extended family. Not unlike my Italian family back in New York. My work entails drama and humor — and sometimes danger, because life isn't all sweet, and a job in drug treatment takes you near the edge of the cliffs. I have friends in high places as well as low. Let me tell you, it's not dull. And it definitely beats overdosing and waking up in the morgue, as I did, with a DOA tag wired to my big toe — Dead on Arrival.

The good life is real. You build it yourself. Just walk through the door and leave the drug hell behind. Bring a friend, too. Welcome to Habilitat.

Vinny

Vinny Marino

Little Italy

I GREW UP ON THE STREETS of New York, and my friends call me Vinny, although my given name is Carmine Vincent Marino. When I entered this world on December 22, 1938, everybody was still stuck in the post-Depression, prewar blues, and the economy was damn near flat on its ass, at least as far as we were concerned. My old man never had any money to speak of.

Poppa Joe "Rocks" Marino was some character. He was born in an Italian ghetto called Little Italy on the Lower East Side of Manhattan in 1912. His dad died a miserable death of cancer a year later, and Pop came up the hard way, on the streets. His mother Rosa was only 24 when her husband died, and she took work as a seamstress in a garment district sweatshop to support my pop and her three other kids.

Right after the Depression, in 1935, when Pop was 23, he had the good fortune to meet the woman who was to become my mother, Miss Gemma D'Onofrio. Pop must have been some special Romeo because Momma went for his pitch and married him in less than sixty days. She was only 17 at the time and gave birth ten months after that. The baby was my older brother, Frank.

To earn us a living, my pop had his own fish pushcart on the streets of Little Italy and would have done all right if it weren't for an insatiable gambling streak running right down the middle of his spine. He risked a hell of a lot on the turn of events, which usually turned out against him. My mom had to beg him for money to buy

5

the bare necessities, and when he had cash he never gave her more than half what she asked for.

Things were so bad when I was a baby that we moved six times in the first eleven months of my life. We shifted from one cold-water tenement flat to the next because the old man could rarely make the $10 to $12 rent for the month. He would storm in and order my mom to "Pack everything up!" Then we would sneak off like thieves to go settle for a while in another broken-down building.

When times got tight in the city, lots of people transformed themselves into lower animals. They would blindly gouge for a buck or eat garbage from the trash cans lined up on the street for collection. Some would literally kill for less than a $50 bill.

Brief flashes of those two-room, cold-water flats we used to call "home" still come up in my memory now and then. All they had was one gas stove for the cooking and to heat water for washing the dishes, doing the laundry, and bathing. One bathroom, usually in the middle of the hallway, was common to eight or ten families. The halls were always filthy with trash and cigarette butts, and the lead-based paint was peeling off the walls. How many kids died in those days from eating poisonous paint chips is known only to God and the slumlords, but there was no conscience in the picture at the time. You survived if you survived, and if you didn't, well, that was too bad because life went right on and never skipped a beat.

Little Italy is a ghetto made up almost entirely of Italians on one side of Canal Street and Chinese on the other. How did these two diverse groups of people end up in the same neighborhood? Probably because most other people thought the "guineas" and the "Chinks" were the lowest forms of human life.

Let me give you the basic ethnic structure my pop was facing as the breadwinner for our family: The Jewish people owned most of the tenement buildings and were referred to as "the man." They also controlled most of the judgeships and DA-type positions in the city. Then in my neighborhood all the firemen and cops were

Irish, and they looked down on Italians with a vengeance, calling us "greaseballs" or "wops" as they arrogantly walked their beats, lifting apples from the street vendors. Of course, the pushcart vendors like Pop didn't pay any rent, so the cops kept tabs on them and "assigned" their locations. In return, the cops took whatever they wanted, and if you didn't play their game, you'd get a citation and be forced to spend a whole day in court fighting the issue instead of earning a living.

Little Italy came together as a defensive move against all the outside forces that were hell-bent on wiping out any group that failed to maintain a constant vigil. The neighborhood had definite boundaries — Canal, Houston, Baxter, and Elizabeth Streets — and on the inside everybody knew everybody else, which imparted an incredible sense of security. My grandma Rosa, for example, took walks any time she wanted, night or day, and she never had any worries about being attacked.

"The Mob" was also born under those conditions — survival. As the Italians saw the way things were, they got so tired of being abused they had no choice but to organize or be destroyed. For this reason no one ever acknowledged the mob's existence for the "official" record.

My pop went away after I celebrated my third birthday, and my momma always told me, "Your daddy is away in the Navy, fighting a war." My older brother heard the same line, and he didn't balk at it, so I figured what Mom said was true. Because Pop was away, Mom had to find some other way to make ends meet. So she started taking in laundry and doing outside work for people who had enough cash to spend on frivolous extras. I saw fine lace, linens, and expensive dress shirts all come and go. My momma had none of these luxuries. For her appearances in church she wore the mandatory minimum — a plain black dress and a kerchief bobby-pinned to her hair.

In those days Little Italy was a mixture of smells from fresh baking bread, pasta, fruits and vegetables, garlic, oregano, anise, provolone cheese, sweet pastries, and various salamis — all hitting your nose at once. That, put together with the blare of Italian music being piped out of the stores, made it hard to feel depressed when you woke up. My mom took Frank and me out on those streets every morning while she shopped for the vegetables. With our tight budget, we usually had some kind of starch at every meal — potatoes and eggs, spaghetti with oil and garlic, macaroni with onions, macaroni with beans, macaroni with peas, and lots and lots of bread. On rare occasions we got some meat, cooked up in a stew so a little went a long way.

Next I remember my introduction to the Roman Catholic Church. I was overwhelmed by the size of that cathedral over on Baxter Street. The ceiling must have been two hundred feet high, and the stained-glass windows broke up the morning light into all sorts of radiant colors. We saw the place more and more often right after Pop joined the Navy because mom found emotional relief in the church.

She got up every morning around 5:30, then she woke Frankie and me to feed us before we went to 6:30 Mass. The cathedral was always jam-packed in the mornings because a lot of neighborhood people wouldn't go to work until they went to church. Frank and I were always dressed up, and trooped around in our Sunday best outfits to all the ceremonies the priests put on in that mighty canyon — benediction on Monday nights, Stations of the Cross on Fridays, a confessional parade in the pews on Saturdays, then the whole neighborhood attended Mass served with Holy Communion on Sunday mornings between 6:30 A.M. and noon.

One hot summer day when I was about 18 months old, Momma put me down by her feet and turned to talk with a neighbor. (Of course, being that young I don't remember this, but I've heard the story many times.) According to Momma, this was the first time I had been outside of my carriage. I had crawled a little distance when without warning a huge dog jumped out from nowhere and pawed my head down to the concrete. He growled angrily and started ripping at my face with his teeth. I tried to scream, but he locked onto my upper lip, biting and tearing the skin wide open all the way to the nose. Finally I screamed and managed to roll over on my stomach before he could bite me again. Blood was all over me.

When my mom saw what that mongrel bulldog had done, she fainted on the spot. The neighbor, Mrs. Anniballi, ran to call an ambulance. It was her goddamn dog that had just permanently altered my face.

I blacked out on the street and woke up in the charity ward of the neighborhood hospital with twenty-eight stitches in my upper lip and a vivid picture of that monster burned in my mind. Since my case was taken by charity, the doctors dealt with it quickly and left me with a permanent disfiguring scar. As a result, some years later I was tagged with the nickname "Scarface," which I've carried around with me ever since.

IN THE WAR YEARS between 1941 and 1944, my mom started taking Frank and me over to Grandma Rosa's place regularly so she could babysit for us, or sometimes Rosa would come to our flat. Once the ritual got going, every Sunday morning right after Mass Grandma Rosa would ring our doorbell, then come storming in with a big smile and two or three shopping bags bulging with fresh food. She would take over our kitchen, singing in Sicilian while frying up delicious Italian meatballs on the stove. There was no better way to start off a Sunday than with Rosa Marino's meatballs smothered in some delectable sauce with a side dish of hot Italian bread straight from the bakery.

Grandma Rosa was one of the most widely admired "stand-up" women — good, honest — in the neighborhood. All sorts of men would nod and tip their hats to pay their respects or offer to do things like help her across the street. Even though my grandmother was in her forties, she was still a beautiful woman, and quite a few guys made proposals to marry her, but she said she could never love another man. She put all her energy into her grandchildren instead. In all of her 94 years, Grandma never bothered much with the English language. All she knew was "Thatsa nice," "Hello," and "Goodbye." The subject that Rosa always made a special point of bringing up was her native Sicily with its natural beauty. Then in the same breath, she would relate the not-so-good parts and finish up with how proud she was to be an American citizen, with the freedom in this country. Those words never left me.

My brother Frank turned out to be the favorite of both my mom and Grandma Rosa. He was 19 months older than me, a bright and outgoing kid. Once when we were older, Frank lied to my mother about where he had been and she slapped him hard across the face. At that point, Grandma Rosa came out of her chair and for no apparent reason she laid an even harder slap on me.

When I was old enough to realize how disfiguring the scar on my upper lip was, I began to wonder if I wasn't getting second-rate treatment because of my physical appearance. The older I got, the worse my mouth began to look. I felt like crying about it, but never showed those feelings. Sure, the tears welled up in my eyes, but then I swallowed hard and held everything inside. That was the beginning of a long and difficult trip into my guts. I had some kind of terrible fear that I couldn't exactly identify and yet it seemed to be everywhere. I saw ugliness when I looked in a mirror, plus the mocking way other people looked at me. I felt loneliness of the worst kind and believed no one really cared, and even if they did, nothing could be done. Then I had a feeling of total emptiness stemming from the lack of love for life itself, family, and friends.

WHEN I THINK BACK to the fall of 1944, when I was 5 years old, I remember feeling confused and depressed. My mom enrolled me in the nearby Catholic elementary school. (They let me in at 5 because I would turn 6 in December and they felt sorry for my mother.) The nuns who taught there were from some French order, and they insisted we address them as "Madam," while the grand dame reigning over the whole school was "Reverend

Mother." They lived in a gloomy old gray building behind the rectory. Just observing the nuns' habits was funny to me — I mean the uniforms they wore, not the way they ate or spoke. The dresses were more like full-on robes that covered them from head to toe in solid black. You couldn't see their faces much because a white circle of cloth sat on the ridge above the eyebrows, covered both ears and fastened underneath the chin. As breastplates they wore a two-foot, moon-shaped piece of stiff white linen, and to top everything off they had a six-foot-long string of wooden beads with Christ the Savior on a cross hanging at the end, a rosary. As a nun walked, her beads banged loud enough to warn those of us raising hell that higher authority was approaching.

The nuns were primary dealers in absolute fear. I remember getting shaken by the shoulders once as a nun screamed in my face, "A young boy like you committed a mortal sin, and God struck him dead with lightning right on the spot!" I wondered, "What kind of God would allow that to happen to innocent kids?" I didn't know quite what to think, but they went on and on with some incredibly illogical sermons. There was one on limbo, a story about how young unbaptized children who died suddenly were doomed to spend all eternity in some never-never land without seeing God.

Most of what they said about religion didn't make any sense to me, and as time went on I discovered that a lot of things related to the church didn't add up in my head. Many times a celibate priest would give my mom instructions about her marital situation, saying things like "It must be God's will, my child, for you to suffer" or "God hurts those he loves." I asked myself, "Who is this God, and if he's so good why are we living like this?"

Frankie was a year ahead of me in school, and the nuns favored him because he was quiet and very obedient. He became the natural star of the books, and I saw no point in trying to compete, so I paid attention to mischief instead. Frank was also getting upset about my dad's long absence. We shared a single bed. Frank would be half asleep, and he would shudder and grab onto me crying, "Dad! Where are you? Come home. We need you!" A variety of feelings would build up behind my eyes, but I just gritted my teeth and kept them in until they went away.

By the time I entered second grade, my reputation for acting out was firmly established, so the nuns got together and decided it was time for me to become an altar boy. I started to serve every day at 6:30 A.M. Mass for nothing but thanks and "God's blessings, my son." The only exception was an occasional Saturday when I got to serve at a wedding, which meant a tip from the groom, but my mom and Grandma Rosa watched me with pride up on the altar at Mass every morning.

One night the tinny doorbell sounded in our tenement flat. I was about to get up and answer it, but Momma got there before me. When she opened it, she beamed and cried out, "Joe! Joe! You're home!" I looked up from my chair and saw a man dressed in a Navy uniform standing in our dimly lit hallway, hugging and kissing my momma. My father had been gone five years and I didn't recognize him, so I just stayed glued to my seat.

Now that he was back from the war, I hoped Pop would help Mom out so she could do a little less work and take better care of her health. She was burning the candle at both ends and then some, what with us and the household and paying strict attention to the Italian family scene with phone calls and visits, then doing a heavy load of outside housework and inside ironing. Plus the parish priest would regularly tap her time for church activities to raise money.

Everyone in the neighborhood came by to welcome Pop home from the high seas. A couple of Sicilian friends even threw a big block party for him a few weeks later. My old man was the war hero of an entire city block downtown.

Pop was always willing to work hard, so he soon got himself another pushcart on the streets and peddled fish every day. In a short time he was making fairly good money, but we didn't see much of it because he gambled it away, just like before. On the rare occasions when he won, things were good, with everyone laughing and the table full of food. But when he lost, he started to get mean and abused Mom — first verbally, then it got physical. Frank and I couldn't stand to listen from the other room where we were huddled together. "Gemma, get off my goddamn back!" followed by another loud crack. Frank and I whispered a vow in the dark to give our mom everything that the old man was depriving her of — someday.

From where I stood, I couldn't see any purpose to life, so I took up creative hell-raising to find out where it might lead. I first met my best friend then. His name was Hooks. It all started at school when a nun assigned us to serve together at 6:30 Mass. After the service and before school got started, we used to pull off a prank that we called "wiring the girls' johns for sound." We placed a piece of plastic wrap tightly over the toilet bowls in the girls' bathroom. When the little girls peed, it ran onto their knees, and if they shit, well, that was it. It only took a second for them to realize what happened and start screaming their lungs out.

We made the classroom scene every bit as much fun. One of our standard numbers would start with Hooks banging his feet on the floor while the nun was busy writing on the blackboard. She would whirl around and demand to know who was disturbing the order of the day. Naturally, no one would say anything as we tried to hold back the giggles. The nun would return to her work, and old Hooks would start banging again. I guess I had a guilty face because I'd usually get a whack across the knuckles with a thin hickory stick. It hurt like hell but only served to make me more devious about our tricks.

Another act was to wait until the nun was writing on the board, then lob a chalk-filled eraser, hitting the slate as close to her as possible. The cloud of white dust would break everybody up since it came down snow-white all over her solemn black outfit. Then the nun would do one of those wet-dog shakes just trying to breathe and dust off. Nobody knew it then, but another kind of white dust had a place in my future, and when it happened, Hooks would be along for the ride.

BY THE TIME 1946 rolled around, home life was fairly well fixed. The old man was out more than he was home, and when he did show it was with heavy words and empty pockets. The nuns were totally dictatorial, citing God Almighty as the source of their authority. Frank found that he was gifted with a voice in the same crooning style as Sinatra — so the whole family got behind his act, and that left me feeling alone out in the cold, wearing hand-me-downs.

Next I noticed Mom was beginning to gain weight, especially around her midsection. It turned out she was pregnant with my younger brother Joe. This was her last-ditch attempt to get my old man away from a gin rummy table and back into family life, but of course it didn't work, and the baby's birth turned out to top it off for me, now the scar-marked middle kid. Any money we had was lavished on Frank, hoping his voice might ring the cash register in the sky that would lift us from abject poverty. And baby Joey picked up all the love and attention, since he was a cute kid, as even I had to admit.

Right around that time I walked out to the front stoop of our building and looked down hard at the concrete, wondering what to do. Mulberry Street in Little Italy had a special cheese flavor, most notably provolone and also mozzarella being cooked up in pizzas. I got some immediate relief from the pressures at home every time I took a walk around the neighborhood. After a while, I took a certain route, picking up a feel for things while I carefully watched the action unfold. I would walk down Mulberry Street to Grand, then around the corner to old man Quatrini's shoemaking shop. He was a friendly codger in his seventies who didn't mind me hanging around watching him. I used to query him on just about everything he did, and one day I asked him to teach me how to duplicate his spit shine. He agreed, and after that I started to give him a hand.

At supper one night, I asked Mom if I could get a shoeshine box and earn money to help put food on the table. She had no objections, and Pop wasn't home, so I was in business for the first time. Those days on the streets shining shoes were far more pragmatic an education than anything the nuns taught me at school. I quickly found a new purpose in life to shoot for, since most of the neighborhood clubs were populated with "men of respect" who were "connected" and had money to burn. One day I glanced down to see an expensive pair of Florsheims on a guy. When I approached, the owner was easy because I said nothing more than "Shine, Mister?" and he said, "Sure, kid, go ahead."

As I bent down to begin, his tiptoe reflection revealed the sharp crease in a pair of fine mohair dress pants. Then, as I worked, I noticed his white-on-white silk shirt, the Countess Mara tie with a diamond stickpin, and a flashy diamond ring on his little finger. I put one hell of a finish on that pair of shoes, and he tipped me a dollar. No kidding, I wanted to holler, but I kept my trap shut and started plotting how one day I was going to emulate that style in fancy dress and money. I swore to myself that no way was I ever going to get into ordinary labor like my old man with his smelly fish cart or the hard hats who riveted all the high-rises together.

Within a few months I had developed a profitable shine route. It included all the wise-guy clubs where gamblers plied their endless lines of bullshit between various games of chance and the three-digit daily bet on the numbers game, the local bars I already mentioned, and then offices and other places like that. Every day after school I hit my beat and got back home by 8:30 with three or four dollars. That may not sound like much, but in those days it was enough to buy some basics and really helped my mom out, while Old Joe "Rocks" was probably sitting in a poker game somewhere, hoping for a one-card draw to an inside straight.

That shoeshine box was my ticket to a whole new world, and I soon had customers who would wait for me because I hustled hard and gave a damn good shine. The weekends really paid off because I had all day both days, except for church on Sunday morning, straight through until five or six in the afternoon. I took in $20, sometimes $25 for just those two days' work.

By the time I had been shining shoes for six months, I started to pick up chances to deliver packages as I went along. I learned fast never to ask what was inside, just tell the recipient who had sent it, take whatever tip was offered, bow out, and whistle all the way to the next stop. I began collecting two to five dollars extra per day in deliveries. Then when winter and snow hit the city, I would grab a shovel and pick up a few extra dollars there.

Back home, the situation brightened at our dinner table with what I added, but there wasn't much relief in sight. Mom got more frequent beatings from the old man and threatened to leave him for good. Frank kept his following by winning two consecutive shows on the "Ted Mack Original Amateur Hour," while little Joe held onto his celebrity position as the baby. Me? I just bit my lower lip until it almost bled and kept on moving.

SHEER SURVIVAL HAD BEEN the name of the game for several generations in our clan. When my people faced the reality of Manhattan, they knew damn well that if they were going to make it, the key would be family ties and a total willingness to act immediately on each situation. An important slogan in Sicilian is *Fata di, fata doi!,* roughly translated as "Mind your own business and nothing else." My business was a shoeshine kit, avoiding the hassles of home life, turning as many devious tricks on the nuns as possible, and learning as much as I could about the methods and connections necessary to become a "made-man" — a man who had "made it" became successful.

For relief from the oppressive summer heat and drudgery, we played stickball in the streets. Outside teams appeared in Little Italy for some heavy competition, guys from Brooklyn, East Harlem, the Bronx, Staten Island, all over. The action was hot enough to attract the attention of bookies, too.

Whole families came loaded down with folding chairs, potato salad, hero sandwiches, ice chests, and beer. A massive horde of people squeezed themselves into a city street twenty feet wide. Then there were tenement steps to contend with. Inevitably somebody from outside always parked his car right where we intended to play, so before the start we would ask the driver in nicely-New-York to "move it" and not-so-nicely if he refused. Some guys who refused hardly recognized the stripped metal hulks we left behind, propped up on milk boxes.

We played by strict rules, since the stakes were high. Someone would stand up and yell, "A hit on the wall in front of Piracci's fire escape, that's a fair ball. Hits on the back wall and she's foul. Automatic double for scoring the Widow Talmotese's clothesline. Home run is a fly ball over the line from the Berlotti Bakery sign to that fire hydrant across the street. You guys ready?"

Were we ever! Those games were so highly charged you could almost see the sparks. After the games, toward evening, the men retired leisurely to the local neighborhood clubs where all sorts of action would begin — horse races on the radio, card games at the round tables. The numbers game also siphoned off a significant piece of he action. As gamblers won a bet on anything, they would throw a portion onto a three-digit pick for the next day. One could choose from the Italian numbers or the Brooklyn numbers. I just cruised around the action, taking in everything, figuring it might do me some good later on.

When night fell, the craps tables opened up and the real action started. Sometimes the clubs called a $300 limit, other times it was $500. It was hard to believe the amount of money that changed hands. The house protected the games since the whole operation was under the control of a made-guy, someone known and trusted. He ensured there would be no back door entries or exits and no stick-ups. The guys who shuffled the daily numbers and payoffs all over town were known as "connected," which meant that they were something to somebody but only within a particular family.

It was one complex world inside another. There were rules and regulations, but most were not written down anywhere and were rarely spoken.

One street character named Bones was a fixture on corners. He was tall and paunchy with cropped hair and a nose that looked as if it had been broken once a week for most of his life. For a fee, Bones handled the neighborhood problems. If you needed somebody "dealt with," you would go find Bones. He would ask what the difficulty was and how you wanted it taken care of. Then he would pull a typed-up list in a plastic window out of his pocket: "Slap on the face, $10. Broken arm, $50. Broken jaw, $200." Bones would eagerly whisper the final treatment, "For $400, I'll take off the guy's ear, wrap it in newspaper, and mail it to you." When Bones spoke, it was all I could do to hold back my laughter, but he was dead serious. Most people from my New York neighborhood were born with a black belt in abuse, verbal or otherwise. And they never hesitated to use it.

By Hook or
by Crookedness

WHEN I WAS 13, we were forced to move again. Once more I felt disjointed, out of place, like everything was coming apart at the seams. My old shoeshine route was too far from our new apartment. We were now in Brooklyn, the Borough Park section, primarily a Jewish and Italian neighborhood, and there weren't many Florsheims in sight, as our dilapidated building had forty-odd families stacked up inside. The old man was the same or a little worse, and Momma was treading water while desperately trying to hold everyone's head up.

The only relief was when the building superintendent agreed to let me and some of my new neighborhood friends use part of the basement as a clubhouse in return for cleaning up the other side. None of us had much money, so the club activities consisted of teenage bullshit and stickball, but we weren't complaining. Anything was better than being upstairs in an apartment crammed full of your average destitute family-in-fight. This was the year I headed down the path to grown-up crime.

LATE ONE AFTERNOON at the end of another family fight, I drifted out the back door and headed toward the basement to check what was happening. Just as I hit the pavement, a sweet little treat named Mary Jane came out of her house across the way. I knew her from school, where she was always teasing me about my face. She leaned against the fence in front of her place and waved with her right hand that I should come over.

As I approached, she gently arched her back to emphasize the sunny-side-up-egg size of her budding breasts. The sight struck a responsive chord, and I popped into a new dimension, though I couldn't name it yet. "You look pretty cool today," I said and stood next to her with my back to the fence.

Mary Jane smiled. "Say, Vinny," she pleaded lightly, touching each button on my shirt, "can you help me out?"

"Sure, Mary Jane. What do you need?"

She grinned and turned toward her building. "Help me find my kitty. I lost him in the basement."

"Sure, Mary Jane." She strutted to the front of the building and took my hand. Once inside, the first thing visible in the dark was a red and yellow glow from a huge coal furnace. Mary Jane led me around to the back of the boiler and then down between some rows of cardboard boxes in storage. She whispered so low that I thought only a cat could hear the call, "Here, kitty. Here kitty, kitty." I asked her what the kitty's name was, and that was all she needed. She turned around and pressed her body full-on against mine as she murmured, "Dick."

I said, "Oh," and before another thought could pattern into words, we fell down together on a cardboard box, and in less than two minutes my first sexual experience was over.

When Mary Jane stopped moving, I felt a streak of embarrass-ment. It was easy enough to get into this, but how do you with-draw? What should I say? I put my hands on her shoulders, urging her to stand up. She did, and kissed me again as I reached down to put "Dick" away, and Mary Jane said, "Vinny, any time I lose my kitty, will you help me find it? You're good at it."

"Any time you need me, let me know," I said as I backed off to the exit. "I'll see you soon, Mary Jane. Keep your eye on your little kitty."

TEN MINUTES LATER, across the street in the basement, the guys and I decided to get more into sports. We sauntered into Davega's Sporting Goods Store on Thirteenth Avenue, where we all split up, each checking out a different section. My buddy Willy dribbled a basketball right out the front door. I grabbed a couple of baseball gloves, somebody else grabbed a half dozen baseballs, another guy grabbed three bats, and before we knew it we were back safely in the basement all excited that we didn't get caught.

The morning after that first experience with stealing, I felt a twinge of conscience from my strict Catholic upbringing, but I quickly substituted two new notions to replace the guilt that was causing short-circuits in my brain. First, I envisioned the whole enterprise as a game with the object being to steal right and not get caught, and secondly, to make sure I stole enough. Meanwhile, we were amassing a small warehouse of sporting goods. For guys who couldn't afford the iron-on letters for T-shirts, we ended up the best-equipped sandlot team in all of Brooklyn.

ONE AFTERNOON IN JUNE, while we were sitting around rapping, a guy named Jocko brought out this brown paper bag of stuff he called "weed." He claimed it would "get us all high." With that, he threw this Mexican-grown leafy stuff onto the table, along with some rolling papers. Like everybody else under the peer pressure gun, I went for it. Taking my first deep drag as instructed, I first felt lightheaded and after that everything seemed humorous as hell, as if some kind of bell had gone off, putting a light touch on all the stinking bullshit in the world. Then I got a gargantuan ape of an appetite and downed nine Creamsicles. On the way down from the high, I felt streaks of paranoia and envisioned cops on my tail about to grab me and take me to jail.

The next day during school lunch break, Hooks (whose family moved five blocks from where my family had moved) and I were hopping on and off various trolley cars. The particular trolley we were on usually stopped at the light just before the street the school was on and we had to get off or be late for the afternoon session. Trouble was, no one was getting off or on, and of course I couldn't reach the buzzer, so I figured I'd jump. Hooks tried to stop me, but as I was about to jump I shouted, "I gotta 'cause if I'm late, they'll call my mother and then the old man's gonna crack my head."

I cracked it for him. Instead of landing on my feet, I fell forward with the momentum and landed flat on my heels, bounced up in the air, and came down on my head hard, rolling under a parked car. An ambulance took me to the hospital, where I lay in a coma for five days. They called it a concussion and sent me home. Within two weeks on a lark, I climbed up a tree, which was rather high, somewhere around twenty-five feet. A branch broke, I went sailing down head first. Luckily, a friend's shoulder broke my fall. Back comes the ambulance and this time I was out again in a two-day coma. Because of the head-bangings and my unusual behavior, my parents began to think I had some kind of brain damage or that I was a "mental case."

When I was 14 and in high school, I remember coming home one day to find my father watching Cleveland play the Yankees on television. I asked him, "What's the score?" He said, "Five-to-one Yankees, bottom of the eighth." Because I was a Yankee fan, I yelled, "Right on!" Pop got off the couch and gave me a kick square in the center of my ass. It turns out he had a bet on Cleveland. From that day forward, any time there was a game on television, I always asked him, "Who do you like?" Whatever team he was for, I became a staunch supporter of, too.

On another day when I came home from school, my father and mother were arguing, as usual, but this time I tried to intercede and stop the argument. My father turned around and cracked me. I stormed out of the house. I was walking around talking to myself, trying to figure out what happened and why I got hit. Suddenly, I bumped into a guy named Tommy the Turk, who we all knew was a heroin addict.

I was so fed up with all the crap in the world around me, I was bound and determined to check out heroin. That day I wouldn't let the Turk get away until he turned me on and I gained my "wings" (street jargon for first use of heroin). The Turk hemmed and hawed, then agreed to let me use a 50-cent cap of his dope. With the deal consummated, we went into the bathroom at a Burgerama joint.

Turk filled the eyedropper after cooking the junk in a bottle cap behind the closed door. Being leery and afraid, I didn't want to mainline heroin, so I told Turk I hadn't slept much the previous night. He agreed to let me just "skin pop" (street vernacular for using heroin intramuscularly). He hit me with the needle on the upper left arm near my vaccination scar.

Nothing happened. My high anticipation turned straight to frustration as we sauntered out the door, with me full of questions as to why nothing happened. Turk told me to hold on. "You'll feel it," he assured me. We drifted into the corner store, where I bought a cold Coke. As I handed the money to the clerk, I felt my stomach turn, halfway between nausea and a hot glowing ball, and then it started to rise toward my gullet, on its way to my heart and my head. Before the clerk could hand me my change, a flash feeling of incredible peace, love, joy, and no pain drained everything else from my mind.

I was away, out on a seacoast somewhere in space where every rush of the tide brought a new wave of happiness. God only knows how I got out of that store or whatever happened to the Coke or my change. Suddenly I had no past and no future, only the present on a plane where all things were possible. Vinny the Scarface was finally the master of all time and space, the land and the sea. I saw myself walking across an ocean of joy where all hands welcomed my presence. I stepped into another age in search of even vaster oceans. I transcended everything and everyone I had ever known, and nothing mattered. I was reaching out to destiny — a sweet sense of overwhelming personal power and the sure gut feeling that Vinny Marino had found *truth*.

And the truth would set me free! I took to it like a duck takes to water.

Within a month of that initial experience with junk, Hooks heard about it, and to stay even with his friend he earned his own set of wings. We discussed the dynamics of teaming up tightly and scoring the maximum that bravado would allow. Late one night, Hooks and I each skin-popped a 50-cent cap and decided as we tripped along that the B.M.T. train station would supply our needs for at least another month if only we could pull it off.

This was to be our first real heist. Hooks and I talked about how we would do it. We decided to ask a third party to accompany us, a guy named Tony who owned a big car we figured we'd need for a fast getaway. Well, at least that part was right. Tony came on like he was the key man in the deal since he had the wheels. Hooks and I didn't particularly care what he thought of himself, as long as he could drive.

As the picture rolled on, we all came to the station on time at exactly 8:45 P.M. with Tony upright and chewing gum like it was going out of style. The plan was to scoot up to the platform and force the agent into turning over the money, and there would be "no trouble."

Tony pulled the Buick up under the steps leading to the platform, dimmed the lights, and let the engine purr. Hooks and I signaled "go" and pranced up the stairs to get in the door before the man locked it. The train was just leaving the station and everything was coming off smooth. When we entered the booth, I waved a knife blade at the man sitting in the corner and yelled, "Give us the money and there won't be any trouble!"

As he stood up, that token seller turned out to be one big Irish character with a pudgy pot belly and a 10-cent cigar in the crunch of his jaw. He looked as if he could do a bunch more than just handle himself as he clenched his fist and barked, "Don't kid around with me! You guys get the fuck outa here!"

Just then I noticed the barrel of a rifle on my right held by Tony and pointed in the general direction of the agent. The goddamn cannon went off with a shattering boom. "Jeezes!" I thought, as the shell whizzed past the agent's ear and tore shit out of a wooden pillar about six inches behind him. We all stood transfixed.

I was the first in the room to come unglued, and I hit the steps out of there on a dead run. Hooks followed my act, and I didn't see Tony, but I could hear the rifle butt banging the steel rungs of the staircase. We crammed into separate doors of the Buick and were off. After a mile or so, safe from the scene, I took a deep breath and jerked the wheel over to the curb, telling this asshole Tony to stop dead. When he did, I hit him with every name in the book and then spent time making up new words to fit the chump. We got no money, and worse, a charge of attempted murder would be on the books. Hooks and I slammed our way out of the car.

My head was banging so hard that I had to push on my eyeballs for relief, and my gut was tied in a knot and pulling tighter. Adrenaline and sweat kept me cold and hot at the same time, and the misery was compounded by the long walk home, nearly three miles in the dark.

After we blew the train station heist with Tony's asshole assistance, we sat down and thoroughly discussed the what-ifs. We were scared absolutely shitless. For instance, what if that idiot had killed the agent? Christ, we could have been arrested for murder. What if we had been caught? The minimum would have been armed robbery. And the ironic thing was that we hadn't gotten a dime.

Hooks and I decided to work together on our own. Then we talked about the smack and whether it could have had a negative effect on our actions. We concluded that it certainly didn't help any, and we made another pact: We would *never* get hooked on the stuff. We were "too intelligent" to allow ourselves to become slaves to a drug or anything else. We were "smart money," and our intention was to become made-men. Right then we flatly declared to restrict our junk highs to weekends, for recreational use. After all, everybody relaxed on weekends. The final pact we made was never to give each other up. No matter what a cop said that one of us had said, we would know the other guy had said nothing.

During the week, Hooks and I became involved in the excitement of petty thievery. We could have bought our dope with soda bottle and milk bottle refund money, because China white was cheap in those days, but the thrill of stealing really turned us on. That we could get something for nothing just made sense to us. The stuff we boosted was relatively easy to sell because a lot of people out there also wanted to get something for next to nothing.

We started boosting cigarettes from A&P stores. Our method was very direct: I just put on a working cap, a pencil behind my ear, walked in, loaded up, and walked out again. If anyone asked a question, I just muttered something like "These are going to the Eighty-sixth Street store," and kept on going. Over the years, our record in stealing cigarettes would warrant an entry in the Guinness book. A&P stock must have dropped twenty points from our cigarette operations alone.

The fact that Hooks and I had been together since we were kids probably made us think and act somewhat alike. Our instincts were totally together, and we usually saw the same opportunities and problems at the same time. From cigarettes we invented a game that eventually became known in criminal circles as "cattle rustling." First we would have a false pocket sewn into an overcoat. Then we'd go into a supermarket and stuff steaks, chops, pork ribs, roast beef, and other premium cuts into the special lining and simply walk out the door. Like modern-day Robin Hoods, we stole from the rich companies and sold cheap to the poor. We became proud of ourselves and our new role in society. It was a real challenge, plus we figured, "What the hell can anybody do, even if we get caught?" After all, we were just kids according to the law — minors. We'd go to juvenile court and get probation or a suspended sentence. Nothing to worry about.

As we started to pull in "regular" money, we also started to use more drugs. We told ourselves it was a bonus for work well done.

Before we knew it, the weekends seemed too far apart, so we figured, "Why not get loaded on Wednesday evenings, just to break up the long stretch." One thing led to another, and in a few months we realized we were pretty heavy into drugs. One night we agreed "to keep up with the stealing, but stop using smack for a while." Of course, this conversation took place right after we had both stuck a needle in our arms.

The following day just after noon I was busy doing nothing when I started to feel something happening with my body. I thought maybe I was coming down with some kind of cold or flu virus. I laid down on my bed but could not sleep. Involuntary twitching spasms prevented that, so I got up and drank some water, brushed my teeth, and took a shower. Nothing I did seemed to help. I was still uneasy and on the brink of some sickness.

That night I climbed into bed early, weary as hell, but I couldn't sleep a wink. I yawned a thousand times, twitching nervously, felt alternate chills and hot flashes, and my stomach was knotted into a ball. Right after dawn the next morning, I got out of bed, dressed, said, "To hell with eating," and went to see Hooks. On the way, I got deep, double-over cramps in my belly and icy chills throughout my body, yet I was sweating at the same time. When I saw Hooks outside his place, his face looked really bad. Before I could say anything, he asked me if I had any trouble sleeping last night. I nodded, and we started comparing notes.

Suddenly it dawned on us. We were hooked on heroin. A shock of terror went straight through my heart. How the hell did we get into this position when we so adamantly agreed we wouldn't? It couldn't happen to us — we knew better. But there was no time to waste sitting around sharing philosophies about the past. My gut was killing me, and sweat was running off Hooks's face. We hailed a cab and went downtown to cop from our connection.

After we scored and got loaded, I was immediately and almost magically relieved. The cramps died down, the chills left, and I stopped sweating. Once again the extremes of feeling warm and mellow swept through my body and took all my troubles away. During the entire twenty-minute cab ride back, Hooks and I didn't say a word. It wasn't necessary. When we got back, the nearest stoop seemed like the place to sit down and relax. It was then that I looked at Hooks in a stupor, and he looked at me. I sensed the fear jolt through both of us. Without talking, we understood the no-win swindle we were up to our necks in. That's how the vicious circle began. Every day stealing, and every day using drugs.

My old man was wrapped up in his gambling losses and didn't bother to notice my stretches of absence from home. My mother thought I was working long hours, and to keep up that front, I gave her some money each week, saying it was "part of my pay." I was having a lot of problems in school — when I bothered to go. It was amazing that the school didn't know, my parents didn't know, my brother Frank didn't know, Mary Jane across the street didn't know, and I wasn't about to tell them. I knew it, however, at the base of my soul: Vinny Marino, age 14, was a full-on, mainline-shooting, heroin-hooked junkie. And I was beginning to wonder how long I would be able to cover my tracks.

A Junkie
with No Relief

BY THIS TIME the Scarface alias was stuck to my countenance in the neighborhood, and people pointed and laughed behind my back. This made me angry and extremely self-conscious, but more and better drugs seemed to temporarily alleviate the problem. Outwardly, my attitude ran from distinctly aloof to downright contemptuous, to the point that my behavior had gotten me thrown out of five different high schools before I was 16. Since you had to be 16 to quit school, the New York State Board of Education simply suspended me for the last year and let me wait it out on the streets.

Being accountable to no one, I hung out with people who would at least give me some recognition for what I was good at — stealing. We sat around and schemed a lot of different scores while shooting a lot of drugs, including "speedballs" (a mixture of cocaine and heroin), which became a favorite pastime. I started to do some ballsy, way-out things, which increased my recognition, and I became a leader of sorts.

One night in the clubhouse, I suggested we go out and rob someone in the park. The other three guys were all sons of a prominent lieutenant in the police department, and they were missing some of the same things at home that I was. At any rate, they were totally willing to play along, so the four of us — me,

Ralph, Richard, and Roland — headed past the iron gates into Prospect Park on a Tuesday evening.

Ralph had lifted his old man's .38 service revolver, thinking we might run into more trouble than we could handle with our bare hands. Inside the wooded area, we passed several people who looked as if they had nothing worth taking, but then we came up behind a couple holding hands on a grass path, very much in love, I figured, looking at the size of the engagement ring on her left hand. I motioned that these were the marks, and Ralph handed me the gun. I felt an abdominal surge of adrenaline enter my bloodstream, and sweat broke out on my forehead.

I reached for the guy's shoulder and spun him around. He was startled and scared all at once, and he jumped at the sight of the gun barrel pointing directly at his midsection. The girl screamed "Oh, God!" with an inhale and moved behind him to protect herself. I told him to freeze and lifted the wallet from his back pocket. Ralph grabbed her hand, and Richard stripped the diamond ring off her finger. We told them to stay quiet under a tree for at least fifteen minutes or risk getting shot.

Slipping off into the darkness, we found ourselves in big trouble almost immediately. The victims ran into a beat cop only half a block from where we had hit them, and he radioed for assistance, calling in four squad cars that surrounded the park in no time. Near panic, the four of us split up. I shoved the gun back into Ralph's hand. I learned later he threw it in the duck pond. Sirens were wailing as if calling for "Vinny!" all over in my head, and I broke into a fast run toward the park perimeter to see if there was any way out of this.

Luckily, I saw an opportunity to make it into an alleyway across a busy street. In one dash I crossed the street, got behind some trash cans, and huddled down out of sight, breathing hard. Since I saw no one running to look for me, I eased out of the alley and ran the better part of two miles home.

When I got there, my father was home watching TV. I looked

like I had just done a marathon, with my shirt hanging out and sweat all over my body. Pop asked where I had been and how come I was out of breath. I gave him some line about a game of kick-the-can, but before he could call me a liar someone knocked at the door. Behind it were two cops, detectives from the local precinct. They told my father I was wanted for suspicion in the park robbery, and Pop whirled to whisper to me in Italian, "Don't say anything! Don't say a word!"

The bulls took me downtown to the lockup. When we got there I saw Richard and he started babbling about me being the guy who had done it all, and he was just along for the cheap thrills of observation. I called him a punk liar, and the cops booked us both.

Within two hours I was out — Pop had come down to the station and signed the papers necessary to get this "juvenile delinquent" released into his custody, standard procedure under the law at the time. On the way home, Pop shocked me as he started talking: "I can't *believe* you would get involved in this nickel-and-dime shit. Maybe you didn't know I spent five years behind bars, but not for loose change! If you're gonna do something, go out and take over a payroll or somethin' worth your while. And do it with people you can trust, not these stupid stool pigeons you're hanging out with!"

I was stunned! My father had opened up to me for the first time in his life, and I felt closer to him for that split second than I ever had before. But why hadn't he told me earlier? Why the whole bit with the Navy uniform and the war stories, being the hero of the block party and preaching to me when he was really just an ex-con?

Whether an earlier revelation would have made any difference to my crazy life is debatable. And besides, he wasn't saying "Don't live this way," he was saying "Live this way but smarter." Not exactly a wake-up call. As it was, I drew a suspended sentence and probation for the mugging, since they failed to turn up any evidence. I had stashed the ring and the wallet in a trash can, so the haul went to the dump. For me it was straight back to the streets for more scheming, stealing, robbing, lying, manipulating, and cheating — all done to get more drugs.

I DECIDED TO OPEN some hunting grounds at school. Three times a week on a regular basis, I would show up and terrorize the other kids, demanding their allowances in return for "protection." Using the tactics of the best Sicilian mobster I could imagine, I painted a verbal picture of the strange and brutal actions they faced if they failed to come across with the cash. They were obviously convinced, because I was raking in a lot of money for those days — about $50 a week — within a month after I put the pressure on.

How wrong I was. They finally had it up to the eyeballs with my demands. One kid told his parents, and from there it went to the cops. I was sitting on a stoop across from my building one afternoon after collecting when two detectives pulled up in an unmarked car. One of them slapped me hard across the face twice before bothering to tell me anything. Then he said, "So you want to be a tough guy, Marino? You want to shake down kids in my precinct? You're under arrest. Stand up and put your hands on the car!" The other guy handcuffed me, then shoved me in the back seat of their car. They drove me to the precinct.

I was scared. That was the first time in my life for booking, fingerprinting, and a mug shot. Not only that — this could mean a jail sentence, especially heavy because the police could line up over twenty personal victims. I had to spend the night in a tank. And what a night it was! My drug habit was coming straight down, all around me, and this was also the first time I had experienced a cell. I was terrified at being locked up in a 6- by 9- by 3-foot space to ride it out.

An hour inside that closed cell and my body began to do its number, like "Get up off your ass and get me some heroin, now!" This time I knew it wasn't flu — it was going to be cold turkey in a jail cell. Crashing bells started going off in my head, and sharp pains shot through my midsection. I couldn't stand to put my head down, because of spasms and chills. Then I vomited uncontrollably until nothing came up. No one noticed. As soon as I finished the vomiting session in the toilet, I turned around and had diarrhea. I hugged myself hard, but there was no comfort coming, only sharper pains. I swore silently, "If I get out of this, no more drugs!"

After a night on the rack, I saw the first light of Saturday morning. Just after 6:00 a hack brought in a cup of black coffee and a roll with butter. Three sips of coffee, and I vomited for the next half hour. My head was swimming with pain, and my gut was wrenched so tight it was hard to breathe. Next thing I saw through my blurred vision was another hack. As he approached the cell, he yelled, "Let's go, Marino!"

You wouldn't believe how happy I was. I imagined it was all a mistake, they were going to cut me loose, and then I'd be able to shoot straight downtown and cop a fix to get my body back in shape. Instead, the guard put handcuffs on me. I said in dismay, "What the fuck is going on?" Everything went foggy until I got a fast backhand slammed into my left ear by a detective, who then had me by the throat. "So you want to play tough, huh, mister? So, what we're gonna do is help you. We're going to send you to a nice tough place called Raymond Street. Stand up."

Raymond Street was in downtown Brooklyn, just a couple of blocks from where Hooks and I used to connect. The building was an old fortress, with stones four feet thick. They signaled a hack to open up the huge iron gate to let us in, and I could tell immediately that clubs were trump in that joint. All the bulls carried big sticks, weighted with lead, I was sure. I was taken into a big room with a sign that said "Receiving."

Twenty-five other guys were in the room when they began the processing. First they took a print of my index finger and told me to empty everything from all pockets. Next was a twenty-minute wait to fill out a 3-by-5 card with my name, address, age, and the charge — robbery. Then they had us all line up and undress.

"Okay, put your hands high in the air and stretch. Okay, now run your hands through your hair. Now lift up your balls. Turn around, bend over and spread 'em." I flashed for a split second on how I'd hate to be the bull assigned to check all the spread-eagled cons, when a gut pain shot me back to reality.

We were escorted into a tiled room full of showers. My body was so racked with pain I would have given anything to leave it there. Again I swore to the gods, "If I ever get out of this mess, no more drugs!" The bulls handed our clothes back after searching through them, and we were told to get dressed. I wanted to sit down, but instead we were led into another room, bright as hell, which was torture to my eyes. The room was labeled "Examination." When I saw the first white gown, I thought, "Goddamn! These guys are gonna know I'm an addict!"

I panicked, but there was nowhere to run. When my name came up, the white gown had me sit down opposite him at the desk and roll up my sleeves. I saw the end coming as he checked out my arms. But he must have been some kind of idiot because he didn't even look at my left wrist under my wristwatch, which was where I got off. Then he asked directly, "Do you use drugs?"

"No."

"Okay. Next."

We went up a flight of stairs, with me huddled over, and entered the "Annex," their place for keeping adolescents. The hack found my cell and led me to it. I walked the three steps in and as the key clicked the lock latch behind me, I was gripped with certain fear that I was going to lose my mind.

It was the worst weekend so far in my life. There was constant, unbearable pain over every inch of my body. Thoughts had trouble getting in, and no way could I concentrate, only think in flashes. "Can Hooks get in here with a fix?" The gut-wrenching pain doubled me over with the question. "Did my parents even know I was in here?" I vomited until the dry heaves left me hanging on the edge of the cold porcelain. "What happened to 'probations' and 'suspended sentences' for juveniles? Shit, these guys were *serious.*" I twitched all over with the absence of junk calling out to my body, screaming in the back of my mind, "Get me some heroin!"

After a while I started to feel my way around the cell with my hands, just to take my mind off the pain — stone walls cold as me or colder. I felt chills as I ran my fingers over the round steel bars. There I was, a groveling caged monster junkie with no relief in sight.

The sink basin had the standard one tap. It seemed that "hot water" was what we were all doing in the joint in the first place so they only ran the cold for us. We each got three wool blankets to use on the steel bunk — no pillows, no mattress. I guessed as I grabbed one that these coarse blankets were straight off the horses' backs the bulls rode in the parks. As I shivered all over, I rolled up in the blankets on the bunk. Then I started to sweat.

I thought getting up might help. It didn't. I hung over the commode and retched again, a dry heave. I felt like climbing into the damn bowl and flushing myself down. Maybe the ride would be a high, circling around in the water. Anything but the misery. "Why won't someone come down and bail me out? I won't do it again! I didn't even mean it! I'll give all the money back! Just let me out!" Then I started to yawn. By an hour later, I must have yawned a hundred times. With the second hour it tripled to three hundred, and before the ordeal ended, I must have done a thousand or more. No sleep, just yawning to the point where my jaw felt like it was going to fall off from the agony, and then a Charley horse locked itself into my jaw muscle.

Back to the toilet to retch more deeply than before, after drinking some cold tap water. I complained loud as hell and rattled the bars of my cage. Nothing came back but the hollow bitching of the other inmates, bouncing without meaning or effect off the bare stone walls.

"What in hell am I gonna do, and what day is it?" Those words went over and over in my mind, the whole time I was cramped over in that cell. At about noon we were brought out into the day room for lunch. After passing along the stainless steel cafeteria line, everyone sat down to eat. All you could draw for utensils was one spoon, which you also had to hand in before leaving, since they figured somebody could easily make a knife.

What I managed to get down on Saturday was two sips of cocoa. On Sunday I got a whole cup of tea down. Other than that, just the thought of food made me nauseous, usually followed by awful retching. The confined space threatened to drive me absolutely crazy, and everything was hell. I held out my hand once to see if it was steady at all, and it jerked so far to the left that I thought it was leaving without me. What a hell of a situation for a 16-year-old guy.

Saturday night after supper slid under the door, they announced Catholic confession followed by Jewish services. Figuring anything to get out of the cell, I went to both services, and no one caught on. The next day I got out for Catholic Mass and the Protestant service. No one seemed to mind that Marino had found religion. I just wanted to move around, anything to get my mind off the incredible body pain.

Back in the cell it was dark, and I folded my arms over my gut, trying to ride the hellish pain and not cry or show what was inside. I thought I would either go insane or get some sleep and forget about the misery for a while. I lay down on the steel bed-slab and closed my eyes. Just when I was about to fall asleep, a shooting pain would hammer home, raising my eyelids and jerking my body to any other position but the one it was in. I went through several hellish hours of catnaps, brief flashes of shut-eye before another blinding pain jolted me. I would get sane to the point of standing up to circle the cell, all doubled over like a hunchback, hugging myself and searching the ceiling for some relief from the drug withdrawal.

The next thing was the smell of freshly brewed coffee drifting into my cell on what turned out to be a Monday morning. Arraignment day, and the damp and cold were seeping into my bones when I woke up. I thought of brushing my teeth but didn't have any gear; no razor either, so I splashed some cold water on my face to revive. Then I went back to the bunk and sat with my head in my hands, totally drained and still in pain.

Soon a hack let me out and led me back to the bull pen, where they called out my name and another guy's, then handcuffed us together. When about fifteen pairs of kids were ready, a bell rang and a whole fleet of hacks came out to transport us to court. By that time I was feeling a little better since some fresh air came in as we moved. When we arrived at the adolescent court, I was overwhelmed to see my mom and dad standing there. I was hand-cuffed, with a three-day growth of stubble and my clothes all crumpled to hell, but I was so relieved to see someone I knew that I managed a big, shit-eating grin. Momma was ashamed and holding back tears. Pop's stare said he didn't like the action at all, I could tell that immediately.

We were escorted into the courtroom, about thirty guys, cuffed in pairs, until all were seated. As soon as they freed my hands, I used them to double up over my stomach in an attempt to hide the pain that kept coming back for more. I wanted to sit up straight, but the knot refused to cooperate. Finally I heard my name called and stood up in front of the judge. They read the charges and asked, "How do you plead?"

"Not guilty, Your Honor," I said. The judge banged his gavel, set a trial date for three months in the future, and set my bail at $2,500. I was in a fog the whole time the judge was talking and banging until he came to the bail part. "Damn," I said to myself, "who has that kind of money?" They took me back to the courthouse bull pen, and a shyster lawyer my pop had hired came in to see me. He said some reassuring words, but somehow I didn't trust him. "Don't worry, Vinny. We'll have you out of here in ten minutes."

Even with my body so full of pain, I felt a surge of excitement. I stood up and told the man representing me, "Please hurry! I have a terrible flu and couldn't get any medicine inside. I gotta go see a doctor!" The actual thought running through my addict consciousness was "How the hell am I gonna get away from my mother and father and get a fix?"

An hour and a half more I sat there with no way of covering the pain and nothing to do before I heard my name called by the bailiff. They brought me up to the receiving area, gave me back my personal stuff, and opened the door to freedom. Mom and Pop were waiting outside in the cold. Mom rushed over and hugged me. Pop stood still, a frozen look deep in his eyes. I thanked Momma for coming and told her it wasn't the way they said it was in the courtroom. I told her that I would tell her all about it and then asked Pop if he had a dollar and a cigarette. "Yeah," he said as he gave me one of each.

"I gotta go see somebody first," I told them, "but then I'll come straight home in less than an hour and we'll talk about everything, and I promise this kinda thing won't ever happen again." While they were hemming and hawing about what they wanted me to do, I excused myself and skipped away backward, then jumped on the next bus. It was a bus that routed right past Hooks's place. At the nearest stop, I was out in a flash, dashing over the street to leap on the stoop and bang loud as hell on the door. More good luck — Hooks was home. As he opened the door, he looked at me and grinned, "Where the fuck have you been?"

I would have cracked him — if only he knew where I'd been. Instead, I just pleaded for mercy: "Hooks, I gotta have dope. You got any?" He nodded in the affirmative. He had just bought a half load the day before and was selling it to friends since it was excellent quality dope. I was in such bad shape with the shakes and chills that Hooks had to do the cooking and loading, and fire the needle into my vein. It was like a flash from heaven when it landed. My stomach turned in that halfway twist, and the ball of warm glow shot straight toward my head. The cramps went out the window, and the weekend was erased from memory. I was alive again, junk running freely in my veins.

After a twenty-minute nod, pure ecstasy, I thought about Mom and Pop. So I shuffled back home within the hour as promised, then begged off to the bathroom to "clean up, and then I'll explain." Once inside the door, I locked it and nodded pleasantly in the never-never land for over an hour, then shaved and showered. It was time to emerge and face the music.

"What the hell did you do?" Pop asked.

"It wasn't like they made it sound, Pop." He pressed further.

"Well, what the hell *did* you do?"

I told him some guys were getting pressure from another neighborhood, so they were looking for help. I was just trying to help for a fee. I promised Pop to get out of doing that kind of stuff and stay out. I promised to behave totally. I would have promised them anything. Pop seemed to at least halfway buy my story, while Momma didn't do much but wring her hands and circle the room, sobbing, "Why, Vinny, why?"

"All right," Pop said, "but you still got a robbery rap to beat. You'll have to go see some guys I know tomorrow. And don't go pulling any shit tonight. Got that?"

The next day Pop's connected friends recommended a real lawyer, and one of them made an introductory call for an appointment. At this point I got a special perspective on the American judicial system. I located the tattered box-shaped building covered with ragged old posters. Inside, dustballs the size of medium rats drifted down the halls. When I saw my lawyer's name on a brass plate, I knocked and he said to enter. Behind the desk was this character about 50, wearing a yellowing shirt and an egg-stained tie loose at the neck. He was chain smoking and losing the ashes in a massive pile of papers strewn over the desk top.

He couldn't locate my case file, so he asked me to tell him what had gone down. After I gave him my story, he lost no valuable time telling me exactly where he stood, which was in a position to know every dirty angle about the law, every corrupt judge, and the proper approach, and then how I had no choice but to pay for his services, assuming I wanted to remain a free man. With a twinge of fright, I recalled the weekend at Raymond Street and asked, "How much?" He weighed the situation for a good twenty seconds before informing me coldly that the fee would be $2,000 cash for "taking care of things," all at once and with no strings. So within ten days I sold everything of value I could find or steal. I even borrowed $300 to cover this legal beagle who was going to bark up the right judge's tree, loaded with money, buying a favor.

It worked. The next thing I knew, with no trial or anything, I ended up convicted of a misdemeanor. The judge sentenced me to "One year on Riker's Island, suspended." The kids I'd "protected" screamed and stomped around in circles at the total injustice of the penalty. I just vowed to stay the hell away from actions that might lead me back to Raymond Street.

BACK ON THE STREETS, Hooks and I got noticed by a local precinct cop named Brannigan. He was Irish, and he haunted us day and night. When he asked questions, Hooks would flip him a dime and tell him to call information. One time Brannigan rolled up in his blue-and-white and told us to get up against the car. After the frisk, he asked, "Where were you two at 10:15 last night?"

"Fuckin' your sister," Hooks came back, earning himself a righteous slap on the side of the head.

Next thing we knew we were on our way down to the station again. Brannigan would routinely hold us without charges for ten or twelve hours, to the point where he had to let us go or get in trouble himself. Meanwhile, we were pulling jobs and heists he knew nothing about.

Once Hooks and I were loaded to the gills, drinking ice-cold sodas at the counter of a greasy spoon. The wind outside was gusty, blowing old newspapers in the air, and one minute it was sunny, the next cloudy. A definite do-nothing kind of day. The rickety diner door opened to admit a decrepit junkie from Queens named Digger, in dire need of a fix. We knew him vaguely but avoided him like the plague because he didn't have any part of his act together. Digger weaseled up and slid his rear over a counter stool next to me. His breath was worse than a soldier's damp socks after a week in the trenches, and I felt like leaving before a word was said. "Listen," Digger came on. "I gotta talk to you two." Digger leaned closer and started licking his lips, getting more excited as he shifted around. The waitress came over, and I ordered him some coffee to cover the foul air that came out with his conniving words.

He edged the smell a little closer and whispered, "Listen, this little old lady, she lives in my apartment house, see. One day last week I'm passin' her door, and it's open a crack, held by the chain. I see she's got her back to me, so I slow down and peek in, you know. Well, she's countin' a lotta money outa this sack, see? Hell, there ain't nothin' but hunnerd-dollar bills for as long as I'm standin' there!"

Hooks shot back, "So what, you asshole. You wanna hit the old lady right in your building?"

Digger shrank back a little, as if to avoid the charge. His eyes were rolling in their sockets. "No, no. You do it. The two of you."

"What's in it for you?" I demanded, knowing the answer.

"I finger her apartment, and we split. Fifty-fifty."

I laughed out loud and pushed him back to an upright position. Looking back at Hooks, I said quietly, "Listen to this man. We take all the risks and he wants 50 percent."

Hooks got up and walked past me, then landed on the stool next to Digger. He yanked the jerk's collar up a bit tighter toward the throat and snarled at Digger, "Get the fuck outa here! You're totally nuts!"

Digger was literally bouncing up and down off the stool at this point, begging, "Please, you guys. It's a helluva lotta money. Thousands! I saw it!"

Hooks looked over at me, signaling his dislike for Digger but said nothing. I told Digger the conditions, flatly. "We get 70, you get 30. And it better be smooth."

"Okay, okay." Digger breathed in relief. "When do we do it?"

"Tonight, after dark," I told him. We agreed to meet him at 8:30 outside the diner.

Hooks and I drifted off to shoot some pool, where we talked about Digger and the upcoming move. Something didn't smell right, but neither of us could nail anything down. Back in my basement we got loaded again and dressed for our evening's work. I wore black shoes, pants, and a leather jacket. Hooks looked straight out of a Dracula flick.

Digger was twenty minutes late and came in totally loaded. Once again we nearly walked away, but instead we took a cab to within a block of his building in Queens, got out, and scouted the area. There were several good getaway alleys nearby. Digger would point out the apartment, then get the hell out of sight. Hooks and I would knock and break in if necessary, wearing stocking masks.

We got into the building unnoticed and went craftily up three flights of stairs. Then we shuffled down the hall, which was much too bright and narrow for my liking. Digger stopped suddenly and pointed at a door in silence. I shoved Digger out of the way and he took off — presumably out of the action. We slipped on the stocking masks and rapped on the door.

"Who is it?" came from inside.

I yelled through the door, "Western Union, telegram!" then pulled out the .38 special message I had for the occasion, while Hooks stood back flat to the wall with a .22 pistol aimed up in the air. The old lady unlocked the door except for the feeble chain, which was fairly useless because it was mounted on old wood. I took a deep breath but couldn't have muttered a word because my mouth was too dry. When we went bursting in the door, my heart was pounding over every inch of me as we tipped the old woman backward just enough so she fell over the coffee table and crashed all the knickknacks. Then she slid off onto the floor and looked up at us.

We waved our guns, but she was already scared out of her wits, you could see it in her eyes. We had no intention of hurting her, but I wanted to be sure she kept her mouth shut. When I warned her about screaming, she went into a tantrum that could have brought the neighborhood for two blocks around. I went straight for the vanity drawer while Hooks tried in vain to calm her down. Madly stuffing the bag I found there inside my belt, I heard a noise. I spun around toward the door, and my heart sank.

Digger came bounding into the room, holding an overcoat halfway across his face like Zorro with a cape and wildly waving his right index finger at a china closet behind me. "Wait! There's more!" he yelled. "In that bureau!" He had never told us about that second stash. Maybe he felt guilty and had come back to redeem himself, or maybe he just forgot since he was so excitable. Now the lady got her first serious look at Digger, and she tripled her decibel output. I heard the clack of a deadbolt opening somewhere nearby.

"Let's go!" I motioned to Hooks, and we sprinted for the open door. Running down the hall full tilt, we passed a tenant who had just stepped out to see what he was hearing, and trailing far behind us like a pure fool was Digger. The tenant was thunderstruck, and I knew right away that Digger was made (fingered). We jumped out a hall window and over a roof with the tenant yelling, "Hey! Hey! Don't let 'em get away!" but I was adrenaline-ready to run into the next day. We raced down a fire escape to a dark alley below. Meanwhile, Digger had disappeared.

Only slowing down to dump the masks along the way, we slid into a cab about four blocks from the scene. "Fuckin' Digger!" Hooks shook from fear. "That guy made him!" In the moving shadows of the cab I counted out the haul, putting it at just over $7,000. I gave the cabbie a fifty and told him to have a nice evening. Hooks and I each stuffed half in our pockets and took off in opposite directions.

The morning newspapers said that ID of Digger, a parolee

junkie, was made clear and clean by both the victim and the tenant. In no time flat Digger was in a cell. Moreover, the street grapevine had it that Digger was spilling his guts. Within a day or two Hooks and I got together once again, quietly, in a bus station out on Staten Island. We stood there, shivering like hell, partly from fear and partly from loathing for Digger. We had no choice but to go on the lam, so we just drifted out of sight, cruising in various parts of the city, but nowhere near Brooklyn. Finally I had my fill of the haunts and the cold hallways. Four months had passed since Digger went down, so I figured to go back home. I never got any closer than the sidewalk out front.

Two cops jumped out of an unmarked car and ran up to me, pulling guns out of holsters. One of them was Brannigan, who loved to point guns at people, never mind the reason. "Get 'em up in the air!" he ordered. "We gotcha this time, Marino!" After they read me my rights, I refused to say anything so we rode to the station. They dumped me in an old waiting room while they scribbled out the standard mountain of police paperwork. As I sat there I could feel the ghosts and emotions of all the people who must have been dragged through the room. I could almost taste the hopelessness associated with those earlier transients straight on their way to long sentences, but I swore the cops weren't going to break me.

I hung up the receiver from my standard one phone call, somewhere between hope and despair, and turned around to see Brannigan and another bull bringing in Hooks wearing handcuffs. Brannigan handed us both separately the "Your pal's a fink" routine. But I knew Hooks was a stand-up guy, my partner, and that he wouldn't admit it was dark outside at midnight. He knew me to be the same, and that ultimately wore them down.

It turned out that the tenant refused to come down and identify us, and the old lady "wasn't sure." Digger was made, though, and he ended up drawing ten years for rushing the china closet, plus he already owed them seven on a previous conviction. Down went Digger.

The day Hooks and I were released, I saw Brannigan standing forlorn on the steps of the courthouse near the lion statue with white pigeon shit all over its cement mane. The only thing I could think about was getting loaded. I never even thought about the old lady we'd cleaned out — or what she was going to do. A junkie is only sorry for himself.

SOME DAYS SEEMED TO COME together like a charm, especially when my junkie mind was hot to score. I got up out of bed one day and all I could think of was a fix to straighten my head. Problem was I had no money — time to hit the streets. Five minutes and three blocks away, I ran across a delivery boy on a bicycle loaded with three sacks of meat from Al's Butcher Shop. I stopped the kid to bullshit for a while and appealed to his greedy side by offering him three bucks to turn his back while I went south with the goods. I told him he could always claim a thief must have hit the bike when he was away pissing in a building or something. He agreed and held out his hand for the money. Naturally, I didn't have any, so I just grabbed two of the bags and told him I'd be right back.

When I got to the apartment indicated on the delivery sheet, I knocked and stood back from the entrance politely. A woman wearing a black dress and a white apron came to the door. She relieved me of the delivery, saying she would be right back with the money. I stood there idly, waiting for her to come back with the $23.50 they owed me. My eyes lit up when I saw the fifty-dollar bill in her hand. I accepted it graciously and told her I didn't have the right change but would run straight down to the store for it and hurry back. She smiled in trust and closed the door.

Back on the street, I stalled the boy and took the last bag in my arms, heading for delivery. The lady of the second house handed me a twenty and a ten to pay for her $26 order. Again I had no small bills, and I couldn't believe it — she told me to keep the change. I smiled warmly and said, "Why, thank you, Ma'am."

Back on the street again, I told the delivery boy to wait just a second longer while I went to a Western Union office to get some change and pay him off. As I entered the door with the twenty in my hand, I motioned to the clerk behind the cage indicating I was interested only in making change. She nodded as I came up to the window.

Standing off slightly to the right I noticed a woman writing an official telegram, and I also noticed a twenty she had laid out to pay for the wire service. She never saw me lift it. I stashed my bill and inserted hers under the cage for the change. Five seconds later when she noticed the missing money and started complaining, I said, "Hey, don't look at me, lady! I came in here with this," and held up my hands in innocence, as if she were pointing a gun. The clerk defended me: "You must be mistaken, Ma'am, I saw him come in here with this twenty, too."

I went out and gave the delivery boy five bucks for his trouble and headed for the train to Harlem. I added up the triple windfall, which had taken all of twenty minutes to rake in: $50 from the first stop, $30 at the second, and a bonus $20 from the Western Union stop, less $5 to the delivery boy. I ended up with a net $95 to buy heroin. I had to laugh all the way to Spanish Harlem, where my connection was located.

DOPE FIENDS ARE typically notorious losers in life. Not only are they usually weak, but within a very short time after the first fix they tend to go down physically as well. Under the influence of junk, nothing seems to matter, and in terms of eating you mostly think of sweets — cold liquids and sweets, like cola or some other soft drink, never alcohol.

Addicts also live from one fix to the next and never think to ask about the quality of what they buy. The junk always varies from buy to buy, from day to day, and from pusher to pusher. Sometimes it's dynamite, other times not, and there's no way to tell beforehand in an alley. The only way to find out is to load up and stick the needle in your vein. Most users "boot" the junk, meaning shoot a little and see what the effect is, then a little more and so forth. But I didn't see any point in wasting time. My way was to fill the eye dropper, put on the spike, and shoot it all in. Come hell or high water, let's go for broke. This attitude always leads to trouble.

Take, for instance, the day I got off the train in Harlem and started looking for a Puerto Rican named Diego — everybody called him Dago for short. He lived on the sixth floor of this broken-down building where everything was coming apart. I would whistle under his kitchen window three times. When Dago heard me and signaled back with a "Yo," I'd tell him how many bags I wanted and he'd lower a tin can on a string to collect the money, up front. He'd send your order back down the same way. Dago had the situation wired because he couldn't get busted from that distance, and even more important, he couldn't be ripped off since all his customers paid cash through the tin can before they saw the goods.

I bought a half load from Dago, fifteen two-dollar bags, and headed for a quiet place to get off and taste the stuff. Then I remembered that I didn't bring any "works" with me so I looked for another guy I knew, named Haysoos. I soon caught sight of him, and he agreed to lend me his works in return for a free bag. With that we slipped into his building and went up to the stairwell above all the residential floors, right next to the roof. I tied off my arm with his black leather strap and loaded the eye dropper. As soon as I found the vein and the heroin hit my stomach, I knew it was dynamite to the point of too much. I also knew I was going out. In that dense fog just before the blackness, I begged Haysoos not to leave me. Next thing I saw was pitch black up ahead and it was coming down fast. I knew there was no way out. I figured I was dying.

WHEN I OPENED my eyes again, it was only slightly. I had no idea how much time had passed, but I made out a huge lamp overhead that flooded the table where I was laid out, drenched in my own sweat. A white sheet covered me and a green tag was attached to

my big toe, left foot. Off to my right and standing against the wall
was a Roman Catholic priest I didn't recognize, holding his holy
missal and wearing a sash around his neck, the same one they
used for the sacramental administration of extreme unction. I
remembered that much but not much else. Turning my head
slightly to the left, a wave of incredible nausea swept over me, and
I thought I was going to lose it completely when I saw Mom and
Pop at the other end of the stark white room. It was the first time
I had ever seen my father cry. Pop came over and took my hand
saying, "Thank God, thank God."

"Where am I, Pop?"

"In the emergency room of St. Luke's Hospital, and damn lucky
to be alive." I could tell Pop was really upset, although I couldn't
see anything clearly.

"How'd I get here?"

Pop loomed over me, enraged. He strained to hold back his
fury, his face white as he spoke. "Vinny, you idiot! Somebody
called an ambulance, and then the hospital called and told us you
were in trouble. When we got here, they had you covered up.
Dead. The priest saw you move while he gave you the last rites."

"Jesus Christ," I murmured, and the priest's ears perked up.
My momma burst into tears. She couldn't bear to face all the
naked grief — her son a heroin addict, overdosing and ending up
in a hospital with a DOA tag on his big toe. I pulled the sheet back
over my head and played dead, wondering about what had happened to the rest of my dope.

Making Doctors
and Cracking Churches

THE BUILDING I had overdosed in was only a short block and a half from St. Luke's emergency room, where they had worked hard to save my life in a hurry. I learned later Haysoos had lifted my half load but called an ambulance for me.

When the light of the next day came streaming into the hospital ward, I was alive enough to realize my body wasn't racked with the blinding pain of withdrawal. I discovered an intravenous needle in my left arm and thought maybe they were taking care of my habit. The bottle turned out to be glucose, but they had me on methadone, too, a drug that permits the painless withdrawal from heroin.

This pretty nurse came in with a broad smile and a tray full of medicine, something for everyone in the ward. Her name was Wanda, I saw by the tag, and I gave her a weak wave, just so she'd know I was alive. Wanda walked over to my bed, examined my chart, and said, "Well, Mr. Marino, you sure are a lucky guy."

I told her I'd give up everything if only she would agree to spend a day with me on a picnic. Her cheeks flushed and she let a smile get past. "We might just do that, as soon as you're on your feet." She poured me some ice water, extended the glass, and said, "Take this methadone with your pills, and you stay right in that bed." I smiled and asked if she wouldn't climb in with me to chat for a while.

I thought about how lucky I was to have made it off the rooftop alive and how easily it might have gone the other way to a real DOA. I thought about my mom and pop and how they would react now that my drug use was out in the open and about reducing my habit to get it under control. I thought about the methadone they were giving me and about Wanda again.

The next day right after breakfast, a social worker named Mrs. Wentworth came into the ward asking for me. As she approached the bed, I could tell immediately that this lady had been straight as an arrow for her entire life. When she spoke it was in maple syrup, those sweet tones that only come from years of trying to help people from a long distance away. She knew most of the jargon associated with disaster but had never been out on the streets for the experience. Mrs. Wentworth described my future in the glowing terms of what would happen as a result of admitting myself for detoxification at Riverside. She said sternly that I had no choice but to get rid of this "horrible habit" because it would eventually kill me.

I told her that I was interested in going straight, cleaning up, freeing myself, starting a career, getting ahead, having a family someday, and other things she wanted to hear. She smiled, deeply satisfied that she had reached yet another derelict kid and headed him on the path toward the great American dream. On her note pad she wrote, "Arrange for Marino to detox at Riverside."

Riverside turned out to be an island in the East River in the Bronx, not far from Riker's Island, the penitentiary. As the ferry pulled away from the pier, I felt like a piece of my life was left behind on the bank. After docking we were ushered into a room with about fifteen small booths inside, each big enough to hold one person. An orderly instructed us to step into one of the booths and strip down. Then he announced we would be getting an enema.

"Shit, an enema," I thought and wondered why. Later I learned from other residents that some junkies would voluntarily sign up to come here and would actually bring dope with them. The trick was called "stalls." They would put the drugs in a condom or one of those rubber fingers doctors use, swallow the bag, and shit out the load for use later. Well, the hospital cut off the stalls at the pass. A nurse came into the booth with a bedpan in hand and placed it face up on the wooden chair. I was invited to sit down and finish my watery business, right in front of God and two female nurses so they could check it.

They told us the program would take three weeks, and they handed everyone a pair of new white pajamas, loose-fitting and comfortable, and a robe. The two nurses led the way to another building and upstairs to the detoxification ward. Inside we were invited to sit down in the main receiving area. One nurse stood up and gave a pleasant, low-key lecture about how they were inter-ested in our health and welfare. The hospital emphasized "good nutrition," she said, and then gave us the location of a 24-hour juice bar. She told us to drink a lot of water and said they would give out pills for sleeping at night and methadone three times a day, in steadily decreasing dosages. She told us to spend time rebuilding our bodies, and they would all help in any way they could.

The three weeks went by without a hitch, almost before I knew it. I must have met thirty different guys while I was there from all five boroughs of the city. We exchanged names, crimes, new meth-ods to work on, all the angles, cons, and capers, sometimes what was in the newspapers, and especially where to score "good shit" in each neighborhood. I was furthering my education at the expense of the state and getting healthy in the process.

Twenty days later I felt like a new man. It was a sunny bright Monday when I had my kiss-off shot of methadone. I enjoyed a farewell lunch with some of the guys and the staff, put on my freshly washed street clothes, shaved, put a shine on my shoes, and got onto the ferry back to the streets of New York. The first thing I did on hitting the streets was to phone Wanda from St. Luke's and ask her about the picnic, but instead we agreed on dinner the next night at eight. I hung up with a grin. I felt clean and good about myself as I got on a train for Brooklyn.

When I appeared at the door, Momma jumped up full of happiness and hugged me warmly. She immediately started whipping up a big meal, and Frank wanted to know all about how I was. Even little Joey was there, following me around and wanting to play. The old man was out losing it somewhere, but that day nobody cared. We joked around and told family stories, and I felt proud to announce, "I'm clean now." They were all so happy I felt like taking a bow.

Then I figured to go over and see how Hooks was doing. With that decision came trouble. I hadn't been out of detox for three hours, and here I was telling myself, "Just one shot to feel good." Naturally I promised myself I would not get hooked, as I sent the junk into my vein. In my drug-filled stupor, I forgot all about the supper Momma was cooking up for me back home. That made her cry hard yet again. She had a long time to go before she'd see me clean, and a lot more crying to do. It takes a lot more than twenty-one days swapping tricks with con artists to clean junk from your body as well as from your head. You need to get clean *and* learn how to stay that way. I was just a clean junkie then, and there's no room for much besides junk in a junkie's brain.

IN 1955 FEDERAL PRESSURE on dope smuggling cut off about half of the heroin coming into the city. The addicts panicked. You would see them rolling around in alleys, vomiting all over. It was at this time that Hooks and I learned the game called "making doctors," getting some croaker to prescribe stuff and staying the hell off the streets.

You probably already know that doctors prescribe dope for ordinary people. All you have to do is prove — or claim — you are terminal with something painful such as cancer and you can get a prescription for a drug called dilaudid. Dilaudid gets you off just like the real thing.

A junkie I knew told me about a doctor known to write scrips (prescriptions) for heavy drugs if the receptionist was paid in cash. I set up an appointment. The woman who answered sounded like she was going to crawl through the wires and get it on with me, she was so sweet and sexy. "God," I thought to myself, "that woman is in the wrong business!"

At 10:50 A.M. the next morning, I was getting off the elevator on the fifth floor of a fancy Park Avenue building. Behind the door of the doctor's office, the receptionist sang out, "May I help you?"

"Marino. I have an appointment for eleven," I answered crisply.

"Oh, yes," she gushed. "That will be $50 for the first consultation, Mr. Marino."

I paid as I wondered what kind of act I should put on to convince the doctor. I walked down the corridor to his office and knocked, and he said to come in. Inside was a little character about 55, with shifty eyes and big horn-rimmed glasses. He looked up from his seat and said he was Doctor Perkins and offered me a chair.

He instructed me to take off my shirt and then checked my blood pressure and heartbeat and looked with a light in my nose, ears, and throat. He told me to put my shirt back on and walked back to his chair behind the desk. As he sat down, I was wondering who was to say what next, but the doctor broke the ice. "What's the problem? What do you need?"

I leaned forward and gripped the handrests of the chair, then looked him straight in the eye. "They tell me I'm dying of cancer, and I'm in constant pain. I need dilaudid."

Doctor Perkins scribbled on a pad as he said, "Certainly. Certainly. No pain. No pain." He handed me a scrip for thirty dilaudids, which was really nice of the guy, so I thanked and backed out the door. When I got back to the waiting room, I noticed Sexy's purse sitting beside her, so I figured I'd go south with it. I told her the doctor wanted to see her in his office for something. In a thoughtless second she went for it and took off down the hall. Lightning fast I lifted her wallet and a new pad of blank scrips, printed with the doc's name, address, and phone number. I was out the main door and into the elevator before she had even reached his office.

My reward came in two doses. The first was cash. I got back my $50 for the office call, plus a bonus of another $125. Not bad for thirty minutes. The next dose had to do with those scrips. I had memorized and practiced the doctor's handwriting and the way the scrip read. The dilaudid was good, but we ran out soon. Hooks and I had done some, sold some, and gave the others away. I was fairly loose at the time, since money was not a particular problem — drugs were the problem.

Hooks volunteered to imitate the doctor's signature, and I strolled into a busy pharmacy at Broadway and Fifty-third in Manhattan with the prescription. The pharmacist behind the counter informed me, "There's going to be at least a thirty-minute wait." All I thought was that was the price you had to pay these days, waiting for your drugs to appear as if by magic from over the counter. I walked across the street and into a pizza joint, where I ordered a slice with pepperoni.

Well, this same druggist had been hit with forged scrips three times in the past ten days, each one for dilaudid. That tripped his warning switch. Then he heard from the receptionist that the prescription was a phony, so guess who met Marino after the pizza and before he could burp? And who was back in the slammer?

I spooked when I learned the penalty for forging a prescription for narcotics was not less than one year in prison. But my lawyer and I were hanging onto two technicalities, hoping to save my ass: the scrip was not in my handwriting, and the detective arrested me *before* I took delivery of the drugs. My lawyer recommended that we cop a plea before the judge.

The judge looked down at me hard. "Mr. Marino, this is serious business. I don't like what I see about your past, and frankly I am not thrilled with the prospect of having you on the streets much longer. So I am going to offer you a choice, Mr. Marino. You can go to Riker's Island Penitentiary for one to three years. Or you can enlist in the Army and learn some proper discipline, in which case I will drop this charge from a felony to a misdemeanor and suspend sentence."

THE NEXT THING I KNEW, I was trading in my street clothes for an olive-green standard uniform issued by the United States Army at Fort Dix, New Jersey. Before reporting in, I had turned all my available cash and goods into more than $700 of the best junk I could find so I could make damn sure the Army didn't get to me. At times it was tough, because I was anything but ready for what was coming down. That was in March 1956. I was 17 years old. Korea was over, and Vietnam hadn't started yet. I was flying high about 90 percent of the time under the influence of junk, so I didn't need to hear all that "Hup, two!" shit in my ears. They wanted me to run around buildings, do pushups, then pick up butts, march some more, run while carrying a gun, fix bayonets, and jump in and out of used tires just for the exercise.

Bored as hell, I crawled away one day, heading for the sick bay. The first time in, I complained of a fever after running the thermometer up to 102 degrees by rubbing it on my pants. In the end, I conned a croaker into giving me what was called an "L-3 Profile," which meant no walking, standing, or marching for more than five minutes at a time. I convinced the guy my feet were flat, and with that I ended up in a bunk where I belonged, while all the other booties were out there in the freezing New Jersey air doing whatever bizarre bullshit the Army thinks up to keep everybody busy.

Since I became a regular on sick call, I never got through the basic parts of what they had scheduled as an eight-week training session. Instead, I got "recycled" (which meant "Send him back through!"), but that didn't bother me because I was usually just occupying a bunk with my veins full of dope. At one point the base commander called my pop in for a discussion. The brass told Pop I was way the hell behind par as far as military bearing went. Pop cracked my face with a backhand and told me to "act like a man." I was cycled through basics for nineteen weeks, before they finally gave up and handed me graduation papers.

At Fort Dix, I saw a lot of easy marks come and go through the basic sessions, and it was easy to get them caught up in a game of craps or cards. Before I left basic training, I wound up winning nearly $2,000 in cash and a 1948 fire-engine red Cadillac convertible. Even Pop's eyes bulged with excitement when I drove up in that Cadillac and parked it on the street in front of our building. I didn't have a driver's license at the time, since I wasn't 18 yet, but that didn't bother Pop.

Frank came running out of the house and asked me if he could drive. He got in behind the wheel and we were off, waving to everyone who was watching and blowing the horn, a little crazy. We were laughing and talking and having a good time. It sure was good to be home. That night I drove over to Hooks's place to see how he was doing, and we both got totally loaded and sat around drinking Cokes.

When I arrived at Fort Eustis, Virginia, two weeks later, I found quite a few other guys were into junk. One was the sergeant of the outfit, who was willing to check me in on Friday night for the whole weekend, when I would actually be on a bus to New York where I would cop for the crew and return Sunday evening. During the week, I figured to repeat the "sick call" routine, but it didn't work very long. By the fifth day, the medics — realizing I was loaded — flat refused to see me. One morning I countered by refusing to respond to reveille.

A sergeant came storming into the barracks and started banging on my bunk, demanding that I "hit it on the double!" Without bothering to come out from under the pillow, I rolled over and told him, "Look, do me a favor. If there's a war on, call me. If there's not, leave me the fuck alone. I ain't runnin' around no buildings today."

Old Sarge couldn't quite believe what he had heard, so he called in a second lieutenant. This guy also came in with the "Okay, Marino, up and at 'em" routine. I told him that if they gave me a gun again, I was gonna figure there was a "war on somewhere and start shootin'!" They didn't think I was very well suited to the Army, so within two days I was mustered out with an undesirable discharge.

I figured everything had come down just fine. After all, the judge didn't say how long I had to stay in the Army, so I was out on that one — and with no parole and no probation.

JUST BEFORE CHRISTMAS of 1956, heroin was catching on like wildfire on the streets of New York. A whole fleet of dope fiends were into the cattle-rustling caper, and some were openly boosting cigarettes, which had been our primary source. One night I had just scored some junk on a street corner near a Roman Catholic church in the Flatbush section of Brooklyn. Since I was in a hurry to get off and check the quality, I asked the church priest if I could use the bathroom in the rectory. He didn't particularly like the idea but finally agreed and showed me the room.

I got behind the door and locked it. After shooting up, I put away the works and was into the familiar warm-glow world as I emerged from the bathroom. The priest hadn't waited around to see me out the door, which turned out to be a fatal mistake. On the wall near the front hallway was a series of pigeon-hole boxes all full of envelopes. I helped myself to about thirty and hustled out the door. When I saw that the haul from them totaled over $400, I couldn't wait to get back and tell Hooks. I had just found a new business.

In working a church, the hardest part was getting inside the rectory. Typically, Hooks would knock first and go into his act for the day. Either he was thinking of killing himself, quitting school, join-

ing the priesthood, or some other drastic move that required immediate attention. The priest would invite him into an office for a discussion. Once Hooks was inside, I would knock, usually to be
received by the caretaker who would ask me to wait since the priest
was "now tied up in a meeting with somebody else." That was like
issuing me a license to steal, and I went straight into action.

Just about every rectory we got into had money all over the
place. Every drawer of the bureaus in the priests' rooms had
either money or jewelry or both. The pigeonholes full of envelopes
destined for favorite causes or charities were everywhere. In
some of the larger parishes they even had special rooms to count
the money, including huge machines that separated coins. Once I
turned on a machine like that and walked out with a sack full of
quarters totaling $1900.

We stayed away from synagogues and Protestant churches. I
figured that even if they caught me red-handed, the priests would
never prosecute an Italian kid from one of their own neighborhood churches. My rationale was that Jesus was a carpenter and
so was his father, but they never bothered to build a church. Yet
there I was, standing in a huge cathedral with expensive stained-
glass windows and matching bells and solid gold chalices when
brass would have done just as well. Besides, I figured, those guys
had an endless supply of money, stocks, bonds, and real estate, all
tax free, so I was just robbing a little from the bigger thieves. Our
little business had nothing to do with God.

Crazed Addict

I T WAS ABOUT that same time in 1956 when I made the final turn into a crazed addict — I was totally gone. Our whole trip was to get into a shell insulated from the outside world, using dope, and to stay there. We mixed heroin with cocaine, we mixed heroin with disoxyn (the poor man's speedball), and whenever we temporarily ran out, we were not above drinking a bottle of cough medicine with codeine to wash down three or four doridens (hypnotic downer).

Addicts refer to overdosing as "falling out," and I fell out in some of the craziest circumstances. Once I went so far as to go out in a "shooting gallery" up in East Harlem. A shooting gallery is a rented room or an abandoned building that some dope fiend opens and then brings in a few sets of works. They rent the works for fifty cents or a dollar to any junkie who wants to use a set. The unwritten law is that you come in, pay up, do your business, and hit the streets. Some busy galleries would entertain as many as a couple hundred "customers" on a daily basis, so there was absolutely no opportunity to sit around and nod out inside the place. But one day in February 1957, first I fell down, then I fell out. I was dragged down to a storeroom to sleep it off in an empty refrigerator carton. And this wasn't the only time I fell out.

I knew a guy named Gino. He was a musician, good enough to form a band and get a gig at a club in Flatbush. The members always had quality dope, so one day Hooks and I headed over to see what we could find. Gino was practicing some songs and waiting for a new load to arrive.

The junk arrived in about an hour, but Hooks had gone out to pick up some cigarettes and soda. Gino and I went into the kitchen and got off. The last thing I remembered Gino saying was "Wow! This is fucking dynamite!" When Hooks got back five or ten minutes later, we were both out cold on the floor. Hooks panicked, since Gino lived with his folks, but he thought fast and took the works, then stashed the rest of the stuff in his pants before carrying me out to a cab. Two blocks away, he stopped the cab to call an ambulance for Gino.

I slept off the night in a heavy fog, and the next day I learned that Gino was dead. They had found him on the kitchen floor, right where we left him. Apparently the ambulance never came.

MY BROTHER FRANK started to come down hard on my case whenever he thought I was stoned, pleading, "Vinny, what do you think you're doing besides killing yourself?"

"Hey, I tried some weird stuff for a kick, like everybody else, but nothing regular," I said. Besides, I intended to end up as a well-connected made-man one day, and soon. Frank came back at me flatly with, "Brother, you know the Organization doesn't have anything to do with dope fiends." I hadn't thought about it that way. I felt heavy inside with the final gut realization of knowing I was not to be a made-man. But I figured, "Fuck the mob and fuck Frank, too."

Two or three days later Frank had to break down our bathroom door because he smelled something foul as hell burning. First he knocked hard and fast but got no response. Then he shouted, "Hey, Vinny! You in there?" The odor got stronger as the minutes passed, and he blasted in, using his shoulder.

Frank couldn't quite believe what he saw. Our bathroom had a steam radiator standing up against the wall about two feet in front of the commode. I had lowered the lid to sit down, and after I got off, I immediately knew the junk was much too powerful. I saw the now-familiar blackness closing in. My first thought was to make it into the bedroom, but it was too late. With the needle still in my vein, all I could manage was a slight lean forward, ending up with my right arm pressed against the radiator, which had just started to warm up.

When Frank picked up the smell, both the shirt and my flesh were smoldering. He almost fainted when he saw the grim scene and the source of the odor. There was Vinny breathing shallow in a deep overdose, with his arm burning and a needle stuck in it at the same time.

He shook me viciously and nothing happened. He cursed me like hell, but I never heard the words. He splashed cold water on my face, and that made no difference. He hoisted me up and walked me around, after which I fell back on the floor. I don't remember any of this. Four and a half hours later, something finally came into my mind — a sharp pain, and it was everywhere. I couldn't move my body and just barely opened my eyes. From off in the distance an angry voice was lashing out full of fury.

"Christ, Vinny," Frank was intense. "Don't you see what you're doing to yourself?" He held up my bad arm to make me look at it, but I wasn't focusing clearly. Frank shook the burnt limb. "Look, burned to shit. You're better off dead than this!"

Through the pounding in my head, I thought, "Frank, why don't we just start with a fix, and then I'll die peacefully, later." But I said nothing out loud and faded off to total blackness. They called a doctor who put some salve on the burn and bandaged my arm.

IN WHAT SEEMED to me like a flash but was actually more than an hour on the clock, Frank busted back into the room and started banging two suitcases around, with Pop right behind him. Even I could see that Frank's emotions were somewhere between total outrage and crying out of love, when he said, "We're going away, Vinny. You and me and Pop, and as soon as we're set up we'll send for Mom and Joey." I couldn't even raise my head, so I said, "I can't go anywhere, Frank. I'm sick."

Frank opened one of the suitcases, then looked up at me and shouted, "Fuck your bullshit, Vinny! We're going!" And he stuffed my belongings into the bag.

I said, "Okay, Frank, let's leave tomorrow. By then I'll feel better."

"No way, Vinny. We're starting a new life, and we're starting it *today*." The beginning of a long and painful trip — cold turkey down the Jersey turnpike.

The next thing I knew Frank was stopping. Somewhere I thought I heard pounding surf. Frank and Pop jerked me on my feet, urging me to get out of the car. We'd hit Miami. Somehow they managed to carry me into the water. When the first wave hit, I could only crawl back up on all fours, like a groveling dog. Before I could shake dry, the next wave crashed in, knocking me down in the sand. Frank was all lit up, bright as hell, and kept saying over and over, "Hey, you guys! A new life! New lifestyles!"

Within three hours of hitting town, Frank came out of a hotel with a big smile on his face. "A living room, two bedrooms, and a kitchen. If we take care of the pool and the grounds, it's ours for only fifteen bucks a week."

Two weeks after we got there, Pop had signed on as a porter at the hotel, Frank was keeping up about half an acre of grounds surrounding the place, and I was off drugs and on duty as the hotel's official lifeguard, swimming instructor, and pool cleaner. Then, at various opportune times, I burglarized the rooms of selected hotel guests, using a plastic card on the lock while they were busy sunbathing at the pool.

Soon I was familiar with most of the big hotels in Miami Beach. Then I first noticed another breed of shark than the ones swimming around in the ocean. These sharks played cards, mostly poker. I started watching over shoulders, and saving my money for a game.

Within five weeks after we set foot in Miami Beach, things were looking up and we all felt pretty bright. I was still clean and had

$325 in my pocket, ready for the poker game. Frank had become a good groundskeeper, and Pop enjoyed the hustle of the bellboy job. After work he usually went off to the dog races at the track. As the eighth week wound up, I was into a winning streak at the game. As the deck got better to me, I neglected the pool more and more, so Frank and Pop did the pinch-sweeping.

One night at poolside under the stars, the deck was hot in my favor. Suddenly I saw this young fox walk in, so full of allure I dumped my hand and begged off to go wash up. When I stood up, she nodded and I caught her with my eyes, indicating a meeting in back. She appeared at the hotel bar five minutes later.

"You're some player," she said smiling, "and my name is Anna."

It was hard to believe how well her name fit this sultry girl. I could tell she was young, but her breasts pushed hard against her flimsy blouse. Reaching for her hand, I kissed the back ever so softly and said, "Anna, my pleasure. I'm Vinny, and we will see just how good a player I am, especially with you." Anna called to the bartender and turned toward me. "Vinny, would you like a drink to relax?"

"I can think of better ways to relax than over a drink here in the open bar," I said in my sweetest Sicilian-plus overtones. Anna came right along, obviously enjoying the charge between us as we played that "first time together" song. She sang in my ear, "Let's meet somewhere away from here."

"Where and what time?"

She wrote down the name of a place and gave me a couple of hours to get there. I edged my hand around her waist, kissing her neck and looking down her blouse. At 9:30 sharp, I got out of the game, with $800 and my pile of chips.

Anna was right where she said she would be, which pleased me and I let her know by saying, "Anna, it's good to see you again." As she reached out to put her arms around me, the sleeves of her blouse pulled up to reveal telltale marks. I couldn't believe it — Anna was a junkie.

Within an hour we had scored off an ex-pimp of hers, and made a beeline for my hotel. In less than three minutes we were cooking up while we kissed each other over the flame in wild anticipation. I loaded the eye dropper and got off. Then I tied her arm, found a vein, and sent it straight in. Next thing Anna and I were in bed, rolling around up in heaven, maybe even a little higher, moving together in a sweet and slow rhythm.

Right then Frank came in. I thought I heard the door open but was so far away with Anna I didn't even roll over when he pulled off the sheet. Even then I still didn't realize Frank had just been added to the room, but he was furious, especially when he saw the works and the bag of dope sitting on a nightstand next to the bed. He picked up the bag and started yelling, "What's this shit!?" And then he threw it at us.

I couldn't do anything but laugh. That did it for Frank. He grabbed a suitcase from the closet, yelling about how much work he had done for me on the pool, plus his own job, and now there I was all fucked up on heroin again. "I'm going home," he yelled. Anna and I made loud murmuring noises, and Frank just kept on packing his bags. We exchanged "Oh, Gods!" and "Oh, babies!" beneath the sheet while Frank changed his shoes on the edge of the bed. The springs squeaked as Frank walked out, and he slammed the door.

The next day I told Pop Frank had pulled out. He didn't seem at all surprised. "I think Frank was homesick, for Momma, Joey, and the city."

"Jesus," I thought, "let's hope so. Surely Frank wouldn't take off just because I slipped up once and got loaded."

But then things came further apart. Junk is sort of like antiglue — it pries apart your connections to the world. It unsticks you from your job and dumps you out of your home. It tears you away from people you might have actually loved — if you'd ever grow up. That's the point. You usually get into junk because you haven't grown up. Maybe because the people who should have taught you how to grow up didn't know how themselves. That's how it was for me — all that Sicilian family pride wasn't enough to show me how to be a man in New York. At 19, I was just a boy, and fucked up at that.

It didn't take long after Frank left for Pop and me to lose our jobs. We packed and got in the car to head home, doing a real father-son trip, discussing games of chance. Round about the Georgia state border, I noticed the speedometer pushing above the seventy mark. Ten miles farther we picked up a highway patrol car.

"Hey, Pop, there's a cop back there!" Without a word, Pop tightened his arms and we roared away from the bull wagon. The blue light came on, flashing in a circle, and I thought I could hear the faint wail of his siren. We were hitting at least ninety with the bull about three-fourths of a mile behind when Pop jerked hard on the wheel toward a gas station up ahead on the right-hand side. The car swerved, bounced once, and then came to a screeching halt. Even before we came to a full stop, Pop bounded out his door, moving faster than I had ever seen him go, headed straight for the men's restroom. I looked back through a ball of red dust to see what was coming.

For a split second I imagined we had lost the cop, but he soon drove up through the dust, sliding into the station next to our car. He struggled to get out, holding onto the roof with his left hand as he pushed his heavy weight up from the seat. As he came toward our car, he grinned with yellow teeth and hitched his holster belt up but failed to get it over his inner-tube belly. He cocked the hat upward and held onto the peak as he asked, "Say, son, are yew thuh driver of this heah car?"

I said the minimum: "No, sir." The bull looked in the window and across the seat at me directly. "Well, wheah thuh hail is he?"

Pop came out of the men's room, and the bull turned to question him. "Were yew drivin' this?"

While hitching up his belt tight, Pop said, looking down, "That's right, Officer." The cop reached for his pad, but before he could get it, Pop broke into an anguished, "Ooooooo!" and held his ass, as if in terrible pain. Then he whirled and raced to the safety of the men's room. The cop looked at me again, puzzled. I threw my hands in the air and shrugged, as if I were a hitchhiker and knew from nothing. I *did* know nothing — what was Pop up to?

Within two minutes, Pop came out again, looking apologetic and fumbling with his belt, as if to buckle up. The bull started to recite the violation. "Yew wuz doin' 87 miles an hour, an' ah can't let that kinda thang happen in mah county." Pop spun again and ran for the restroom, holding onto his pants and moaning. Pop came out the third time, pulling his belt tight with one hand, the other covering his backside.

Before the cop could say anything, Pop cut in with, "Bad case of diarrhea, sir. Just making a run for the men's room."

The cop deflated like a pricked balloon. "Huh?" was all he could manage before Pop went into his wail one more time and bolted for the restroom, slamming the door. Meanwhile behind the windshield I was cracking up. It was all I could do to contain a burst of open laughter. The bull started shifting his weight from one cow-leg to the other, not really knowing what to do. Bang on the door? No. Shoot through it? No. He finally just took off his trooper hat and the dark glasses, then proceeded to wipe the sweat off his face with a bandanna.

Pop came out into the open air again and looked straight at the bull. "Well, Officer, you see why we were in such a hurry." Pop displayed his most convincing smile, his eyes pleading for mercy to a fellow man who might understand this human condition.

The cop had no real comeback so he muttered, "Wail, no mo' speedin'. Yew okay now?" he asked Pop.

Pop said he "was better" and then asked the cop where he could get some Jockey shorts in the area since his were ruined by the runs. Incredibly, the bull gave Pop some directions to the next town, and sped off. Pop and I doubled up in laughter.

If You Can't Do the Time

THE FALL OF 1958 the streets of New York were hotter than Miami's with pressure coming down from the feds about drugs. Hooks and I decided to get off the streets altogether. We went into the business of buying written scrips and stealing blank pads full time. Dilaudid was better than the street heroin at that time and a whole lot easier to score. We would shoot for the greedy side of a pharmacist and see what happened. I would take the first legitimate scrip in, and the pharmacist would usually call to verify it with the doctor. Then when he filled the prescription, costing four or five dollars, I would drop a twenty-dollar bill and leave the change.

Next day I would come back with the empty bottle and no scrip, saying, "The doctor wasn't in yet, but I need this filled right away. The scrip for it will be ready later today." Again I'd leave a twenty to pay for a five-dollar prescription. The third time I'd tell him, "I lost the scrip, but could you please fill it one more time," as I waved the twenty before placing it under the bottle. From then on, I would simply walk in and tell him to fill it up.

In the drug world, whenever a caper started to work for a few people, word would spread like lightning. It was like that with our cattle rustling and cigarette boosting, and now with forging prescriptions. Official blank pads were getting stolen like hotcakes. In

67

the beginning, you could cash in a forged prescription like you would a traveler's check. They were as good as gold.

I PREFERRED THE GAME OF "making doctors." One day a junkie told me about a certain doctor who was inclined to write heavy drug prescriptions, but you had to have a story and pay the nurse up front. The next afternoon I opened the door to Doctor Leachman's office in Manhattan. A young receptionist smiled and offered me a seat. She asked my name, address, and phone number, and told me, "The initial visit will be $75." A white-capped nurse emerged from a door and said, "Mr. Marino."

I followed her into a cubicle, where she asked me to have a seat on the examining table and told me, "The doctor will be right in." Within five minutes the doctor appeared and sat down opposite me. "What seems to be the trouble, Mr. Marino?" I figured my story had better be real good, with seventy-five bucks riding on the outcome, so I grabbed the edge of the bed and leaned toward him.

"Well, Doc, it all started in Korea. I was in a foxhole with my three buddies. All of a sudden a mortar shell came in and exploded right on the edge of the hole. All three of my buddies were blown to bits." I wrung my hands and dropped my head, shaking it from side to side.

"Yeah, I was badly wounded, Doc, but no one could reach me for two days. I had a severe concussion and was in tremendous pain. All they could do was give me morphine since they couldn't evacuate me to a hospital for another three days, and they had to keep me quiet because the enemy was all around us. I was in a stupor. The pain was awful, so they kept giving me more morphine." I went on, "I got hooked on morphine. I need some help. I can't go to one of the institutions because I have a wife and three kids. Doc, what am I going to *do?*"

The croaker had heard enough. He picked up his pad and wrote me a prescription for thirty-six dilaudids and gave me a nice little talk about the "debt America owed her veterans." As I walked out, I saw the perfect chance to pick up the prescription pad on his desk.

Three weeks later I showed up with a new sheet off Leachman's pad at a pharmacy I had never been in before. What I didn't know was that it had become popular with other paper-hanging junkies, and two detectives were hiding in the wings, checking out every prescription. Naturally I had the wrong number. I was arrested. The cops circulated my mug shot to every pharmacy in all five boroughs. No less than ninety-nine pharmacists positively identified me. So, ninety-nine counts of "forgery in the third degree: prescriptions for narcotics."

This time, my lawyer told me there was no way out. Get ready to serve some time. I made a plea bargain with the DA's office to cop to "attempted forgery in the third degree," including "all known and unknown counts." That meant that any other scrip they said I forged prior to my sentencing they couldn't prosecute me for later.

It was also obvious that there was no sense going into the can with a bad habit. I knew from experience that the joint was no place to kick a jones — they had no tolerance for addicts. So I went through a quickie detox program. And then I was ready to go.

The judge slammed his hammer and came down with a call for, "An indeterminate sentence of one to three years at Riker's Island Penitentiary." That meant one year minimum and, depending on behavior, up to three years maximum.

I was looking square in the face of three years behind bars. The feeling was close to that black wall called overdose, and my mouth was dry as I walked to the bull pen ahead of the bailiff. Time to ship out for the island in the middle of the East River and the beginning of my three-year bit on the "Rock."

It was freezing cold that Monday morning. I had nothing to wear but a light sports coat and a white shirt. Handcuffed and waiting for the ferry, the chill ran right through me. As soon as the ferry was away from the dock, they had to open the doors of the van we were in and take the cuffs off. Once a ferry had sunk in the middle of a trip, and twenty inmates drowned because they were handcuffed together inside a van. With that first blast of frigid air out on the open water, silence was king in the air.

After the boat tied up, everyone was told to sit down and wait for the standard processing. They sprayed us with delousing liquid, then off to the showers. After the showers, uniforms.

As I got dressed, it hit me that Vinny Marino was gone — replaced with #102129. By then I was starving and colder than hell. The hacks came out and announced lentil soup was available. My stomach ruled and I went for it, wolfing down the whole thing. Even the cut-up frankfurters on the bottom tasted good.

Now I found myself with seven other young guys being escorted to check in at the adolescent dormitories. The only way to reach our dorm was to pass through the main cell block, and that moment was one of the scariest of my life. The sounds were weird and eerie, like four or five hundred guys crying. And it built to a crescendo of moans and low groans, as if everybody was being tortured. I thanked all the gods for not sending me to serve my stretch there.

The first thing each man had to do was find a job within the facility so that the hacks could give you "marks." Marks were assigned after you were on the job for 90 to 120 days, and depended on your involvement, performance, behavior, and attitude. If you were sentenced to three years, the marks you got indicated your maximum and minimum stay.

A job was open for a captain's clerk. When it came time to interview, I only had one thing in the experience column: I had memorized the standard typing test line "Now is the time for all good men to come to the aid of their party." I could rap that out like an electric transmitter — but nothing else. Well, the captain didn't dictate anything original, so I got the position based on that.

Like most hacks, all Watson wanted was no trouble, so he gave me a free hand and I took over. Within a month, I had changed all the bunk assignments in the four dorms to reflect what the guys wanted, which was strict segregation. There was one group of blacks, another of Puerto Ricans, and then white guys. We also sat in these groups in the mess hall at separate tables, and everything was going real smooth. It wasn't long, however, before a certain hack told us to "cut out this separation and mix it up." He gave that order one night at supper. After the meal the leaders of each group met and everybody agreed, "Let's go on strike in the morning."

We sent out word. The plan was to line up for breakfast as usual — blacks with blacks, whites with whites, and so on. If the hacks gave us trouble, we would refuse to eat. We came out of the dorms at seven and fell into the unspoken color codes. The hack spotted the segregation and started raising hell, demanding that we "mix up the colors." We did, and passed the word to skip the meal.

Each guy passed through the food line, picked up a tray and a spoon but nothing to eat. Ten minutes later, the bells went off. We were mustered out of the mess area and taken on the march back to the dorms to sit and wait for the trouble we knew was on its way.

Just after eight, a full-blown riot squad came barging into Dormitory Number 3. Next stop, King's County Hospital. Maximum security psychiatric ward. I was there for "observation," as the ringleader of the riot.

A lot of weird people were in that maximum security psychiatric lockup. They must have had at least ten murderers. One was a guy named Cavanaugh, about 24 and so strange they kept him in a straitjacket all the time. Even with that, he would shake violently back and forth. His story was that he once asked his mother for ice cream money, and she refused him or didn't have it. Either way, he didn't like it, so he picked up a ball-peen hammer and bashed her over the head until she was dead.

One night after supper they brought us all into the day room for a movie. When we were seated, they brought out the "hard cases," including Cavanaugh. An orderly opened the back straps of Cavanaugh's jacket, allowing him to move his arms. The movie credits rolled, *White Heat* starring James Cagney. Just as Cagney was proclaiming, "Look, Ma, I'm on top of the world!" I got a blind-side blast from Cavanaugh. He knocked me off the bench and hard onto the floor. I looked up to see no less than six massive hacks coming down on Cavanaugh, holding him absolutely still, although he was shouting at the top of his lungs about "killing everybody." A nurse hit him with a quick shot, and within three minutes his lights went out and they carried him away.

I spent three weeks in that ward and never did find out what they were looking for or what they found. But nobody messed with your head, and the food was better than Riker's.

On my thirtieth day in King's County, the same two plain-clothesmen came back to pick me up. As the boat to Riker's pulled in, I wondered how life was going to be back in the dorms. But I was driven directly to the bing. The next two days, coffee and bread, tea and bread, and cocoa and bread. On the third day I got three square meals. Showers were once a week, and I didn't even bother to shave. Who the hell was I gonna see?

On the morning of the twenty-second day, they brought me up out of the hole. I was thinking about which bunk in the dorm I would have, when we stopped right in the middle of Cell Block One-A. The hack opened the door and edged me in, signaling the other hack to close it. I wasn't going back to the dorms.

I found out quickly that my new cell block was reserved for the more defiant adolescents, and most had heard of me as the "riot ringleader." That earned me some respect.

We drifted along with the boring routine. The hacks picked on more and more trivial stuff all the time — we weren't staying in a straight line, going fast enough, or some other bullshit. One hack decided to start attacking segregation again. I saw the handwriting on the wall this time, and I wanted no part of the action.

That night about one or two in the morning, I took my razor and cut open an artery on my upper left arm, enough to produce some obvious bleeding but no permanent damage. To finish the scene, I put in a weak call, "Off-i-cer, off-i-cer." One finally approached; "Whaddaya want, Marino?" I showed him my wound and whispered, "I'm dying. You gotta help me."

The hack signaled for a stretcher to the hospital. They tied a bandage around my arm and pushed me through a door marked "Mental Observation." At least I was out of the cell block and what looked like certain trouble.

The time I spent in MO wasn't all that bad, considering the alternatives. As time went on, I landed myself a job as an orderly. The bonus was that some drugs were available from time to time, especially valium and librium.

After a while on Riker's I got good at transferring between the cell block and the mental ward. When the cell block got dull, I told the psychiatrist that I was hearing voices. Next thing I was back on the sixth floor as an orderly, then playing cards on valium after hours. Every once in a while some junk would come in.

I was assigned a job in the commissary, which was pure insanity since every con working there was a thief. But that didn't seem to matter — everyone was stealing from the state in one way or another, including the boss hack. We worked out a deal to stow cartons of cigarettes and cases of candy bars in the trash cans, then retrieve them later and share the haul after we finished working our shift. All things come to an end, however, and that caper was done for when the prison warden ordered an inventory. The cons got transferred to other blocks, and the boss was convicted for embezzling $80,000 worth of goods.

We were treated on rare occasions to junk, pot, or booze, all provided by hacks. Also as your seniority built, it was not unusual to gather several valuables that couldn't be bought — a pillow, bedspread, a decent hairbrush, or a bigger mirror. These were officially ignored if you paid your way with cigarettes. The same was true about good food.

We all played cards regularly, but just kept track of the money on paper. I once beat a smartass named Kelley, and he ended up owing me twenty dollars. He put the word out that I could go to hell for what he owed me. So I approached a hack I knew. I told him straight, "I have a beef with a guy I want to take care of myself, so could you stay out of the back of the block in the square for ten minutes?" He didn't seem to mind: "Marino, no weapons, no blood, and make it quick."

So I sent a friend to tell Kelley I wanted to see him. Kelley walked up and said, "You wanted to see m..." I cut him off with a roundhouse right under the chin — which stopped him cold but broke my hand. Then I went in with a story that I broke it playing handball on the back wall. They sent me to the prison ward at Bellevue and I complained so loud they treated me to a free shot of morphine before they set it. I felt like I was sailing around in heaven somewhere.

THE MONTHS PASSED BY. I assumed I was getting out at the two-year mark. Two days before I thought I was going out the front door, I got a call to report to the preparole division. I found myself facing three men each about sixty years old with a big pot belly and a suit way too small. "Mr. Marino, because of your improper behavior, most notably participating in a riot, your marks have been extended by three months." I slammed the door hard behind me. Another week in the bing was my specially designed sting for slamming their door.

As my time on Riker's Island finally dwindled down to the last sixty days, I got myself one of those cheap ball chains you normally wear around your neck. Each day I clipped one of the little balls off. I kept my mouth shut and stayed in line so there was no chance that they'd extend me again. My inner clock was off and running already, and I had a clear picture of myself on the outside, looking in — a free man after almost twenty-seven months.

But I wasn't going to be a free man. I was still going to be myself, smart Vinny Marino, with a monkey on my back. Nothing in prison taught me what I needed to know.

A Cornered Rat

WHEN I WAS RELEASED from prison, officially an ex-convict at the age of 22, I was on parole — no drugs, no associating with ex-felons, addicts, or drunkards. Midnight curfew, unless you got written permission. Check in every week at 10 sharp Monday morning; after you find a job, check in every two weeks. How to find that job?

First thing off the ferry, see Momma in the hospital for some minor surgery. She had divorced Pop by now, so she was doing better. Was she glad to see me! Then out the door and down to 99th Street for a fix and a whore. Then a fix with Hooks, and we teamed up again, hustling cigarettes, rustling meat from stores, a few burglaries, robbing churches.

By the time I had been home from Riker's for three weeks, I had a habit that cost me $50 a day. My parole officer never even noticed the skin-colored makeup I rubbed over the tracks in my arms. I knew I was headed back for Riker's. Pop was worried too, and put pressure on me to get a job.

Well, I got one. It was May, and the resorts in upstate New York were hiring. One of them advertised for a lifeguard and a water ski instructor. I snowed the interviewer, landed the job, and prepared to leave New York for some fresh air — with a suitcase full of snazzy new clothes. Me, a lifeguard, with dark shades and tracks. I headed upstate in a Greyhound bus, and checked in, got shown around. I always did like looking at blue water and pretty waitresses.

I spent the orientation week thinking a little about canoes and boats and water skis, none of which I knew how to handle, and avoiding direct confrontation with reality. Stoned out of my mind one day I stepped into a canoe and rolled it over in front of fifty guests. That was ridiculous, but my next move was a disaster. A young teacher asked me to teach him to water ski — and I agreed. He got on the skis, I got in the boat — sky high on doriden — and took off. But I had never steered a boat and couldn't have steered anything in that state, anyway. The angle at which I slapped the poor guy against a low-lying tree snapped his leg.

His wife was screaming bloody murder all over as some people came down and pulled him out of the water, while I headed the boat back to the dock and cut the engine. I figured to bluff my way out of this one. I screamed, "What the hell happened? I told you to let go. Don't you know how to listen at all?" The guy kept moaning as someone left saying, "I'll call a doctor and an ambulance." At the same time, the owner of the resort, Katzef, who had obviously heard about my canoe caper, got wind of the crash down at the edge of the water. He came huffing along as fast as he could.

Katzef almost fainted with the sight of the blood and the bones sticking out of the man on the ground. Luckily for him, the ambulance arrived and took his attention away from the wound. The crew did some first aid, then took the guy away for emergency treatment. Katzef took me aside for some private questioning. "Vinny, how on earth could this possibly happen?"

I looked at him as straight as I could. "By God in heaven, I swear that the guy didn't know what the hell he was doing on skis."

He looked down, then directly at me. "I thought you were teaching him to ski. Vinny, how long have you been water skiing, may I ask?"

I never hesitated. "For years, Mr. Katzef."

He didn't hesitate either. "Well then, Vinny, you wouldn't mind giving me a demonstration?"

There was no way out, so I came back with, "No, not at all.

Who's going to drive the boat?" My heart sank down to my ankles, and the drugs were past giving me any assistance.

I took off my cabana jacket and hung it on the ski rack. I closed my eyes, hoping for a miracle, but none came as I waded in knee deep with the skis and splashed around getting them on. A smart-ass waiter who had poked fun at my canoe turnover gunned her twice and the roar hit me as a warning, but I couldn't back out. I tucked my knees up under my chin and yelled, "Yo!" The curtain was up on my act. I shot straight up out of the water about two feet and straight back down, head first. The boat dragged me about fifty or sixty yards before I let go of the bar and went under. When I surfaced again, I knew it was all over. Half of the staff and more than two hundred guests were watching with a giggle from the shore.

Old Mr. Katzef was looking, too, shaking his head. As I dragged my amateur act out of the water, Katzef approached with my formal walking papers. "We won't be needing your 'services' any longer, Vinny. Please pick up your pay envelope and be off the premises before ten o'clock tonight." Feeling all washed up, I walked weak-kneed to my room and ate three more doridens to even things out while I packed — after less than a week on the job.

Once the bus pulled away from the little mountain town, I started coming down hard as the full weight of the day's disasters landed in my head. I thought, "How could you be such a fuck-up?" That wasn't enough, so it went on. "A peach job and you blow it, asshole." Conscience was riding me hard and finished with, "What the hell do you expect to get out of being back in the streets?" In a desperate attempt to avoid that kind of inner conflict, I put my arm under my head and leaned against the bus window, trying to sleep for the rest of the ride.

I WAS DOWN AT THE BOTTOM, and there was no light coming in under the door. This stretch of my life, before I made my first real stab at recovery, was what I think of as dirty. You know, when you're a kid you have some kind of future no matter what — you're on your way somewhere, pulling shenanigans for now, but planning to be a big guy someday, somehow. But over the years you lose that bit of brightness, that phony hope. You're an adult now — sort of — and not very cute anymore. Not smart enough; nothing you do succeeds. You sink and no one wants to help you any more; you can see in their eyes they no longer trust you. You're not able to raise that smile on their faces. And you're wearing your life on your face more — it shows, like sickness, even through the façade of slick dresser that I cultivated. It shows in the mirror, too.

My mom got my godfather Uncle Bobby to talk with me, and he agreed. He also gave me $200, which got me a fix fifteen minutes after I thanked him and took off. With the rest I rented a rathole of a room on Forty-second Street in Manhattan.

Hooks and I scrambled around to put a new scam together, to feed our habits. Too many junkies had copied the meat-stealing routine and the church rectory thefts for us to use those tricks any more. People wise up and lock down, so you have to get creative. The new scam was paying a guy in the post office to get us credit cards that were being sent to people, with no signatures on them yet. I had all the cashmere coats I wanted, plus every once in a while I'd charge a case of whiskey and sell it cheap to the winos down in the Bowery. We weren't greedy at first — we'd ring up $500 to $1000 and then dump the card. But then I got to thinking about jewelry, and a clerk made a behind-the-counter telephone call that brought the cops running and sent me back to the Tombs. It dawned on me that I'd broken parole, so no bail was allowed. I was going to sit my cold turkey out in the can.

A group of us got ushered into an elevator, headed for the "cattle floor," where they put dope fiends when they got arrested. As the doors slid open, I could not believe what I saw and heard. My stomach crawled with the human misery all around. It was God-awful, and I was so scared I couldn't move. I tried to back up into the elevator, but the hack pushed me out with the butt of his stick. There must have been two hundred men on that floor, about 90 percent of them kicking habits. Guys were bent over in pain, others were yelling, crying for help or their mothers. The place smelled like a sewer, and it didn't matter whether a man threw up on the floor, urinated in his pants, or whatever, it stayed right there. The hacks didn't even seem to notice, and they were not about to do anything to help. I got sick to my stomach because I knew that in just a few hours I would be right in there with them, kicking cold turkey.

On the way to my cell, I saw a huge rat walk down the corridor as if he were the warden. Once inside, I looked around for more vermin. The dirt on the floor must have been there for years, and cockroaches as big as your index finger were running everywhere. When you slammed one, they all stopped as if to mark the memory of Cousin Bill the Roach, but not for very long. I also found lice in the blankets, but no one was interested in my discoveries. I was so dejected I sat down on the steel bunk and ripped my silk shirt wide open, popping the buttons.

Then the pain came, and it stayed. I was doubled up on the cold steel for hours, then down on the floor with all my animal friends. They didn't care and I didn't care. How could anyone care when you were freezing with pain, and at the same time it was too hot for blankets? I dragged myself up off the floor and slumped over the white porcelain commode, looking down at the water. I felt this strange urge to sneeze and vomit at the same time, and then it happened. The spasms caused me to throw up violently for at least two hours. It seemed like eternity before my gut relaxed.

At suppertime, they shoved a tray of mush under my cell door, with plain white bread and black coffee on the side. I pushed it back out in the corridor, figuring to let the rats eat the shit since I couldn't bear to look at it. Within minutes the roaches had found the dish. They were crawling all over the food, and four of them drowned in the coffee. The sight made me vomit uncontrollably for the next half hour. Then I started pacing in circles around the cell, holding my gut and squeezing hard, trying to get rid of this horrible monkey kicking the shit out of me.

Suddenly, this character in the next cell started shouting, "Get me outa here! I can't stand it, I'm dying! God, somebody help me!" A hack yelled for him to shut up. The guy was screaming and moaning. It was taking my mind off the pain of my body, so I just listened. The guy picked up his plate and banged the bars of the cell with it. The hack had heard enough, so he came over to the cage and warned the junkie, "Shut the fuck up or I'm gonna tap your head with this," and he cracked a row of bars with his billy stick.

I figured this must have been the jerk's first pinch or he's not from New York, because he told the hack, "Fuck you and your tap dances, I'm dying!" The hack's eyes lit up with a mean streak you could actually see, and he shoved the stick through the bars into my neighbor's gut, knocking the air out of his system and landing him on the cell floor. The guy shut up.

Later that night, he started talking to me. "Hey. You over there." I asked if he meant me since we couldn't see each other with the steel partition between us. I didn't want to cause any more trouble than I already had on my hands, but whispered, "Yeah, what?"

He paused for a moment and then said, "Aw, nothin'! I'm gonna hang up now."

I said, "Yeah, right." Five minutes later I heard his throat gurgle for a split second and then the sound of a rhythmic thump thump thump against the bars of his cell.

I figured, "This fucking maniac is for real!" and called out loud, "Officer! Hang up!" The hack who responded was bent out of shape with having to walk fifteen feet probably for nothing. "Yeah, where the hell is it?" he said as he approached, slapping the club into his palm. His face went white as a sheet when he saw the guy next door hanging by his neck, dead. I turned away and didn't look when they brought a sheet and a stretcher to cart him off to the morgue. Within an hour, they brought another junkie up to fill the dead man's space, and it was as if nothing had gone down.

I was charged with attempted grand larceny and remanded into custody without bail until the trial, set for three weeks later. I told the lawyer to get in touch with Goodman, my parole officer, and tell him I was in. Goodman suggested that we might get a reduced sentence if I would voluntarily commit myself for treatment at a federal facility in Lexington, Kentucky. Hooks had been there once, so I sent word to have Hooks come tell me about the place.

When Hooks finally showed up, I was surprised that they didn't arrest him on the spot. Jesus, he looked awful. His face was sunken and shallow, his weight was down to maybe 110 pounds, and his nails were bitten to the knuckles. Hooks told me a very interesting piece of information. Even though Lexington was a federal penitentiary, when an addict came in on a voluntary basis, all you needed to get out was to give forty-eight hours notice, and they opened the gates.

The next morning I went to Lexington, and two days after I checked in I put in a request to get out because I felt like getting high. After all, the parole board had said nothing about how long I had to stay in Lexington; they just said I had to go there. At the end of the fourth day, I checked out and got on a bus back to New York.

A week after my return, I set out to find Hooks. His folks proudly told me he had voluntarily checked into Riverside for detoxification. Two days later, Hooks showed up at my room, soaking wet and panting harshly. When I asked him what the hell was going on, he told me he had just made it off North Brother's Island by swimming. I told him that he had to be full of shit or high as hell, which he denied. He stuck to his story of swimming away. The next day his version was confirmed by the newspapers with a third-page story. "Man swims from Riverside Hospital on North Brother's Island — Fate Unknown."

I was amazed that Hooks had made it, looking as bad as he did. His eyes were sunk so far back in his head I didn't know how he managed to see anything clearly. Neither one of us was seeing any-thing clearly. We were thieves and con artists being ridden by our drug habits. I was 23 years old and beginning to run out of tricks.

Sometimes when you are down far enough, you can learn les-sons that otherwise you might have missed. I was flashy and quick, and as long as I was still up, it was hard for me to learn self-discipline. But that's a lesson you have to learn to grow up.

One day I was busted again, and dumped back in the Tombs to fry. That night in the Tombs taught me something new about self-discipline and willpower. At first I felt the guy lying right above me might be dangerous, and couldn't take my eyes off him. It helped to imagine myself as a hack or his shrink, sitting there with him as my patient. Then I thought how I might be his father or his brother, just watching to see that the pain didn't get out of hand. My cellmate started heaving, and I knew in an instant he'd be toss-ing his cookies, but I didn't want the mess or the smell, so I told him straight, "Make the crapper, man!" He got louder with the moaning, so I said it again. "Yo! Make the crapper, not on the floor!"

He slid down off the top bunk and went on all fours to the crap-per in the corner, where he draped his arms over the sides with his head partways down in the bowl. He retched for over an hour, and all the sounds were magnified by the flushing bowl. At one point I felt like telling him to "Move over!" so both of us could hang in there. I hung my head in my hands and thought it must be like this down in hell itself.

As morning came on, it struck me that a whole night had passed but I hadn't lost it like I thought I would. I had gone through some horrible physical pain, mainly in my stomach, plus chills, hot flashes, dry heaves, and spasms, but I found that I could ride most of it out mentally and leave a lot of the drama behind. I saw right then that most times in the past I had put on the physi-cal act to make a point, especially if it could do me some good, like in a hospital where you could get methadone or some other drug.

But the Tombs didn't carry methadone; all they had was hacks with big sticks. I was better off concentrating on my cellmate, neglecting my own situation as much as possible. To my amazement, it worked. Later, when I was on my way to recovery, that lesson was repeated: If you can focus on someone besides yourself, you've got a lot better chance at success. Growing up requires a lot of focusing on other people, seeing their struggles, and even helping out.

Synanon

I N 1964, I WAS CLOSE TO 24 years old and had used heroin full or part-time for more than ten years. I was feeling the toll. Most days dragged on in a round of blurry stupors. A security guard slammed me up side the head with his stick, and when the blood and swelling cleared I had 20/200 vision. Now I had a black patch over my eye, which made me look suspicious right from the start. Whatever novelty the lifestyle had at one time died a nasty death and went straight to hell. My sense of humor was buried in junk, and it took a lot of stealing to support the dead-end swindle of my daily habit. Whenever anything happened, the local cops would come looking for me.

Most times they found me high as a kite, standing on a corner or sitting on a stoop, which made me an easy target. I was always good for a couple of free cracks across the face. Then there was always the option of handcuffing me and hauling me off to the station for ten or twelve hours in their bull pen. I was getting sicker and more tired of the doped-up routine every minute, especially since I couldn't see any end to it.

I could only see one thing clearly — eventually I would do a life sentence behind bars, only on the installment plan. The gut realization hit me hard — I wanted to give up drugs, but my habit had me wired. It seemed I had no choice if I wanted to keep on living. The only solid thing I could think of was to get the hell out of the neighborhood for a while, if only to avoid hassles with the heat. So

I drifted to Manhattan and located a hole with four walls at a cheap hotel on the West Side.

In a dense fog one day while I was loaded, I thought of pulling a quick caper, just like in any other neighborhood. I called Hooks and asked him to meet me on Broadway and Seventy-second Street. He drove up about an hour later in a borrowed car, and we went uptown. I had him stop at an A&P, and I got out of the car and walked in. I grabbed an empty toilet paper box, filled it with about 20 cartons of cigarettes, and walked right out to the street with it. No less than six people saw me, including the manager. Somebody even wrote down our license plate number before we took off. Less than a mile away, two squad cars boxed us in, so we gave up. I copped to taking the cigarettes and said Hooks wasn't in on it.

They let Hooks go on the spot and took me to the police station. I was booked and later released on $1,500 bail after spending one night in the tank sick as a dog. Within a week I tried to make the same move with cigarettes and got nabbed in the process. That bail was set at $2,500, and once again my bondsman Tony was there. Within three more days, I robbed four churches and paid him off.

My mother was talking to everyone she knew about me and what they could do, "anything to help my son Vinny." In desperation, she remembered an old neighborhood friend of mine named Mark Varrichio, who was now an up-and-coming lawyer with a downtown office. Momma arranged for a meeting.

Mark asked questions instead of having all the answers, and I liked him for that straightaway. He didn't lecture me on the past, but he was intent when it came to focusing on the future, which was something I could listen to for a change. My past was full of shit, as far as I was concerned. Show me the way out, was what I wanted. Mark agreed to handle the latest two busts.

When the first case came up three weeks later, Mark was at my side, armed with his briefcase and dressed up in a Brooks Brothers suit. After the formalities, Mark sent me into shock as he started to talk.

"Your Honor, my client is not really a thief, in that he comes from a very decent family in this city, and he really wants to become a responsible citizen, but he is sick. He is a drug addict. We admit that, and we also admit to the horror of a human being caught in this position. This man has seriously tried to detoxify, Your Honor, at several facilities. None of them has worked, but Mr. Marino is not willing to give up yet.

"We have learned of a new rehabilitation center called Synanon, which was started in California and has a very high success record. My client wants to go there and commit himself to their program, and frankly, Your Honor, it is my professional opinion that the City of New York will be infinitely better off if we get this man off the streets and into the hands of an organization that can truly help him find the way. This Synanon program, I should mention, is one that lasts a lifetime, and so if it does work for my client, it is undoubtedly the best solution we can offer the court at this time."

A *lifetime?* I was stunned.

The judged looked down and asked, "Mr. Marino, are you serious about this?"

I said, "Yes, Your Honor," and looked up at him with my one good eye.

"Very well, then, Mr. Marino, if you do get into Synanon, I will suspend sentence."

As I walked out of the courtroom, once again a free man, I had no intention of doing anything except shooting off to Harlem and scoring. But my mother was there, and Mark was hanging on my right arm from the time we left the bench. The two of them damn near forced me into a nearby restaurant, where we got a booth. Mark proceeded to pick me apart relentlessly. He talked about my past and drew the inevitable conclusion that I would die soon if I continued my lifestyle. Well, that was clear to anyone — even, dimly, to me. Then he went on to say that Synanon was the only real alternative to prison and that was why he had come up with the idea. I was so run down I could only nod.

Momma made a passionate plea. "Vinny, my son, I don't know how or why you got into this, but please, for me, do this and get out." So I said, "Okay, I'll go."

I was thinking at the time that I could kick the junk cold, but I didn't know what to do with the doriden habit. I had already had three convulsions — I never knew those pills could be so dangerous. Maybe Synanon could work.

Mark gave me a last piece of positive reassurance. "Look, Vinny. They say a lifetime, but just go in and get yourself straightened out, stay a year, maybe two. Then if you choose, come out and lead a normal life."

Again, the easiest way with all that pressure was to agree. Momma insisted that I accompany her and spend the night at her apartment. I agreed but first went to my place to pick up a change of clothes, some junk and the works, and a few dolophines and doridens. After we got home, Momma fixed me some spaghetti and meatballs. Later, she laid out a pillow and blankets on the couch, and I went into the bathroom, got off, then crashed for the night.

At ten minutes to nine the next morning, Momma was shaking me awake. She brought me a glass of fresh orange juice, which I used to wash down a couple doridens and dolophines when she left the room. I could smell the good food as I brushed my teeth and shaved. When I came out of the bathroom, Mark was there eating breakfast, and obviously enjoying it tremendously. I didn't know what the hell was going on. After we enjoyed Mom's cooking, Mark asked me if I had what I needed packed up and ready to go.

I was caught short and asked, "Where are we going?"

"To Synanon, like we said to the judge," he came back.

We went back to my place to pack a suitcase full of my belongings. Then the three of us sped down the West Side Highway and onto the Connecticut Freeway. We were heading for Westport, a community of white-collar commuters. In less than two hours, we pulled up in front of a huge three-story old Colonial house on the outskirts of Westport. Mark said, "Let's go in," as my heart sank to my knees. I made a quick move and swallowed the last three dolphines I had.

A guy named Ted Brown and his wife, May, were in charge of that particular place, and the minute I laid eyes on them I knew they were good people. Brown was simple yet firm with everything he said, and I liked him right off. He invited me to come into his office alone and started in with very direct questions. "How long have you been using drugs?"

"Ten years, give or take," I told him.

"Why do you want into Synanon?"

"I have no place else to go, and I need help."

He tried to push my buttons as he replied, "You don't know what the word means, Marino. You say you need 'help,' and I say go to a fucking employment agency. This is our *home,* and here you come barging in like a wise-ass kid holding your mommy's hand with your lawyer on the other side. You're a baby, Marino, an asshole, and you're not worth a shit."

Well, Brown had me dead to right. I said humbly, "Look, I've tried everything, and I know I need help."

Brown was not kind as he came back with, "Bullshit, Marino, you haven't 'tried' anything. All I see is a loser on the run, calling himself a big man, sticking needles in his arm, and stealing anything he can find to keep his habit flowing."

I knew deep down that no way was I going to be able to bullshit these people. I settled into the conversation, and Brown went on to tell me the "ground rules" at Synanon — no drugs or alcohol, no negative talk, no violent behavior, no sex, no coming or going without permission, and no discussions of the highs or the lows associated with past drug trips.

I nodded my head in agreement. What subjects could possibly come up once all the above have been eliminated? Maybe I'd just clam up.

Momma smiled and took my hand when Brown said, "We think Vinny can help himself here at Synanon, Mrs. Marino, and we have accepted him." A wave of relief swept over my body, but still I wasn't feeling good, and it was getting worse by the minute. Brown sensed something. "By the way, aside from heroin do you use any stumblebuttons, idiot pills?"

I decided if I was going into Synanon, I might as well be honest, so I said, "Dolophines and doridens."

Brown shook his head. "Oops, around here we have people kick cold turkey right on that couch, but we do not mess with barbiturates or hypnotics. You could have a convulsion. You're going to have to go into a hospital first and clean up that pill habit."

Momma asked, "Isn't there a hospital nearby that can help him?"

Brown put a call through to Fairmont Sanitarium, where we hit a jackpot. They could take me right away, and I was eligible for federal rehabilitation money. That saved $1,200 a month, which we didn't have anyway.

On the way I was getting dizzy and beginning to feel like hell. A nurse showed me to my room and as soon as I entered, I had a violent convulsion. My body cracked in a giant uncontrollable spasm, and then I blacked out.

I woke up enough to see where I was again three days later. Tubes were in just about every pore of my body, and bottles were hanging overhead. A pleasant middle-aged nurse was the first person I recall. Mrs. Beatty's job was to keep all the tubes open and my juices flowing.

When she thought I was well enough to absorb some solid information, she told me how lucky I was getting to the hospital when I did. If I had had the convulsion at Synanon, I would probably be dead or else a vegetable. I was choking on my tongue, and it took more than nine hours of constant treatment before I was out of intensive care. Most of the staff had never seen a convulsion that severe, and it had everybody around talking for days.

Around the fourth day there, I was getting the sense that something they were giving me was just like the high of junk or doridens. I asked Mrs. Beatty about it. She picked up my chart and said, "You're getting methadone and doriden on a daily basis." Then she looked up, "I would guess they can't let you go off all at once, not with the condition your body is in."

When I was all dried out, the director called Brown and said I was ready. Two residents came over to pick me up on a bright Monday morning in May of 1964.

As the car pulled up in front of the Synanon residence, I saw the hugeness of the place. These people were living in a mansion. The huge living room had a fireplace with a marble mantel. The dining room was decorated with a formal chandelier that had about a thousand pieces of cut crystal. I thought, "The Duke of Synanon must eat in here," as my guide led me through the dining room and out into the kitchen, where there was space for more food than an army could eat in a year. Two huge refrigerator-freezer combinations stood against one wall, and two ten-gallon coffee urns brewed on a counter next to the chillboxes.

They took me upstairs to the sleeping area, which was made up mainly of large and small bedrooms. "These are the male dormitories, and the other side of the house is where the females sleep." There were single beds and bunkbeds. My guide, Tommy, pointed to a top bunk and said, "You can call this home."

Then he told me a little of Synanon's history while we passed by the single rooms occupied by staff. "A guy named Chuck Dederich started the organization in Santa Monica, California. Now we have houses in San Francisco, Oakland, Tomales Bay in Marin County, Reno, New York, Detroit, and, of course, this one here in Westport." I asked him if the different houses worked together in any way. He told me the units were all self-sufficient, but residents might be reassigned to different locations at times for different reasons, like when individual talents were needed. This provided a change of scenery and experience.

Tommy told me I had half an hour to clean up before meeting everyone in the living room. I showered and then lay down on my bunk, when it occurred to me that my suitcase wasn't around. As

I walked into the main room, twenty-five minutes later, about fifty people were sitting around the room. Most were smoking cigarettes, and they all seemed glad to see me. They had heard about the trauma I had gone through at the sanitarium, and they were happy I had made it. Each one stood up and said who he or she was, but I only remembered three or four names at first. Then I remembered that these people could only speak in positive words, so no wonder they were all smiles and handshakes.

Next I saw my suitcase in the middle of the room. Tommy told me again about the cardinal rules, and that the penalty if the staff chose to excommunicate you was instant exile from the program. He explained about "my" clothes and said, "We don't have 'personal' possessions in Synanon since everything is community property. You can use all those fancy colognes along with everyone else in the male bathrooms, Vinny, but forget about the clothes."

My heart sank. I must have laid out a thousand dollars worth of the best threads available in New York, and the thought of losing everything hit me hard. I wanted to ask for my favorite cashmere sweater but kept quiet and figured maybe I'd be able to buy it back later when I saw someone wearing it. Tommy told me I could draw clothing from the free community store.

The next step was "Please come up to the attic with us for your formal initiation."

"Uh-oh," I thought, but halfway up the stairwell I remembered one of the ground rules was no violence. That calmed me down somewhat. The attic was empty except for one solid old oak chair, sitting smack in the middle. Tommy invited me to have a seat.

"We want your wig." With that, a guy named Eddie plugged a cord into an outlet and turned on the barber clippers he had in his hand. I got a military crewcut in less than five minutes and was then unceremoniously handed a broom and dustpan with the instructions "Clean up your mess."

The first couple of days were real tough. I got fed up with the positive bullshit all the time, since there was next to nothing positive about me, and I knew it. Almost everything I said brought the same response: "We don't do that here." I would meet a guy from the Bronx, shake his hand and say, "Hey, I used to cop in the Bronx," and two people would shoot in with "We don't say that here." My whole past life was out of bounds from Synanon conversations, and I felt like an orphan. But there was a point to it, I soon saw. It cut off the hooks to your past, and although that withdrawal was painful, it was necessary to destroy the cues to drug use.

The night after I arrived I was busy doing my after-supper duties as dishwasher and general cleaner-upper for fifty-two people when Tommy walked through the entire house shouting, "General meeting at seven o'clock." I looked at my wet, soapy hands and thought, "Now what? I was planning to watch TV," but I went upstairs to shower and change clothes before the meeting started.

Everyone showed up a few minutes before seven in the living room, and I noticed right away that no one was talking, as if something serious was about to happen. Ted Brown stood up to announce each person's room assignment for an "encounter group." I wondered what the hell an encounter group was as I followed fifteen people into a room. Inside, all the chairs were in a circle. I sat down in the only seat left and looked around silently, waiting. What was next?

Well, no way could I believe the words I heard. The rule was that "anyone could say anything at anytime," but I wasn't used to that kind of talk, not coming from the streets of New York. If that kind of thing came down on me out there, I would have had to break the person's jaw. You simply did not talk to anyone like that without asking for trouble. In the group, people were verbally tearing each other up like dogs on the street, and I didn't get it. It was scary, the way someone would attack a person verbally, along with everything that person seemed to stand for.

After an hour or so of watching this abuse being thrown around, I started to get the message. Aha! The game was beating people up with accusations and putting them down with nothing more in mind than having them take a careful look at what was said. A person could say anything, and it didn't matter as long as you listened to it and didn't get violent. Then I noticed that most people looked no different after their turn in the hot seat, so I got more used to the idea. But I had no history in the place yet, and no one was ripping at Marino during that first encounter session. Under it all, I began to see a dimension that was totally missing from the streets — some kind of genuine caring. The comments were all made to help.

One guy named Reed announced his intention of leaving Synanon the next morning. Absolutely no one could come or go without permission. It was a lifetime bit, so if Reed did leave the next day, he was out.

The founder of Synanon emphasized how we were to view the place: "Synanon is an island of sanity and the world is an ocean of insanity. If you step off this island of sanity, you die." It was obvious the others cared about what was going to happen to this guy out there. I didn't have much to say during that first encounter session, but I sure was listening hard. It was a good feeling when I got the idea people there still cared about another human being. I remembered being in various hospital detox wards when someone would say, "I want to leave," and the official response was more or less, "Yeah, go ahead."

I warmed up to the idea of caring for other people, and I found I liked most of the residents. Then I started to like the place itself and the lifestyle. It wasn't long before my sense of humor was back in full swing.

I started to believe deep down that this place could work. What I didn't realize at the time was that I was on what they called a "honeymoon," which was somewhat easier treatment granted to the newcomers. I guess they knew that heavy pressure on someone just off the streets might cause a person to bolt out the door.

Once after I had been there two weeks, the entire house went on an outing, down by a very beautiful lake nearby. After we got out of the vehicles and started strolling around at the water's edge, I noticed a Synanon guy dressed in funny clothes, sporting a shaved head, who was doing all the work. Since I was already on the service crew at the facility, I figured to give the poor guy a hand. But Tommy told me, "He's considered spare parts, leave him alone." I guessed that he was more or less serving their equivalent of time in the bing. Then I learned later that he was on what they called a "contract" and would have to do anything he was told to do from 6 in the morning until around midnight. It was a punishment with a purpose: People who break rules without suffering some kind of consequences don't learn. It's true for training dogs and raising kids, too. You grow up when your actions have consequences.

Inside the facility, they made a special point of breaking up the day to avoid boredom. First was breakfast, after which we would go back to the dorm and clean up. That was followed by the morning meeting where they talked about the schedule for the day, people who might be up for transfer (or, as they called it, rotation) to another facility on the West Coast. Then we would do something like sing songs, tell jokes, or do skits. One of my favorite activities at those morning sessions was the "liar's contest." You would have to tell a total lie, and the winner was the most believable person. Before lunch, my duties as part of the service crew were to do the dishes, sweep, mop, and clean the shitters.

Lunch was around noon, and then a seminar was held. Sometimes we had guest speakers from the local community, or one of the directors would simply throw a subject open for discussion, such as euthanasia, abortion, or the ideas of famous people — anything so long as it wasn't drugs. After dinner on Monday, Wednesday, and Friday evenings we had encounter groups, or "games" as they were called. On off nights we usually had some kind of special event. On Saturday nights we hosted an open house for the folks from Westport and surrounding communities.

Sandwiches and coffee were served, and one or two residents would relate their horrendous past history and then speak brightly about the future as a result of entering Synanon. The guests, or "squares" as they were referred to, were generally impressed with the turnarounds. The term *square* was used for nonresidents, but it was not meant in a derogatory way.

Of course, at times I had second and third thoughts about the whole trip. In addition to "no drugs," they also told us "you will never have a drink again in your lives." I remember thinking "Am I ready for this?" I wondered if anyone there ever got loaded on the side. I wondered if I could commit myself to Synanon for a lifetime.

Most of the trouble in my head at that time, however, came from the no-sex rule. I was more than just a little horny, particularly since I had recently kicked. That was fairly normal after withdrawal because so many sexual feelings were repressed when you were on drugs.

The same was true of eating. On the tenth or eleventh day of a dry-out period, a junkie usually gets what we called "the chucks," which means you feel like eating everything in sight. During that time you take your ribs out of hock and make up for all the skipped meals.

Women were on my mind, too. I met a beautiful black woman from Manhattan named Barbara. We had coffee together, and soon she asked me if I wanted to get into a trap with her.

I asked an older guy named Manny, "How long do you have to be around to get a trap?"

"To be eligible for a trap," he began, "you have to be around for about a year, and so would the female. Then, if you've got eyes for someone and she's got eyes for you, you go to the male director and ask for permission to get hooked up. She goes to the female director and asks her permission. Then the directors get together and weigh up your progress. If they think it would be healthy for each of you, they give you what is called a courtship. That means you're recognized as having a relationship but no sex yet — no petting, no touching, but you would be allowed a respectable kiss when you walk her to the girls' dorm at night. This courtship goes on for about a month.

"During that time, you'll go out with older traps to movies and such. Then if both your attitudes are okay after a month, you'll be given a trap. That means you get to go to what is called the guest room. In the beginning it's once a week for four hours. Then it goes to twice a week, then it goes to twice a week overnight. Of course, prior to giving you the trap, a female would have to go to family planning for some form of contraception.

"To tell you the truth, Vinny, you're really wasting a lot of psychic energy worrying about things that will happen naturally down the road. Why don't you put more emphasis on doing what we do here? That would be a lot more important."

"Okay, Manny," I said and thanked him. What a nice guy he was.

JUST AFTER MY FIRST MONTH Ted told six of us we were being rotated to the San Francisco facility called Seawall. He showed us six one-way plane tickets, nonnegotiable. The flight was scheduled for the next morning. Barbara was one of the six. I was elated.

Ted said, "Okay, we're going to ask you to raise your right hand to swear allegiance to Synanon before you make the trip."

I thought it was bullshit, but said the words anyway: "I swear to abide by Synanon's rules. I have no intention of leaving and no intention of using drugs or alcohol ever again." Ted then appointed me as the leader. He knew I was the craziest guy in the place, so he probably figured if I was the leader, I'd keep myself in check.

But when we got to San Francisco, the director needed a guy who had done time in prison, to help with cons at the Nevada State Prison in Reno. Me. I'm thinking, "Where the hell is Reno, in the desert?"

Reno Clean

FIRST LIGHT THE NEXT DAY, I got out of bed and packed my bag again. After breakfast, I got into a van with some others going to Reno. As we pulled away from Synanon San Francisco, the driver announced "We'll be stopping at the Tomales Bay facility in Marin County before we head out for Reno. Our founder, Chuck Dederich, and his wife, Betty, are there now, so you'll have a chance to meet them."

Right then we started to cross the Golden Gate Bridge, and the panoramic view hit my insides with a wide open feeling of wonder. The driver turned off the freeway to swing by Muir Woods, beautiful old redwood trees standing tall. I said to myself, "Look at you, Marino. Seeing the sights, having a good time, and no drugs."

We turned in the driveway to a huge estate and we headed up a circular driveway to what looked like a grand old southern plantation house, except that it was painted powder-blue and was faded and peeling. A hundred people or more were at work on painting, construction, cement, and yard work. I wasn't anxious to get into that kind of labor.

As the van stopped and we got off, the driver said, "That's Chuck Dederich." I decided, "What the hell," and walked over. I said, "You know, this is a very nice place, and I'm glad I came to Synanon for help."

He pointed his finger at my face. "We *know* it's nice, but I'll tell you the trick to Synanon. The trick is to *stay* here. It'll be a hard life until you get the hang of it, but then it's heaven." Then Dederich turned and walked away toward the Pacific with his wife. The Roman Catholics never told me God was married.

ANOTHER BEAUTIFUL MORNING brought the van around again, and four of us boarded it and headed for Reno. After five or six hours of incredible scenery, we came to Donner Pass and an hour down from the peak, we could see the city of Reno. As we drove in, the town seemed small. Another twenty minutes past the downtown area, the main house looked a lot like Synanon Westport, with a cottage-type building off to the right. Maybe a couple of acres of grounds.

As we entered the front door, the driver was telling me, "Only sixteen people are in residence here. Private and peaceful." In the kitchen we ran into the directors, a married couple named Clapp. He shook my hand, saying, "I'm Dick. Welcome to Reno."

In no time dinner was on the table. That first meal consisted of thick porterhouse steak, a baked potato, and fresh green salad, plus all the corn-on-the-cob I cared to eat. Later I discovered that the hotels and casinos threw almost everything away after a day or two if they hadn't used it. Clapp arranged for the Synanon truck to pick up their "trash" before it hit the can.

I was given a formal assignment to the kitchen crew, which I figured would be a good move, being next to all that good food. I swept and then mopped up the floor in the kitchen, set the tables for meals, happily bused the dishes and washed them up, took out the trash and performed the other peon jobs required from time to time.

Within thirty days at Reno, I was gaining weight and looking good, even to myself in the mirror. It had been three months since I stopped wearing the black patch. But I was bored in the kitchen. I looked around, concluding that the easiest way out of my boredom was to step up and cook. Until then my experience with cooking was limited to what I had seen over Mom's or Grandma's shoulders. But I was determined and started to spend evenings after group meetings reading all the recipes in the cookbooks and watching in the kitchen.

One night I got a shot at some practice when the whole house returned from an outing. I volunteered, "How about some egg sandwiches?" A chick named Shelley said, "Why don't you make them for us, Vinny?" I jumped out of my chair and headed for the fridge. Now egg sandwiches take no Harvard graduate, for sure, but I added some spice on the sly, and several people commented, "I didn't know you knew how to cook!"

I was delighted. I started making special gravies and then the pastas — macaroni, spaghetti, lasagna. I played with spices and finally became damn near a master at improvisation. I was enjoying myself, impressed that I could be there, have fun, feel good, and get high *without* drugs. Three months earlier, this scene would have seemed impossible to me.

But after a couple of months, the cooking routine began to get boring, too. I wanted an assignment to the prison project, just to break up my day and get out of the house. I told Clapp I was interested in getting into the prison project, "anywhere you see fit." He started out by giving me a tour of the honor farm, the minimum security, and the place they called "the Cave," for maximum-security inmates.

I got a weird feeling the first time we went into the Cave. Not all the inmates were involved with Synanon — most thought we were a bunch of stool pigeons or worse. To get to where we had to go, we walked through a long yard with a chainlink fence. The convicts would catcall and chirp as we walked by, and crowd up against the fence. I felt real fear, thinking, "If these guys catch me in the wrong place, there's no telling what they might do."

Soon Clapp was making me his regular companion on prison trips, where I would attend the encounter sessions with the cons. Almost none of the cons in the Cave trusted me at all when they found out I had only been at Synanon a few months. Most were old-timers, doing long bits for manslaughter or murder, assault, armed robbery — heavy stuff, not the two-bit things I had been doing back in New York. They would say, "How can you sit there and tell me what to do, when I don't even know you're gonna make it?" I would answer, "I'm not here for you to find out whether I'm going to make it. I'm only giving you the same information Synanon has given me, and it might just pay you to listen."

Before another month had passed, Clapp let me facilitate my own groups. At first, that only made the old-timers push me harder. I would say, "Look, you can beat me up all day, I don't care. But when the day's over, I get up and leave here. You go back to your cell. So the question is, what's going to help *you* get the hell out of here and stay out of places like this?" Before long I proved myself, and I enjoyed the work.

Of all three prison facilities, the honor farm drew most of my attention. Inmates got there from other prisons based on their good behavior. The farm had no locks, and they were pretty much free to move around. The cons lived in mobile homes converted into dormitories, and they did some farming, woodworking, metal work, and construction, and learned other useful trades. Most of the guys there were already interested in helping themselves, so my job was a whole lot easier than at the other two joints. Since most of them were due to be released, the honor-farm inmates were trying to learn as much as they could to stay out.

No one understood that motive better than Marino from New York, but when I sensed I wasn't coming across with them, I would call in Gary, who was from the Midwest and had been in Synanon three years. In the Midwest, they called drug addicts "hypes" (short for *hypodermic*). Gary had done some heavy things and drawn time in various joints, so the Nevada cons listened when he spoke.

As time went on, I again started to see signs of boredom creeping in through the cracks of my act. Almost all sixteen residents of the Reno house were from the Midwest, and I had some real trouble relating to them.

I thought about putting in for a rotation to San Francisco. Thinking of the neighborhood and the folks back home brought to mind letters I was getting. Momma wrote how proud she was. Frankie said he couldn't wait to see me, and Joey wrote, "Come home, Vinny." Even Pop sent me notes a couple of times. After these letters I would start to miss the streets and especially Hooks. I wondered how he was getting along, and whether he was still using or in the joint. I made a mental note to write him soon. One night a line from Pop about a situation in Brooklyn had me outside for a walk on the grounds under a full moon, thinking, "What about my family? Am I ready to take this separation for a lifetime?"

To counter my boredom and the cons from the Cave who were giving me shit, I took up acting. I got so good I could get a charade described in half a minute. Then we started to play mental gymnastics. You would be introduced to a subject just as you stood up: "Okay, Marino, talk about equal rights." The person speaking would assume either a pro or a con position on the subject assigned for the first half hour. At that point, a bell would ring, and you would have to switch your viewpoint and argue the opposite side for another half hour.

The whole point was believability, and the audience would critique your "act": "Your eye contact was good, but watch what you do with your hands." I learned a lot about myself, especially where I was stuck in some rigid thinking, like tunnel vision, which addicts are prone to. But I was also learning that the acting ability that had made me a good thief was useful elsewhere, in straight life. And it really was part of my personality, a good trait.

I also found some things in my head I didn't know were there. For one, because I hadn't finished school I had thought of myself as dumb. I developed real confidence in myself as I cleared some of these ideas out of the way. Finally, I realized how much I enjoy standing in front of a group, holding people's attention with what I'm saying.

As I passed my six-month mark at Reno, I felt pretty good about myself, especially that I was learning and growing. But I was still wondering seriously about my future in those Nevada mountains. I figured I needed a new challenge, so I started to spend my late evening hours reading. The collection of books wasn't all that extensive, but it was deep. At first I had trouble because I didn't know enough about words. To correct that, I got myself a dictionary and looked up the meanings whenever I was stumped. Then I came across a book titled *Six Weeks to Words of Power.* I was determined to master it, and I did.

The first book I read was *The Prince* by Machiavelli, and one of his ironic comments struck home: It's not important what you do, it's what people *think* you are capable of doing that creates the doubt, the fear, or whatever effect you may want. I tucked that information away and went on to read Emerson, Thoreau, and Sartre. Then I got into self-help psychology books. Sometimes I would fall asleep with a book in my lap and wake up suddenly, wondering if I had overdosed. I would look down, see the book, and laugh to myself.

As my vocabulary became more extensive, I started to use it on the people in the facility, sometimes to annoy them. I would say something like "Why do you consistently repudiate your humanity with arrogant and immature actions?" I was just having some fun, but the others got indignant. Invariably, I would get the shit kicked out of me verbally by everyone else in every encounter group.

Later one evening I stepped out on the front porch for some serious thinking. I had been at Synanon for almost a year. I felt good about the inmates who had responded to me and about everything I was learning. I felt best about being clean for that long. But another thought shot in: "Yeah, you're clean, but there's got to be more to life than just being clean. Lots of people are clean. What is your *purpose*?" I couldn't answer my self-imposed question and that bothered me.

I knew I didn't belong in those mountains. And was I ready to live on Synanon's maximum salary of $50 a month, *when* I was finally eligible, for the rest of my life?

I began to withdraw more and more. The people in the house were boring, and I was getting more into books. I came across a book called *Rules for Radicals* by Saul Alinsky. His message was that I could be doing the same shit I was doing here out on the streets, but for positive, genuine purposes. What I needed was something ethical to get behind with all my might. I liked Alinsky so much that I decided to read his other book, *Reveille for a Radical,* too.

Meanwhile, I still had to attend all the regular house functions and follow all the rules. One night I went into another encounter game with no particular interest in participating, since I was only about halfway through Alinsky's second book. Someone started to rap about being "a martyr" for the rest of us, like he was the only one paddling to keep the boat away from the reef. I unloaded on that unfortunate bastard with the most cynical, abusive verbal blast I had ever administered.

Right after the game was over, Ellie stopped me and called me into Dick's office. Inside I saw her husband Dick and Gary, my coordinator at the prison. Sure enough, all three of them landed on me to conduct a verbal "haircut." "Marino, you're a dummy in deep shit around here. Your attitude simply sucks. You've managed to turn off everyone in the house with your dictionary words and fancy phrases. You've isolated yourself, and you don't do what you're told.

"The only thing that seems to interest you is your work at the prison. In fact, you excel at running groups there. Because you like the prison project so much, we're taking it away from you. From tomorrow on, you're confined to the facility. As of right now you're in the dishpan!

"'The dishpan' means that where there's water, there's Marino. It starts after breakfast when you add water to the dishes and wash them. Then you put clean water in a bucket and mop the floor in the kitchen. Next you go straight upstairs and clean every shitter. After that, you come back and knock on my door, and we'll figure out where you go from there."

As I washed up, I wondered whether things could or should be patched up. They would probably hold me down from prison work for maybe two or three weeks, but if I was leaving, why wait? By the time I got to mopping floors, I thought, "Well, let's just sit on it for the time being and see what happens." I pressed through the rest of my duties in an hour, and reported back.

As soon as Ellie opened the door, I smelled trouble. "Marino, something's wrong with the cesspool. I called Rotorooter, but they can't be here until four o'clock this afternoon. Take a shovel and a bucket and go out and fix the problem." I walked to the kitchen pantry and grabbed an old five-gallon white plastic bucket, figuring I would at least go out in the yard and size up the problem. As I closed the back door, I got wind of a foul odor, but I held my nose and headed in the general direction. When I actually looked at the mess, I knew in a flash that this was it. Synanon could consider me gone.

That night at the general meeting after dinner, I walked in with a smile on my face and sat down. Clapp opened up, "Okay, Marino, what the fuck are you so happy about? You just lost your job, you're in the dishpan, and you're gonna stay as a spare part, cleaning up dog shit, cat shit, and cesspools until you straighten out your act. Now what is so goddamned funny?"

I grinned as I said, "Dick, I have finally made a decision."

He looked flustered. "What the hell does that mean?"

I smiled again. "It means that I've made up my mind."

"Does that mean you're going to leave?"

I smiled. I was thinking about packing in the morning. As I headed for bed, I saw the moon and wondered if it was shining on my old neighborhood. My mind ran through pictures of my family, thinking of all the things I had been missing for over a year.

I WAS UP BY 6:30, WHISTLING as I shaved. I sang to myself in the shower and did some calisthenics while drying off. I looked in the mirror and felt great as I ran a comb through my hair. Then I remembered the box of clothing my family had sent. I picked out a nifty shirt, a pair of beige gabardine slacks, and a $300 black leather jacket I had stolen from Bonwit Teller's a long time ago.

I packed the rest in my suitcase, and then I went to see Dick in his office. "Dick, I just want to tell you, because I think I owe you the courtesy, that Synanon is a nice organization, and the Reno facility is great, too. I like it here, and the organization has helped a lot of people. I myself have learned a lot of things, but now I have to go.

"Dick, I'm not angry with anyone. I just think a year is enough. I have the information now, and I have to go out and apply it, or life is just not going to work for me."

"We don't want you on the streets around here, Vinny," Dick said. "We're too visible already. So you can leave, but we will put you on a bus to San Francisco. Gary will drive you to the station and buy you a ticket."

Two hours later, I was sitting on a bus to San Francisco with my ticket all paid for. But who said I wanted to go? As we started down the street full of casinos and flashing lights, I thought, "Hey, this might be something to see." So I went to the front and signaled the driver at the first traffic light.

When he looked up, I acted totally anxious. "Jesus, I just remembered I left my wallet at home on Dickerson Drive. Can I have my ticket back, please? I'll have to catch a later bus." The driver looked at me dumbfounded, but he didn't argue or say a word, he just handed it over and opened the door. I jumped off the bus before the light changed.

I went straight back to the ticket window at the station and got a refund: "I just realized I lost my wallet, so I can't afford to go anywhere." At 8:35 in the morning, Reno time, that would make it

10:35, 11:35 back in New York? Who would be home at that time? I immediately thought of my old girlfriend Angela. I pulled out my phone book, pumped a dime into the phone, dialed for the operator, and asked to call collect.

Angela answered. "My God, Vinny, how are you? I called your mom and she told me you were in Synanon on the West Coast."

I laughed and said, "You're beautiful, Angie. I can't wait to see you. I'm leaving Reno in a couple of days, but in the meantime I need some money for the trip across the country. You got any spare change, honey?"

"I can always get some for you. How much?"

"Three hundred would be nice."

"Where do you want it sent?"

"Western Union in Reno."

I managed to kill a few more hours, then I headed toward the Western Union office. The cashier handed me the wire. At another window they cashed it for $300. I hustled over to Harrah's, where I took a room.

I got dressed and headed down to the casino for an hour or two of blackjack. It was my lucky night — at the end of an hour and a half I had $200 more than I had started with, and the night was still young.

As I got up to cash in my chips, I felt good about everything. I got the money and looked around for the nearest bar. On my way, I remembered something the people at Synanon had told me over and over: "First you'll end up with a drink in your hand, and before you know it you'll be back on junk, and then you'll fall down dead, alone in the gutter, or wind up in the slammer for the rest of your entire life."

I slid onto a barstool and ordered a Coke. I had a look around the room and on the first swing, I spotted a cute little blonde sitting alone at a table having a drink.

We spent most of the next four days in the hotel room, naked and ordering from room service — something to eat "and another bottle of vodka, some tonic, ice and a plateful of lemon twists on the side." We had sex as often as either one of us thought about it, and we had fun getting drunk and then sobering up sleeping in each other's arms.

After our first night together, Terri insisted on paying for nearly all the extras we were getting. She showed me a roll of $100 bills, which I thought was $2000 or more when I first saw it. I just sat back and watched her spend it all down to nothing. One morning she said quietly, "Vinny, Ah have to go back to Texas today," as she kissed me on the chin.

I woke up on the sixth morning outside of Synanon with a hellish hangover, and I couldn't remember what had happened just before I went to sleep. I dragged my ass out of the bed and looked in my pants pockets for a cigarette and to make sure I hadn't lost all my money somewhere along the vodka trail. Incredibly, I had $300 left.

With more than a little trouble, I located my toothbrush, the tube of paste, and brushed up before starting to shave. As I looked in the mirror, the thought hit me again: "Leave Synanon and you die. *No one has ever left and been successful.* First they hit the bottle, then they hit the junk, and last they hit the morgue or draw a telephone-number stretch in the joint." I looked hard at myself. "Is that what I'm doing?"

Why did I have to get loaded in some way to feel good? What about the year I spent in Reno, clean all the way, feeling great about washing dishes, cooking, mopping floors, raking leaves, taking all the shit, and yet in some kind of way still happy. "Why not go back and spend another year or two with Synanon? By that time, you'll be on top of the world."

It occurred to me that I hadn't called Momma since leaving Synanon, so I picked up the phone. "Ma, it's me, Vinny. How are you, Ma?"

"Vinny, my God, where are you? Are you all right? The people at Synanon called and said you left."

"Ma, don't worry. I'm in Reno still, but I'm leaving today to come home and see you."

It caught me off guard to hear her say, "No, Vinny, don't do that. You go back to Synanon and do what they tell you." I didn't like the idea of being rejected.

"Ma, look. I got all the information they had to offer, and it's time for me to apply it now. I'm not using drugs, Ma, I promise. I just want to see you."

What I didn't know was that the Synanon people had in fact called my mom and told her that I was doing fine and making progress. They explained that one year is a crucial time, and this happens to a lot of people. "Above all, if your son should happen to call you, urge him to return to Synanon, and no matter what you do, send him no money or plane tickets."

Mom was trying to think of what to say next to persuade me. "Vinny, you listen to me. The Synanon people tell me you were doin' real good and I want you to go back and finish what you started with them."

Suddenly it hit me, "Mom's right, idiot, so tell her you agree." I followed my conscience and said, "Momma, I'm going to do what you say. I'm going back to Synanon today."

"Oh, Vinny, thank God. You promise?"

"Yeah, Ma, I know you're right, and what I'm doing is stupid, so I'm going back, as soon as I pack up." She sighed in relief and made me promise to have Synanon call collect when I was back safely, and we said our goodbyes.

I looked at the bottle of Smirnoff, poured a short one, and called my brother Frank. When he answered the phone, the response was the same. "Vinny, don't be stupid. Why throw away all that good time? Go back, Vinny, it's the best thing."

So I hung up and had another drink to drown out the thought of calling Synanon with my hat in my hand. Halfway through the second ring, Dick picked up the phone with "Good afternoon, Synanon."

"Yo, Dick, Vinny Marino. I've had some time to think, and now

I'm thinking I made a mistake by leaving. I shouldn't have done it, and I'd like to come back."

Dick didn't hesitate. "Where are you now?"

"Downtown Reno."

"Good. Tell me where, and we'll pick you up in twenty minutes."

"Harrah's Casino."

"Be outside the main casino in twenty minutes. Look for the van." The phone went dead, so I looked around the room, then decided I had to pack. I poured another drink, chugged nearly half, then sat it down and started opening drawers. Just before leaving, I poured the rest of the vodka down the drain, brushed my teeth, picked up my bag, and headed for checkout. I paid my tab and took a last shot at the crap table and went broke except for three dollars. Then I went out the front door to wait.

Within five minutes Gary pulled up. I swung the door open on my side and chirped, as if nothing had happened, "Hey, Gary, how are things back at the ranch?" Gary said nothing and stared straight ahead all the way back to the house. Stepping inside, I saw Dick, ready with orders: "Vinny, go sit in that corner and face the wall. Say nothing to anyone for any reason."

I said, "Okay," and did what he said. The house went to dinner and I sat. Then they went through cleanup and I sat. Finally, after nearly five hours, Dick called a general meeting and when everyone else was in the room, he came out and told me to come in. I followed him in and took one of the remaining seats.

"Stand up, Vinny." I did and held my head humble with my eyes closed. Dick asked a question, "Okay, sucker, what do you want?"

I couldn't look at anyone as I said toward the ground, "Well, I'd like to come back and get another chance."

Dick cut into me. "Why, Vinny? You tell me why we should take you? You're nothin' but a pain in the ass to everyone, ever since you came, so why should we think any different of you now?" Dick went on and on into the harassment, including such charges as "You're an asshole…a spare parts piece of shit…a running scum bag."

I suddenly thought again to myself, "Why am I putting up with this verbal abuse? It's all bullshit, and it's coming from assholes I wouldn't even associate with back in New York. They could never make it in my neighborhood, which is exactly where I belong."

Dick's wife and codirector, Ellie, stood up next. "Vinny, we want your wig, and we're gonna put on some special wax when you're bald to make your head shine. And then you're gonna wear a sandwich sign everywhere you go that'll say, 'What an asshole I am.'"

At that point, the meeting turned into a free-for-all, when some long-timer said, "I want his jacket," and pointed out the fancy leather one I was wearing. Another shot in with "I want that sweater," and one of them spoke out for my suitcase sitting in the middle of the floor.

A thought shot through my brain, and I acted on it impulsively. I stood up, snarled "I'm leaving," grabbed my suitcase and split right out the front door again.

The Revolving Door

THE BEST THING I CAN SAY about that time of my life is that as I began that revolving door routine with treatment centers, I picked up a little more knowledge each time I went in. And each time I went back out on the streets I learned a little more about myself there too. I was growing up, none too soon or too quickly, but it often felt like dying. And that is true; when you change, a little bit of your old self dies off to make way for the new.

The drug treatment centers tried to cut me off from my self as I had been, my junkie self. And I couldn't tell the difference between my junkie self and my real self anyway — shit, I'd been a junkie most of my life. So when they tried to cut off my junkie self, I felt like my throat was cut. Deep in my heart I knew that some of what they were doing was right. But just as deeply I knew the core of me, the little hustler who made good as a shoeshine boy to help Ma out, was just fine. I wasn't just "spare parts," "dogshit," as the Synanon folks liked to say in the encounter games. It took me a long time to figure out what parts of these programs helped and what parts harmed me. When you feel like shit about yourself, it's hard to sort out other people's shit about you from the truth. That's why encounter groups really do work. You learn, the hard way, one step at a time.

RIGHT AFTER I STOOD UP for myself in Reno, I hitched a ride that happened to be going to San Francisco. So that's where I drifted.

111

For money to eat on, I robbed a guy. Then I hopped a cab to the Tenderloin district, which simmers with drugs and crime. Within a day I'd found junkies and junk, and in two days I had a hooker girlfriend and a little .25-caliber Beretta. We set up business — Penny worked the hotels, the desk clerks would call me when she got in, and I'd come busting in and stick the guy up for hitting on "my wife." Scared shitless, they paid up.

It takes no time at all to hit bottom. A caper at the Mark Hopkins Hotel went foul one day, and I ditched Penny there to take the heat, glad that she didn't know my name. Slid up against the greasy wall in yet another fleabag hotel, I do recall waking up to the smell of burning flesh and cloth. Then I felt pain in two places: my left hand and my prick. I looked down but couldn't move right away to correct what I saw. A cigarette was burning down between my fingers, plus there was smoke from my pants right next to the zipper. I slowly thought, "Hey, my cock's on fire!" as I finally managed to start beating out the smoldering with my good hand. After a couple of minutes it was still smoking, so I managed to get out of the pants and my underwear, and drop them in the sink. Still stuck in a fog, I looked at the burns on my fingers and felt totally disgusted with myself as I fell down on the bed to sleep it off for another seven hours.

When morning came, I looked around at the mess I had created. Cigarette ashes were everywhere along with ten or twelve soggy butts. My cooker had been knocked over, dammit, and the bags of junk were loose on the floor along with the works. My expensive pants in the sink had a big hole, which rendered them useless. I held up my left hand and wished I had some salve to soothe the burns. I went back to the bed, holding my head. I was sinking and there was no way out that I could see. Luckily, I didn't burn my family jewels.

When I woke up again, it dawned on me from nowhere, "You have to change your habits and take on a challenge or you'll go right down the tubes." And then the answer came: "Ditch the junk and knock off the booze, then hitchhike across country and go see your family."

HITCHHIKING IS ABOUT PEOPLE. I got a ride from Joe, a trucker with a heart of gold, who fed me and talked to me, and handed me a $20 when we split, to go home and see my ailing ma. I got a ride from a spoiled college kid with money to burn. Me and the other riders he picked up, we helped him burn it. When they got too loud to escape notice, I slipped out one night, and hitched a ride with a guy who made a pass at me. I strong-armed him for $75, and split, looking for a bus to New York.

After I bought my ticket, I sat around the station for what seemed like forever. As soon as the driver opened the bus, I gave him my ticket and got on, looking all the way in the back for a seat. When I found one that suited my anxious mood, I settled in next to the window, leaning my head against the smoky glass. Suddenly I was hit with a rush of fear and pictured a state trooper hauling me off to the local lockup. I slid even farther down in the seat, trying to get more incognito into the picture and less Marino. I thought for a moment of actually getting under the seat to hide from my own worries about "Damn! That faggot kid going to the cops."

The driver finally started up. As the lights of the town disappeared, I felt relieved enough to breathe freely. I couldn't believe that I had gotten away one more time. I wished for one more shot of junk but settled for three more dolophines to last me the night. I went back to my seat and dozed until I saw the lights of the Lincoln Tunnel.

First, I had to hit Harlem to check out what was happening and cop some dolophines and doridens so I could be fairly straight in front of the family. On my way over to Mom's, I could stop at Hooks's parents' place to see if they had his current address.

The first guy I recognized was standing on the corner of 101st and Second Avenue — old Haysoos, the Puerto Rican. We stood around shooting the shit.

I said, "Haysoos, can we cop here?" He looked at me and grinned.

As Haysoos disappeared up the steps, I paid close attention. It's hard to describe Harlem. One thing is you can never know anything about anything for sure, so you have to watch everything all the time. Once I was up there to cop with Hooks along for the ride and stoned out of his mind. We were walking around 105th and First and saw two guys arguing loudly. I nudged Hooks to be on the lookout as we moved closer to the buildings in order to pass them without any trouble. When we came within five feet, it was clear they were hassling over drug prices. One guy was selling doridens for forty cents a pill, undercutting the other guy by ten cents.

Just as we got next to them, one of them shoved the other and he got angry. He pulled a switchblade, flicked it open, and growled out "Muthafucker" as he nailed his opponent deep in the chest, overhand. It was so real and so sudden, I couldn't believe it — a man with the look of shock and death on his face even before he realized what had happened. He tried to grab the blade and pull it out of his body but fell over backward first, with blood pouring out his mouth. Half-stoned, Hooks and I ran like jackrabbits to get away from any involvement. Next day the headlines read, "Harlem Stabbing Death. No Suspects."

Haysoos and I copped some pills, and then I wasted no more time getting to Mom's place. When I got to her door, I straightened out both me and my outfit and knocked three times, standing upright as best I could, since the chemicals were peaking inside. Mom opened the door and took me by the hand, leading me inside. Then she turned around, crying as she threw her arms around me. "Vinny, oh Vinny, my son," was all she could get out. While we were still hugging, Frank and Joey came out of the kitchen and started slapping me on the shoulders, saying, "Hey, Vinny! Good to see you!"

We all sat down and I offered my version of the last fifteen months. I got it together enough so they didn't suspect anything, but none of them was looking very closely, either. It amazes me, because now nothing is more obvious to me than someone who is stoned on drugs. I told them about my responsibilities as a "facilitator" at the prison and what it was like living at Synanon. When Mom asked me directly about the lifetime commitment, I gave her a variation of the same line I had given Clapp in Reno, "I have all the information they had to offer, so now I have to go out in the real world and apply it." She looked a little skeptical, but her scrumptious dinner was nearly ready, which she didn't want to spoil with a hasty accusation. We all sat down to one of the best meals ever.

THE NEXT DAY, AFTER I had gotten off, I settled down to consider some action for the day. I had forgotten to stop at Hooks's folks, so I slowly got dressed for the trip to Brooklyn.

His pop didn't seem happy to see me, but he invited me in and told me Hooks was "away for a while." I pressed him a little harder: "Is he in any kind of trouble?" Hooks's old man glanced at me, saying, "Both you and him should have your asses kicked all over Brooklyn for using that stuff!"

Then he pointed his finger directly at my face. "How could two young guys with brains be so fucking stupid?" Hooks and I had been using for ten years, give or take, and the heartache for him and his wife had been the same as the grief my family had to face.

He looked at me and said, "He tried to stick up a cabbie right out front here, in broad daylight."

I said, "Oh, no. Was he loaded at the time?"

He looked at me like I was crazy and said, "Loaded? You mean using that stuff? When the hell *wasn't* he loaded? Of course he was all screwed up. He didn't even know where he was."

"Can you tell me what else happened?"

"Yeah, Vinny, sure I'll tell you. So you can go out tomorrow and pull the same caper, eh? He stuck a knife to the cabbie's throat and said, 'Gimme all the money!' The cabbie wrestled the knife away from him. So Hooks just scrambled out of the cab and came back up here as if nothing happened. In fact, he went to bed."

"Oh, Christ."

"Next thing, a whole squad of cops came barging in here from all directions, which scared the living shit out of his mother, and she hasn't been the same since."

"I can't believe it. I'm sorry," I said.

He didn't have much patience left for me. "Yeah, yeah, he says he's sorry too. Meanwhile, his mother is still a wreck, and he's doing five years at Greenhaven."

It was time to go. His final line to me was "So now you're back, huh? I heard in the neighborhood you were doing real good in that program. Is that true, Vinny? Are you a new man?"

I was standing in the hallway, as I said, "Well, not exactly new, but certainly better than I was. Goodbye." I wondered about where all this bullshit was leading me. Why had I left Synanon? For this?

BUT I WAS STILL ON THE STREETS, and again a junkie, so I needed drugs and money, big time. I picked up a hooker named Patti, and for a while I just did robberies, and kept her at home. After a while I put her back to work on her back for me, the same gig I'd worked with Penny in San Francisco. She'd go into a room with some john, and I'd burst in and wave my piece around, smash him upside the wall till he froze with fear, and we'd take off with the loot.

We were banging in $300 to $400 a day in a short time, but the circle was vicious and I soon smelled rotten from my insides as well as up in my head. On the rare occasions I could see myself in the mirror, the questions would start: "Why do you need chemicals in your blood to feel good? How do you really feel about yourself? What the hell do you think is happening? You're a quitter. If you had continued in Reno, where would you be now, if you had stayed clean? You damn well know what you're doing and you know why you're doing it. And you know that you're the idiot to blame for it." It all sounded Synanon familiar to me.

When those conscientious hard times came up, I would walk away from the mirror in utter disgust with what I had seen, cook up a double load and send it in with God-awful vengeance, desperately trying to block out all the thinking I had just done. Then I would run my "tough guy" act as the peak of the high came on: "Those Synanon assholes actually had the balls to call me a baby. Well, you show me a baby who goes out every day on the streets, puts his life on the line, his balls on the line, his freedom on the line to earn money." With that I would either head out to the streets or nod out in the room.

About a quarter to ten one night, Patti went out loaded and made some dumb move with a narcotics detective on the street, and he followed her home. She took the heat for me. Patti got busted on the spot and taken to the precinct on a charge of narcotics and paraphernalia possession. When she finally came up for sentencing, the judge gave her sixty days detention.

But that left me with no old lady and no more money and a helluva junk habit. So I let it be known among the hookers that I was "open for business." The business, of course, was protecting them on the streets, arranging for hotels and bail if need be, copping their junk, taking all their money, and sleeping with them every once in a while. I was losing it completely — getting strung out staying up for three or four days at a time, shooting heroin and speedballs. Something had to go.

UP AND DOWN, IN AND OUT. I found a kid named Jimmy, a diamond thief, and he and I detoxed in a hospital to get some of our health back. But we left early, and within two hours I picked up my first hooker to "protect" — a junkie fem, Nicki, whose pimp was in prison. Two weeks later I picked up another, Mousie. In a month I was making deals for the girls in six different hotels, and watching them go sliding down the junk tubes.

It was Mousie that set me up. She headed me down a dark alley in Brooklyn, to meet a new connection. When we were deep into the shadows, a guy stepped out, and I scored four bags of junk. But then I heard a car door slam behind me, and whirled to outrun the narcs I knew instantly were headed my way. As I ran, I swallowed the bags; and then they caught up with me. I busted out of one chokehold, and swallowed the last bag, just as they caught me again and rammed me into a window, full force.

I was bleeding all over the place, and all that blood and broken glass shocked the cops too. Then the cop who'd choked me, a guy named McClean, from the old neighborhood, came at me again, this time grabbing my shirt and pushing me backward, yelling, "So you wanna fuck around with junk, Marino, and you wanna fuck around with tough guys? Then you look to swallow the shit, fuckin' punk, then you look to hit *me*, asshole." He reached into his pocket and came up with a bundle of junk, proclaiming, "See this, fucker? It's yours. You had it on you. And when we load you in the back of the car, cocksucker, you wanna eat that, fine. Go ahead. Because when we get to the station, I'll bring more to you, on a goddamn plate by the pound, with a nice big spoon, and you can eat the shit until you fuckin' die. But you're under arrest, punk, so get up against the wall, hands first. Lean forward."

SO THEY GOT ME TO THE JAIL. But when I got into court, the judge dismissed, saying the evidence had to be suppressed along the guidelines of *Miranda* — they hadn't read me my rights. I shook my head in disbelief. Here I was totally junked out, a pimp living off women's bodies, a thief, and I got to walk free because the system worried about civil rights. You know, it would have been some sort of justice if I'd gone to prison anyway. But it's good there are protections for civil rights, no matter who you are, or other people's rights would get trampled in the stampede to get me put away. It's something to think about; even something to give you a little faith in people and the system.

Mousie split, of course; and the next week Nicki disappeared. I didn't know what happened to her and I didn't give a shit. I was sick, strung out, and tired of living.

My "working girls" were gone, I looked like a bum, and the heat from the narcs was coming down heavy all over town. The only caper I was really ready for was more cigarettes, since my cattle-rustling coat was in storage at Hooks's place, and I had long ago lost the finesse necessary for the diamond exchange.

In a fog, I tried to make a move on an A&P, but the manager actually stopped me right in the store and held me there until the cops came. They cuffed me and threw me in a car for the ride to the station. Mom got right on the phone to Mark Varrichio again.

I was released on bail, and Mom and Mark threatened me directly, "Vinny, we're going to commit you to an institution."

I couldn't think of anything but my freedom for the day, so I said, "Maybe that's what I need. You tell me where, Mark, and I'll go. I have to straighten out." They both seemed relieved. Mark called Synanon in Westport and told Ted Brown I wanted to return. Ted asked to speak to me: "Vinny, is it true that you want to come back to Synanon?"

I blinked without thinking and said, "Yeah, Ted, that's right. I'm not going to make it this way."

Ted said flatly, "Well now, we're going to have to interview you again, and there will also be a 'good faith' donation to Synanon of $1,500."

I asked Mark, "Where will I get $1,500 for Synanon? I don't have any money."

He didn't hesitate at all. "Vinny, if you're serious and they accept you, I'll loan you the money, and you get it back to me when you can." Then he handed me $200 and begged, "No, Vinny, take it. Just do me a favor and stay out of trouble until we can get you off the streets, okay?"

No sooner had I hit the streets in front of Mark's building when the $200 he had given me was burning a hole in the pocket of my muddled brain. I could only think of Harlem, my second home — the place where dreams got started at the end of a dirty needle.

I flagged down a cab and gave him the same old directions. Soon I'd copped twenty-five five-dollar bags and cabbed it back to the seclusion of my room in the hotel. I thought I was getting away with something as I cooked, tied up, and sent it all in. Within two minutes I knew what junk had done: It kept me from getting sick for the moment, but there was nothing high about what I was looking at — four walls of a broken-down hotel in midtown New York and me at the end of a string ready to drop in the gutter.

Three days later I pulled off a heist in broad daylight in the Fifties somewhere. And then another attempted petty larceny charge, another night sick in the tank with five or six other junkies. And then I was going to have to face Mark Varrichio once again. As I was released on bail, it hit me: "Damn, today I was scheduled for that Synanon interview."

Standing there alone on the sidewalk outside the jail, I had no idea which way to turn. It occurred to me to sit on the curb, but I decided not to stoop that low — at least not yet. I set myself in motion, trying to forget the gut pain and take some time to think about whether it was worth going on and if so, in what direction? I knew that if I kept using heroin, I'd be a dead man in no time. Either I'd fall under a wheel loaded or overdose fatally or some cop would connect with his club or a gun. Something had to happen, as stoned as I was.

The next day, scared, I checked into Metropolitan Hospital's detox ward. While I was there, I heard that a guy named Tommy LaCosta I had met in Synanon had left them and gone to a new organization located out on Staten Island called Daytop Village. So I looked up their number in the phone book, and dialed it. "Good morning, Daytop." But they told me to call back at one, and at one they told me to call at nine in the morning. But at nine I was sitting in court with Mark, listening to him swap a judge my commitment to Synanon for the time in prison I had so richly earned. It was a done deal. Mark didn't smile or shake my hand; I chased him down the court hall. "Look, Mark," I tugged lightly on his sleeve. "Please stop. Listen, I was working hard on getting into Daytop, that's why I didn't call. I'm sorry. And I'm going to do something about it."

Mark spun around on his heels and bellowed, "God damn it, Vinny, don't talk to me about anything you're 'going to do.' You want the truth? I can't trust you, so I don't want to hear any more about it. Just *do it* for once. You asshole, you're stuck in 'Tomorrow I'll do it!' You wanna know what I think, Vinny? I think that's what junk does. It takes you to the experience of tomorrow today. But that's a dream, and you're a great dreamer, and you're never going to collect on that dream because you can't get there from here. You can only trick your body into thinking it can get to tomorrow before it comes up naturally because in your soul you know, deep down, that you'll *kill* yourself by punching holes in your arms with those needles, and I hope to God, *if* he exists, that some higher court somewhere — if there is such a thing — finds you guilty as charged of murdering Vinny Marino, you evil, rotten sonofabitch! Vinny was a *friend* of mine! Now get the hell out of my sight!" He turned and walked away.

Daytop Rehab Center

I CAUGHT A CAB AND headed back to the hospital. As soon as I got on the ward, I took my shot of methadone and went straight to the phone to call Jack Karola, the director of Daytop. "He's in a meeting… He's not on the facility… He went out to lunch… went out to dinner," and I was consistently told what time to call back. This went on through the week — Thursday, Friday, Saturday, Sunday, and Monday. Finally, late Monday afternoon, when I actually got him on the phone, I pleaded with him.

"Jack, if I'm not in Daytop by Wednesday, I'm definitely going to prison. I've called you religiously, I've never been late. What more do you want? I really need help. I'm tired of running, I'm tired of using junk, and I'm scared of prison." Karola set an interview for the next day. I came too early, I was so worried they wouldn't let me in. They were worried, too: Was I worth it, and what were my intentions?

I told them in all candor, "Look, I have to be serious because if I stay out on the streets I know I'm a dead man, and if Daytop doesn't accept me, I'm going straight to prison."

The guy called Rudy started yelling at me. "Look, asshole, we know you've always been full of shit! You never did anything in your life. You're a baby and you're really afraid of going to prison! Come on, let's hear it, sucker!"

"You're right. I am a baby. I am an asshole, and I'm scared of going to prison. I couldn't make it on the streets, and I need some help."

They told me to scream for help, and I did, at the top of my lungs, for five minutes. And then they welcomed me to Daytop. Tommy LaCosta took me back to the kitchen, got me some coffee, and sat me down to clue me in. Daytop had been started by a guy from Synanon and was structured much the same. The house rules were more rigid, and various "expediters" were appointed to bust you for breaking rules. "And they do that deliberately with inductees — put you off for a week or so. They figure the candy-asses melt in the street and the serious people get in. I try not to pay too much attention to the bullshit."

I asked him, "Can you see yourself staying here?"

He thought about it for a few seconds and said, "Tough question, Vinny. You know, with this program you can *graduate* after two or three years, then either work for the organization or go back outside. I take it day by day."

Tommy went to court with me to ask the judge to accept Daytop instead of Synanon. And I went directly from court to the facility, with only enough time to thank a stone-faced Mark Varrichio.

AFTER DINNER THAT EVENING, I was given a job on the service crew and told about the routine. It was basically parallel to Synanon, except the structure was much more rigid and the penalties more ludicrous and lengthy. An example were the rules on shaving. Each person was issued his or her own Wilkinson blade, at the rate of one a week. To get a new one, you had to turn in your old one. If you left your blade lying around, you had to wear a four-foot wooden model of a blade around your neck everywhere you went for maybe three, four, or five days. I had a habit of leaving my blade perched on the sink after I shaved. It got so that seeing me without the sign would be a novelty.

They were very big on signs — sandwich signs that said "I'm a dog" or "Don't trust me." If they thought you were acting like a baby, they'd hang a plastic baby bottle around your neck and make you wear a diaper. The only time people didn't have to wear any signs was during open house on Saturday evenings when community people came in to see what we were doing. These kinds of degradations really didn't seem constructive.

Daytop was also very much into physical haircuts. They would shave your head if you were a male and females were given stocking caps. I don't know what was supposed to be accomplished by that except maybe some sick needs taken out by the people in power there.

One activity really caught my fancy, though. Inside a separate building two punching bags had been set up. When I put on the gloves for the first time, I vented a thousand angry frustrations, slamming the hell out of the bag. Until the day when I first stood in front of the bag and considered it my worst adversary, I never knew I had so much anger buried inside me. "Bam!" I would slam Brannigan for his bullshit. "Whack!" I would crack Pop for his gambling, and on down through the roster of tough guys and raw deals I felt life had handed me. I would get so exhausted I could only hug the bag and hang on, since I couldn't lift my arms to punch anymore.

Hitting that bag was better therapy than I had gotten from the legion of shrinks who had "listened" to my problems. With each hit, I would yell, "Yo!" and let everything out. I would fantasize about being in boxing matches with various assholes that ran the facility. I discovered over time that I could tolerate the daily routine much better, and I was slowly gaining weight in the right places. It felt good to be involved with something physical, and I was amazed at the way I could free my mind from everything else and yet still think clearly.

Aside from the punching bag, the first week I was at Daytop I found that the everyday routine got to me fast. Nothing was new or exciting about the inside of a toilet bowl, and I already knew every angle there was about slinging soapsuds in different directions and whistling while I worked. Within three or four days I started drawing designs on the bathroom floor with a wet mop, picturing myself as a fruitcake Picasso. When people would walk on my wet masterpiece, I bitched at them for "screwing up an artist's work" and sometimes chased the guilty party, shaking my mop. Of course it was all an act, but lots of people would get angry and stay that way. I couldn't be bothered thinking about their reactions; I was just trying to break up the grueling monotony any way I could.

At the end of my first week, Art, the director, announced what sounded like a new experience. At a general meeting one night, he said, "One hour from now, at 8:00 P.M., the house will be totally closed down and we will be going through a seven-day marathon. Put on something comfortable before we meet in the dining room." I remember thinking, "I can see myself getting bored at the end of Day One. How in the hell am I going to get through *seven* days?" I felt relieved to hear we were free to move from group to group or from room to room.

As soon as the game began, I knew I didn't want to play. I got bored with the same old stories we heard at the general meetings, which only lasted two or three hours. When the first spotlight hit me, I begged the question and took off for another room to hide in. In the second room, I figured it was close enough when the girl next to me got the "hot seat," so I left then. All in all, I managed an entire day without ever answering a single question. I started to see myself as a fly on the wall: present, but upside-down on the ceiling. All those people sure looked strange.

Eventually the groups were all called together. Art started the action: "Okay, the game is called 'emotion,' and here is how we play. Go around the room and one by one tell each person how lonely you are, how much you need a friend, and how you want that person to love you. The object is for you to convince each person to love you. Got it? You go first, Alex."

As Alex moved around the room with his appeal for friendship and love, I found it humorous at first. But it got boring after he told maybe forty people the same story. By the time he got to me, I had decided not to play. After he made a dull plea about loving me, I looked him straight in the eye. "Alex, I'm sorry, but I don't even know you, so forget about 'love you.' What did you say your last name was? Now, as we get to know each other, we might become friends, but for right now if I were you, I'd pass on me."

In a flash, the entire group sent boos and hisses at me, and I shot them a bird in response. A coordinator finally cut in. "Come on, Vinny, why the hell are you stalling? You've been in Brand X; you know what this is all about."

I thought, "What the hell, nothing matters at these meetings anyway," so I told him the truth. "Yeah, I might have spent a year at Brand X, but I'm brand *new* here. And on the one hand you keep preaching 'Don't do *anything* according to Brand X,' and then in the next breath you want me to switch to being a Brand X old-timer and give everybody a lesson. Well fuck it. From now on I don't know nothin' from nothin' until I get it firsthand from you."

The coordinator looked at me and barked, "That's a selfish, shitty point of view. The object of the game is to share experiences, so that everyone can benefit."

I got a cold and rotten, distant feeling. "Look, I'm not here for anyone else's benefit. I'm here *only* for Vinny Marino. I couldn't give a shit about your benefit, her benefit, or the benefit of anyone else in this house."

Cries of anguish from all directions. The coordinator was first: "You ungrateful asshole, *we* kept you out of jail."

I looked at him directly. "Hold it. *You* didn't keep me out of jail, Tommy LaCosta did, with an act that you couldn't even *think* about duplicating. So let's get off this 'we' shit, Lone Ranger." I got up and left the room. "Who needs this?" I thought, bored out of my skull, and angry underneath.

The marathon went on and on, while I got nothing more out of it. I figured that the whole object of the week-long game was to dissipate people to the point where they would say or admit to almost anything. Painful episodes poured out of personal memories in front of the whole group. People hugged each other, cried a lot, and exposed their inner feelings in myriad ways. I couldn't believe human life was so diverse in terms of experience — especially with women. I was amazed at the number of hookers who had come from homes where they were getting messed with by their fathers, and their mothers knew nothing about it. By the time they reached a place like Daytop, 90 percent of the women hated *all* men, and most of them with a vengeance.

One consistent element ran through the whole marathon, and it hit me like a flash. The pain. Most of the residents had been through some highly charged emotional situations involving physical or mental pain. To pay it back, they had inflicted pain on themselves, with junk, and pain on their families and their friends, with their addicted condition and the subsequent lifestyle of crime, prostitution, and drugs. At least I could see that pattern clearly operating in my case, and it seemed to hold true for most of the other residents as well.

After we came out of the marathon, the whole place started to get childish. They dubbed me Noodlehead for the first thirty days, and people who made small mistakes had to wear dunce caps for a week. If you forgot to turn off a light, you got a fluorescent tube to carry around like a soldier. It might sound funny now, but it proved to be ultimately stupid because during the first month I was there, seven or eight people couldn't handle it and split. One was a young kid of 18, a pretty girl named Sandy, who died ten days after she walked out the front door — overdosed in midtown. I thought it was a damned shame, but I kept my distance since I had to stay right where I was or face up to prison.

Before long, some of us "renegades" formed a new "tip," and we would sit around knocking all the petty bullshit. Tommy LaCosta was the main prankster besides me, and we teamed up to pull off a number of practical jokes, plus we worked out together on the punching bags. Most people thought we were weird, but it served a useful and positive purpose for us. We were cracking the shell of the nuthouse just to let some air in. And it was fun.

Basically, however, time was dragging for me and my insides were getting restless for a change of pace. I discovered to my dismay that there were no outside projects, and no one worked outside for a living. Daytop essentially begged for its money, and I didn't like the idea at all.

The only carrot they had to offer was a position on the staff, eventually, assuming the place grew in popularity with disgusted junkies from the streets. I didn't know if it would be worth my time to spend two or three years there only to become a staff member, since I couldn't go for their "baby" routines, and there wasn't a single staff member I respected. The low-lifes out on the streets would come into a community like this and would run around abusing people with any little bit of power they could scrape up.

I was getting more and more upset with having to keep my mouth shut and do what I was told. The capper came down one day when I left my razor blade in the bathroom. My penance was I had to clean the caulking between every tile in a 30- by 50-foot john with a toothbrush. As I sat there scrubbing, I decided I had to escape soon so I put in a request to the director for what they called a "special." This was an emergency encounter session, and you could pick your own participants.

For my special, I listed everybody in any kind of status or staff position, plus a couple of the most obnoxious low-lifes. The staff member who was facilitating said, "Okay, play."

I got on the edge of my chair and looked at each person. I spoke slowly. "Look, I've been here almost two months now, and I want you people to know where I'm coming from. And where I'm coming from is not Brand X or wooden razor blades, dunce caps, fluorescent bulbs, or any of that shit you clowns use.

"Where I'm coming from is a guy named Vinny Marino, and I'm asking for some common sense to apply to this house. You people have the power to control my future and my freedom, and I don't want it misused. I also don't want to be forced back to the streets or into prison just because I couldn't stand to wear a diaper for a week or sit still for ten hours with a dunce cap on my head. And so, if you guys make sense with your orders, I'll follow them. And if you try to fuck with my head using nonsense, you're going to hear about it. You see, I am just not like those guys running around downstairs and I'm definitely not one of you. Now, let me run it, and why not start at the top, with you, Art."

I turned to face Art and proceeded to lay out what I saw in him and his act, what I didn't like about him, the way he handled his job, how his shit was coming out sideways and on which issues, and how he was handling the power associated with his position.

It took me almost five hours to get around the room, one by one. I finally sat back in my chair and wound up. "That's all I have to say. And now that I've said it, I need some help." It was astounding to see what happened. Everyone spoke in plain English for once. Each one had something constructive to say about what I should do in order to make life easier all around, and none of them argued with my assessments. It took them nearly two more hours to finish.

Happily for everyone, the general drift of things changed almost immediately. The rules lightened up a little, and the "eyes and ears" of the place — the expediters — stopped acting like storm troopers. Then the weather outside turned warmer and we started playing baseball in the diamond on the grounds, plus Art scheduled a picnic or an outing once a week that included everyone.

Inside the facility, I got the break I wanted after about four months when I was taking my one day a week off to play "seek and assume." This meant that you would look around for something you wanted to do and then on your day off just assume you had the position. I found the kitchen the most appealing place, and I started cooking breakfast. Within three weeks I made second lunch cook, then lunch cook. By the time my seventh month rolled around, I was the senior dinner cook for 108 people. I used to sit around with a paper and pencil, adding up potatoes, tomatoes, and pounds of meat. I spent a lot of time figuring quantities when I wasn't fooling around with some new recipe. I started fussing for hours with each batch of spaghetti sauce. Then I got a big white chef's hat, and I felt like old Tim Mixem Marino, but my six-gun was a two-barrel electric eggbeater.

After a long day of slinging pots and pans, I couldn't do much more than read, so I started cracking books instead of the punching bag. My primary objective was to sharpen and expand my vocabulary, like an intellectual word game. Before long, I began to practice on the residents, just like at Synanon. People would listen to me, then start scratching their heads. They would come down on me like dive bombers when we got into an encounter session. They would point their fingers and scream, "Who the fuck do you think you are, with those fancy bits of wisdom? No one in this place can relate to you!"

I watched with interest as my wanderlust built up, and I could see myself working up enough traction to hit the trail. I looked long and hard at the people in power, and I knew I didn't belong here. The simple fact was that I was on probation, with the strict condition that I "remain at Daytop until clinically released." I couldn't go anywhere even if I wanted to without violating my probation and ending up doing time in the joint. I had to take one afternoon off each month and travel to the Tombs in Manhattan to see my probation officer, Ray Hamilton. I could say I was "clean," no kidding, I was a cook, and "Yes, sir, I am learning everything I need to get a job and earn my own living." I felt especially great about looking people like him straight in the eye and not wondering which lie I was building up on. On the streets, trying to remember what I had said would almost drive me nuts sometimes.

After I marked my nine-month anniversary I decided to hop into the fire by requesting a job change before there was a crisis in terms of how-long-can-I-put-up-with-this-bullshit. So I began to shop around for an opening in public relations.

I got to the right place at the right time because the Daytop people were intending to branch out more into the community and start up an aggressive guest speaker program. Finally I made the transfer and started getting on the phone to bankers and brokers, pitching them on us and inviting them over for lunch or open house to speak.

In my new position I learned all about the places we were scoring our free goods and who the biggest donors were. I started to work on the parent and family meetings, which my mom and Frank attended regularly, and I helped arrange special events, such as the yearly "clean" celebrations for residents and the open houses.

Not long after, four of us were in the kitchen drinking coffee when something came on the news concerning the war in Vietnam and a massacre at My Lai. We left our coffee and hustled to the TV in the living room. Five minutes later, one of our expediters walked into the kitchen and found the cups out of place. He got on the loudspeaker and asked that the people last in the kitchen come to the coordinator's office immediately.

When all four of us had taken a seat, this expediter named Butch read us the riot act, saying we were "worse than pigs, and for being such slobs, we're going to shave your heads."

Without thinking, I said, "The hell with this," and got up heading for the door.

Butch grabbed me by the sleeve and pulled on it. "What did you say, Marino?"

I picked his hand off my shirt and shoved it hard into his pants pocket. "I said 'To hell with this,' and now I'm saying, 'Keep your fucking hands to yourself, asshole.'"

His jaw dropped six inches. I slammed the door and thought about what to do next. I'll never forget the flash in my mind that came up. "Get loaded first, then figure things out. That's why you bolted."

NEARLY ELEVEN MONTHS of clean time, and all I could think of was heroin. Angie came up with some money for me, and gave me the name of a connection, a guy named Dink. When I found him, his eyes were half-closed and totally sunken, and drool was running from the corner of his mouth. He looked in my direction but had a lot of trouble focusing. "Hey, it's Vinny Marino. What? Am I dreamin'?"

I held onto his right arm to be sure he didn't fall down. "Yeah, Dink. You got any dope?" He was so out of it that even when we got to his apartment, he couldn't find the keys for four or five minutes, and I was anxious as hell. Finally he dipped into his back pocket for the key, and I helped him zero in on the lock.

I opened the door and walked straight into shock. The filth was appalling, and the place smelled like a mixture of urine and burnt matches. More than a hundred paper plates from take-out places were scattered all over the room so you couldn't even see the furniture. The cockroaches were as big as your finger and having a ball, and green mold was growing on all that dead food. I almost retched until I saw the tinfoil of junk. It stood out like a diamond, and I went for it blindly, picking up one bag for inspection.

I turned back to Dink. "Here's the money." I handed him $20 for four bags as I asked, "Where's the cooker and your works?"

Dink didn't answer; he just started throwing paper plates around and finally came up with everything we needed. I tied up my arm as I queried Dink further. "Hey, I've been clean for a year. How much of this will I need?"

He shrugged at me. "I dunno, Vinny. Take one bag and see."

So I loaded the cooker and added some water, then lit a match to get it all going. "This is insane," I was thinking, just as the glow hit my stomach, causing the familiar nauseous feeling. I didn't even get the needle out of my vein before I heard myself saying, "Here you go, doing exactly what they said you would. Right back on the same lousy track, and you're still on probation. You left Daytop before they released you, dummy, and you're going to get a violation for it." A bolt of fear shot through my body.

The thought of slipping back into the madness of the streets sent me out the door as fast as I could manage. Panic-stricken, my only thought was getting back to Daytop as fast as I could. I jumped in a cab and had the driver take me to the ferry where I boarded a boat for Staten Island. Inside an hour and a half I was standing at the front door of the Daytop house, and a wave of relief hit my body. I thought, "I'm home."

I BANGED ON THE DOOR and stood back to wait with a grin on my face. I was laughing out loud when Art got to me. "All right, Vinny, what the hell did you do?"

I looked up at him. "Art, I took a walk, and I'm sorry. I want to come back."

He told me flatly, "Give me your money and the cigarettes. Sit in that chair, and don't move off it without my permission. And don't talk to anyone. You got that?"

I nodded in agreement, then sat back to float with the heroin.

They left me in that damn prospect chair for over fifteen hours, and I nearly went nuts sitting there. First I was high, but then it turned to depression and paranoia. I felt as if I would have to stay inside an institution for the rest of my life because I couldn't be trusted out on the streets. Leave me alone for ten minutes out there, and I would find a needle like a magnet in a haystack. I was weak and dangerous.

At six in the morning, Karola came down. "Go upstairs, shave, and take a shower, then hit the basement. You have fifteen minutes, and don't talk to anyone." I nodded, stood up to stretch, feeling the pain of being in one position for so long.

The "Mohawk" specialist cut off all my hair except for a triangular tuft in the front, making me look like a total idiot. Karola grabbed a container of baby powder and dumped about half of it on my head. I couldn't see for the dust, and I wondered if there was any point in the humiliation, but I stayed there and kept my mouth shut.

Karola told me where it was at, saying "You're a baby, so we're going to treat you like one. Stay right here."

Next Karola got me a complete female wardrobe. "Put these on, little girl," he said, handing me a skirt and a blouse. I did what he said. The blouse wouldn't button, it was too small. I had to leave the zipper open on the skirt, so everything looked ridiculous. But Karola wasn't finished.

"Okay, Vinny, come on upstairs. We're having some special signs made, just for you."

Karola dragged the prospect chair into the middle of the living room and told me to sit in it, just as all the residents started to gather for my special session. I felt like crawling under the rug but stopped myself short. When everyone had gathered, Art started off. "Okay, Vinny, would you mind telling everyone what the hell you're doing here?"

I kept it low and humble. "I wasn't thinking when I left, and now I want to come back."

Art hit me again, "Why did you leave?"

"I made a mistake."

Art looked around at everyone in the room and said, "What do you people think of this baby? Should we take him back?"

Well, everyone I had ever stuck before with a play on words or a practical joke came at me. "Why should we take you, asshole? You ain't worth a shit, yet you think yours doesn't stink, using all them big words. You want everyone to think you're an intellectual of some kind and then go out like a baby and stick a needle in your arm."

This went on for nearly two hours before one of the coordinators stopped it. "Alright now, Vinny. What do you want from us?"

I looked at him and made a plea: "I need your help. I want to come back."

Karola cut in. "Okay, tell you what. Jenny, you go up to the attic and sit there. Vinny, you get down on your knees and scream at the top of your lungs 'I need help, please somebody help me!' until Jenny hears you. Jenny, don't come down until you hear him. Got that?"

She said yes and took off up the stairs, while I thought about making a mad dash for the door. Karola stopped me, saying, "Down on your knees, Vinny."

As I knelt down, I felt nauseous and said to myself, "Look at the position you got yourself in this time. Look at this childishness, the embarrassment. This is sick, and you're stuck in the middle." Then I screamed for nearly five minutes before Jenny came down with a grin on her face.

"Vinny, we're going to take you back, but only on a stiff contract. First of all, you are nothing but spare parts until we tell you otherwise. You are on duty twenty-four hours a day. Take your meals to the basement to eat. You sleep on the couch in this room from midnight until six. One cigarette every two hours, but only after you ask Ellen for it. Other than that, you don't talk to anybody."

I considered walking out the door but pulled myself up when I thought about the shaved head and violating probation. I went to the bathroom and started cleaning up.

It quickly became a matter of whether or not I was going to break under the pressure. I made up my mind to grit my teeth. First I cut way back on smoking. I had been up to a pack or so a day, but now I would only approach Ellen for a smoke two or three times a day. Next, I made up my mind to do all the work absolutely right. I cleaned the barbeque grill until the damn thing shone. Even the boss commented on how nice it was. Then he had me take a toothbrush and get up a ladder on the front porch to scrub the decorative trellis.

I thought of taking off many times, but strict survival kept me going. I said nothing and did my work. The same thing was true of the games, general meetings, and seminars. I said the absolute minimum. Of course everyone came down hard on me for being quiet, but that didn't change my mind. I was learning a lot about conditioning myself as a discipline. It seemed a good way to inject some self-restraint into my system. I felt okay about the way I was standing up under the workload and the humiliation.

ABOUT TWO WEEKS into the exercise, though, I ran into trouble. I bruised my back badly, bouncing over bumps in the back of an old pickup we used, so I got a little Darvon and bed rest. But then right after I got back to work Butch the bully ordered me to take out two heavy garbage cans. I refused, citing my injury. Well, to tell the truth, I offered to bounce them off his thick skull.

Butch, of course, was delighted, and next thing I knew the whole crew of staff hornets was buzzing around me, telling me I was busted back to spare parts, and to get my head shaved pronto.

I felt something snap in my head. I walked straight over to Butch and stood not six inches from his chair. "My little man, you are not going to shave my head. If anything, you might get your jaw broken, but that's all. On the streets you were a piece of shit and a fucking weasel. Now in here you hide behind the rubber-bullet bullshit power they gave you. Well, I say fuck you, fuck every other asshole in the room, and fuck Daytop."

I mock saluted, did an about face, and goose-stepped out of the room, slamming the door as I left. I had no clothes to speak of, so I dispensed with packing and headed straight for the front door. I snapped at the woman at the desk, "I'm going to New York. Hang my tag under the 'permanent outs,' will you?"

End of my time with Daytop.

ON THE STATEN ISLAND FERRY, it dawned on me that Daytop would be making phone calls to everyone, including my probation officer, telling them I had split again. So I called Hamilton as soon as we docked. He didn't think twice. "Vinny, if you walk out the door, that very minute I'll violate you and have you locked up within the hour."

I swallowed hard. "Ray, fuck you and your probation too. I'm hangin' up and if by chance we should meet, *then* we'll discuss how much time I owe or I don't owe."

I sat down on a bench and started to think about where to go and who to see. Frank and Momma were definitely out of the question, because both the cops and Daytop knew where they lived. I knew that there would be warrants out on me within two or three hours.

What about Pop? I figured I would give him a call. He might have a couple of job leads. Above all, I knew if I started up with the junk again, I'd have to start stealing, and sooner or later I'd get busted. I intended to keep my act clean and stay out of sight as much as humanly possible.

Pop did find me a friend who gave me a job: selling dirty magazines and "marital aids." I caught three of the clerks stealing from Jackie, who was a wise guy, so I became his right-hand man, his trusty. I never stole from the store, but I got to be downright excellent at short-changing the furtive customers, who had other things on their ratlike little brains than counting their change.

So, cool — but you already know, I get bored easy. It wasn't enough of a charge that the hard porn risked bringing the cops around. I looked around for something new to add to the excitement, and hit it easy. I let the word get out that I was open for fencing swag, stolen merchandise. By the end of six months I was making $2000 a week selling swag out of the store, had a swank apartment, girlfriends, and I was still clean. Momma was glad to see me these days, although she worried about the warrants out for my probation violation.

BUT ALL I NEEDED TO TUMBLE was a handshake back to hell.

A Handshake Back to Hell

ONE NIGHT AROUND CLOSING TIME, I was counting some cash behind the register, when in walked a legendary character from the neighborhood. Max was the only 62-year-old junkie I ever knew. He always had a smile on his face, though everything on his back was at least ten years old and he looked like a tattered rag doll. Everybody liked him and the girls on the street would always give him money for something to eat. Most of the restaurant owners would give him leftover food, so Max used the money to keep a little junk flowing in his veins.

Since it was only Max, I relaxed my guard and went back to counting the money after waving to him. He came forward, extending his right hand as if to shake mine, but instead of taking my hand, he just grinned and dropped two pills into my palm. I thought they were doridens, but I didn't even look closely. Instead, I just followed that old reflex and swallowed them right on the spot. Four or five seconds later I realized what I had done. "Max, what the hell were those pills?"

He grinned sheepishly. "Baby aspirin."

I looked at him hard. "Come on, Max. What were they?"

Max didn't feel like sticking around for any kind of pressure from me over his gift, so he started shuffling around on his feet while he said, "See you later, Vinny," and out the door he went.

I was so tired I didn't think any more about the pills. I just returned to the cash register. Locking the money in the safe, I switched the lights off and went to the door, when — *Bam!* — the top of my head blew off from the pills. They were doridens, and I was sailing away on that smooth, mellow plane I had forgotten for damn near two years.

Ten minutes of drug daze and I decided that instead of a drink, "Why not just one more shot of junk?" It felt like a magnet was pulling me, and I couldn't muster any self-restraint. I turned up the street and went looking. I found a hooker who sold me two bags, and got a kid to bring his works to my place. When Harvey knocked I let him in immediately, and as he dumped the works on the kitchen table, he asked, "Say, Vinny, are you sure that you wanna do this?"

"That's a stupid question. Here, cook it up," and I threw the bags on the table.

"Vinny, what did you take tonight?"

"A couple of doridens, why?"

"You mean to say that this is your first shot, in how long?"

"A little over a year."

"Vinny, you really shouldn't take too much of this, 'cause it might be dynamite. I'd say half a bag at first, then see." I put the contents of one bag in the cooker, added water, and lit a match while I watched it bubble up. I tied up while Harvey loaded roughly half into the dropper. Well, I got off into space the instant it hit me, but I couldn't get rid of the thought, "Here you go again, right down the tubes." My response was "No way. This was a treat for tonight only." I went into a frenzy and paced all over the room, finally telling Harvey, "Take the rest from the cooker and take the other bag with you." Harvey didn't understand, but he didn't argue either.

When the light of the next day finally got to me, it was already late, and I cursed the stupidity of the night before. I looked in the mirror, and said, "Well, what now? Do you keep going or stop?"

Over the next several weeks, I answered the question halfway as I took up what was known as "joy-popping." I might shoot up on Saturday night, then lay off until Wednesday, do it again on Friday, and so forth.

As I stepped back into the street scene while operating out of the porno stores, the traffic in swag (stolen goods) kept building. At the end of the tenth month, my habit was back in the range of $100 a day and things were getting crazier all the time.

By June 1967, the vicious circle was tightening into a hang-man's noose, but I was going so fast I didn't see it. Fourth of July was a feast for junkies because so many wealthy people left town for Long Island beach cottages or second homes in the country. Also the number of on-duty cops was significantly reduced. That was the night, with the storeroom dangerously full of swag, when my boss's partner walked in. When he saw that room, Abe's jaw dropped so far his Havana cigar fell out and hit the floor. He went wild. "You're gonna get me arrested, you dumb sonofabitch!"

I tried to calm him down, telling him Jackie had given me the green light. Abe flew off the handle. "Look, Vinny, your ass is fired as of right now!" and he slammed the front door as he left.

My brothers and I moved the swag overnight. My boss, Jackie, met me for breakfast, and handed me five $100 bills. He said, apologetically, "You did a good job, kid. I'm sorry it came out like this."

WHEN I LOST MY JOB, I said, "Fuck it all, I'm a misfit, and I'll take what comes my way. Daytop was shit, Synanon was shit, and here I am drowning in junk just like they said I would. So fuck it." After I got fired, I jammed so much junk in my arms, trying desperately to block out the thinking, that I blew my entire bankroll of more than $25,000 cash in less than eight weeks. The heat started coming hard, both on junk and the swag it took to support my habit.

My brother Frank got married. Standing next to Frank at the altar, I flashed on the fact that I was 28 and I had never even seriously thought about getting married. Frank was doing real good as usual with a solid job, while brother Vinny was busy sticking needles in his arm five times a day, looking for relief.

I thought about those two clean years with Synanon and Daytop, and I knew who was responsible, yet I couldn't answer the question of why I was still running. Then I remembered I had Tommy LaCosta's card. I fished it from my wallet and headed for a phone. Tommy told me that he'd left Daytop because of the pettiness, and joined an outfit called Phoenix House. Much less rigid and not overcrowded. "So you can get aboard and help shape the policy, Vinny. How's that sound as an alternative to a diaper?"

"Anything's got to be better than this dead-end street shit, Tommy. What do I have to do next?"

He told me Phoenix House had a screening facility for prospective residents called Samaritan House Day Center located in Queens. I would have to attend the center on a daily basis for about three weeks, and by then I should be accepted as a resident into the program. I told him I wanted to start the next day.

He looked me straight in the eye. "Vinny, I think this place will work *for* you and what you want, instead of against you while you're trying to get there. Welcome to Phoenix. We rose from the ashes, you know?"

I kicked my habit cold in Phoenix's temporary Samaritan center, and then was sent to a permanent bunk at Hart Island. The state now had a program for committing junkies, and Phoenix House was getting ready to accept hundreds of these people at the Hart Island facility. Jimmy Selman, the director, kept a stern eye on me as he assigned me to a service crew. He knew all about my revolving-door record with Synanon and Daytop.

I was assigned to clean the toilets. It was dull, but I resigned myself and began to take pride in shining porcelain bowls. I set my own schedule and ran right through it, and I was ready for a white-finger inspection anytime.

But after a few weeks on the island, I ran into trouble on the third floor, where most of the resident staff and status people were staying. One morning I noticed a turd perched on the rim of a bowl and toothpaste smeared all over a mirror, but I went ahead with my clean-up. The second day I cleaned it up again. The third day in a row I decided to bring up the subject next morning.

"Look, whoever lives up on the third floor, I would appreciate it if you guys would clean up after yourselves a little better. I don't mind cleaning the shitters, but you guys are missing the target, so I have to clean up your shit, and I don't like it. How about a little consideration for the cleaning crew?" No one said anything, so I went back to the morning routine. Sure enough, the same turd and the toothpaste were already in place.

Next I requested a "special" encounter session, for everyone on the third floor.

The expediter told me my special was set for one o'clock. Suddenly it dawned on me that I had done this sort of thing before, making my presence known in a facility right away. Now that I look back, I guess my action had something to do with knowing that the staff would inevitably make it harder on me as a result of my confrontation. I must have felt I needed that to stay in line because the higher the intensity, the more I would grow from the experience. I went ahead: "Look, I don't care about position and titles or anything else. What I care about is that I have to clean up after a bunch of pigs living on the third floor. A lot of guys in here are not like me — I can leave, but they got sentenced to Hart Island so if they leave because of your bullshit, it's back to the joint. I don't buy it."

So far, so good. Selman backed me up at the meeting, and so did a few other guys. But sure as shooting, who got assigned to do the dirty work at the next new dorm? Yeah — pay-back time.

The new dorm crew wasn't bad, though. We all worked well together, and it was okay on Hart Island until a change of regime took place at the highest levels. A group of ex-Synanon people had just been hired by Phoenix House with a plan for major expansion. A doctor by the name of Mitch Rosenthal was at the head of the new push, and his two main henchmen were a guy named Frank Natale from Brooklyn and a black guy named Candy.

By my seventh month the population had grown from less than 50 people to roughly 250 and new people were arriving at the rate of 40 to 50 per week. We were extremely busy, and everything was changing rapidly. Selman, the director, approached me one day: "Vinny, effective today they made me responsible for the whole island. I am naming you troubleshooter for Hart Island and you will have fourteen senior residents to get the job done."

Mayor John Lindsay had created his own operation for dealing with addicts, called ASA, Addiction Services Agency. Our chairman, Rosenthal, suggested that Phoenix House train the ASA people in our methods, and the city would refer addicts to us for treatment on Hart Island.

We soon learned about this plan to bring these ASA squares in, with their college degrees and making $17,000 to $25,000 per year for "training in how to deal with the addicted personality." We had busted our asses to redo Hart Island for no salary, and every time we asked about a salaried position, the word came back that there was "nothing open." To top it all off, we were being asked to show these squares from ASA how everything worked so they could go out and get even fatter salaries from the city.

Within nine months of residency, I was named senior coordinator for the whole island. And that meant working to induct the ASA "squares" at a special marathon encounter group. Twelve hours into the exercise, it was clear that none of them had their lives straightened out, and yet they were going to be in authority over me and everyone else in Phoenix House. When we broke for a meal, I was so disgusted I started to pack up and leave Phoenix for good. I figured that if that was what I was working toward — becoming a square — I'd rather be a dope fiend. I started to pack.

A group of maybe eight to ten guys subdued me physically and sat me on a chair. Everyone sat still, waiting. I could only think, "Well, asshole, what do you really want out of life? Here you go again, back to the streets, and for what?" Then it dawned on me that what I wanted out of life was to be a part of it, to be accepted, needed, maybe even loved, for myself — not because I had balls or I could steal good but just for being me. It was as if another person inside me had come alive and was burning to get out in the open. I couldn't resist crying. I cried for the anguish of living twenty-nine years with nothing but a tough skin to show for it. I cried for what I had done to my family and what my family had done to me. I cried for more than three hours. Until that moment, I never knew I had those feelings bottled up inside me.

When the session ended, I felt like a new person and the thought of leaving disappeared. The experience changed my outlook on where I was, which way I wanted to go, and who I wanted to be. From that point on, I gave up fighting the system and started planning on becoming the straight person I knew I could be.

As my time on Hart Island approached the one-year mark, I knew it wouldn't be long until I was ready for reentry. I could start working toward either a salaried job with Phoenix or a return to the outside world. One morning Jimmy called me into his office and said with a smile, "Well, Vinny, you're coming up on one year. I want to discuss a job that's perfect for you on Riker's Island running groups for us?"

Talk about coming around full circle! It was strange to be running those groups back there. I thought I had it made — but I wasn't out of the woods yet, as it turned out.

The first sign of trouble in Phoenix came from a racial problem, and I found myself caught in the middle. It was the same old scene, I see now. One minute I was doing good, maybe getting a little too cocky. Then someone gave me a hard time, pushing me — and pushing my buttons. Zap! Furious, my impulses ripped up my self-restraint and I was back out there, slamming the door and headed to the streets for narcotics. This time, as a dealer. But this time I knew the problem within a month: I had learned too much at Phoenix and before that, at Daytop and Synanon. There was just no going back for me, and I couldn't identify at all with the people around me or in the old neighborhood.

A stab wound sent me back to Metropolitan Hospital. While I was recovering, I decided to go back to Phoenix House and — once and for all — complete what I had started a few years back.

BACK AT PHOENIX, one of the directors got straight to the point: "Vinny, we're putting you on a strict contract and shaving your head. You've had over three years of this conceptual training under your belt, so there isn't much you would learn from it. What you need is a lesson in how to *apply* the information, so don't think you're getting away with anything."

The director took me into a general meeting and pointed to me. "You know who this is back with us, and he's on a strict contract. No one talks to him, and whatever you do, don't listen to anything he has to say because every word of it is counterfeit. This asshole is full of shit because he has no ability to apply information, he can only soak it up like a mop and spit it back at you verbally. His tongue is so glib that it's dangerous, so I want everyone to steer clear of him until we tell you otherwise. Has everyone got that?"

I knew they had me dead to rights, so I just looked at the floor, thinking, "It's true. What the hell am I gonna do this time?" Right then I knew this was my last shot — the final run — because if I didn't make it, I didn't want to live any longer. Life just wasn't worth it. Finally I got the courage up to look at the people in the room, and as I stared carefully at each of them, I knew I had what it would take to be running the facility in less than six months if I put my mind to it and didn't let anything get in my way. And I did.

I went to see my director and I told him that I had forgotten that I was on probation when I left Daytop. I completely blocked it out. Because I was doing so well, he wrote my probation officer a letter and they terminated my probation and tore up the bench warrant. Finally, I was a free man.

So before I forget, thank you to Synanon and Daytop and Phoenix House. You taught me what I needed to know, and you took me back over and over again. So now when I say some of the stuff in your rules and philosophy is pure shit, let me also say that some of the other stuff was pure gold.

What Goes Around, Comes Around

PEOPLE WHO HAVEN'T HIT BOTTOM in their lives, or those who never get back up again, sometimes talk about "bouncing back." Well, the truth is, it takes a long time to "hit bottom" — it's more like a sliding down, so far and hard you feel like you're ground into the pavement. And as for bouncing back, that's bullshit too. It takes time and hard work; the light doesn't just flash one day and illuminate your life and smooth out all paths before you. In real life, when you hit bottom you get up slowly and put one step in front of another for a long time, cultivating your sense of humor like a lifeline.

When Phoenix House let me back in, that marked the last time I went rushing impulsively out through the revolving door to the streets and back again. I now had a solid foundation of information about how to live my life, and I could see clearly that I had the talent to run the operations I was now a resident in. I had a real good grip on my life by now, but I hadn't yet made a clear *commitment* to anything. Without that kind of goal, I could drift, and drifting is dangerous for people like me — we get bored, and bolt, and take wild risks for some excitement. I found that commitment during a very odd episode in my life — my arrest and trial for armed robbery.

Exactly two weeks after a three-day marathon, I was mopping the steps of Phoenix House when the director, Louie Zinzarella, stopped me on the stairs. He told me my brother Frank had called to say that the cops were looking for me. "They just wanted to know where you were."

Two days later the directors (Mitch Rosenthal, Frank Natale, and Candy Latson) called me in. "Sit down, Vinny. We just had a meeting with three cops. You're a suspect in an armed robbery that took place during the marathon."

I asked, "Is this bullshit or what?" Rosenthal told me he had refused to let them see me, since I was definitely in the marathon, and a whole slew of residents could testify to the fact.

"Vinny, we're behind you on this 100 percent. We're going to hire the best lawyers we can get."

"Thanks a lot," I said, and I meant it! I asked Mitch if I could go out to the library to look up the newspaper account of the robbery. There were three counts of armed robbery and felonious assault with a deadly weapon. I later saw an Associated Press wire that had been sent out while I was still asleep during the marathon break.

NEW YORK (19 APRIL 1969): At approximately 7:30 P.M. this evening, two armed gunmen confronted the elevator operator at an exclusive Fifth Avenue apartment building. Threatening his execution, the perpetrators ordered the man to take them to a specific apartment on the eighth floor. When the maid answered the door, the robbers pushed it into her face, smashing her nose and knocking her unconscious. The lady of the house heard the noise and screamed when she saw the guns and the men, then ran into the master bedroom and locked the door. The man of the house was shaving at the time and upon hearing his wife in hysterics, entered the living room and tried to jump one of the gunmen. He was savagely pistol-whipped for his efforts, then handcuffed with the elevator operator to a radiator. The two children, aged ten and twelve, were threatened with violence and forced to enter a closet, which the criminals locked. Next the gunmen gained entry to the master bedroom by shooting off the lock, and they handcuffed the lady to the bed and told her she would be shot if she made any noise. The robbers ransacked the apartment and made off with an undetermined amount of cash and approximately $45,000 worth of jewelry. One of the culprits was reportedly disguised with a false rubber nose and dark glasses. Police are looking for clues and no suspects have been arrested.

The newspaper article said one of the gunmen had dark wavy hair (no mention of scars). My mop was only about half an inch long, from the shaved head I got when I came back to Phoenix. I walked out of the library, puzzled.

Two days later Zinzarella yelled at me up a flight of stairs. "Yo, Vinny! Three cops at the front door, looking for you! Go hide in the fifth-floor bathroom and hurry!"

"Damn," I was thinking as I hustled up the stairs, "even when I'm innocent I'm running." As I got behind the door of the crapper and locked it, I remembered that three cops always meant they *knew* who they were after and were going to arrest him. They're not "investigating" or "questioning" anymore — someone is going downtown in handcuffs.

The bulls handed Mitch the warrant for my arrest, and he objected vehemently. "It's impossible for Vinny Marino to have committed this crime. We can account for every minute of a thirty-six–hour period, and over a hundred people can testify to that."

The biggest of the cops said, "Look, Dr. Rosenthal, we're just doing our jobs and what this here warrant says is that he's wanted in a lineup at the precinct tomorrow. If I were you, I'd have him there."

So Zinzarella and I showed up with my lawyer, Cap Beatty, ten minutes before we were due in the lineup. Seven plainclothes cops were already on the stage, and one beckoned to us. Numbers running from 1 to 8 were painted in black on the wall behind each one of us, and I went to the end of the line and stood in front of number 7, just for luck.

I didn't know that on the other side of the mirror were the man and woman who had been robbed, the maid, the elevator operators, the maintenance man, and another guy who had seen the bandits as they hit the street. The man on the street said he didn't get a clear look at anyone. The maid and the elevator operator said it was one of the cops, and the maintenance man said it was "definitely no one in the lineup." And God Almighty, the primary victims — a man and his wife in their forties — both pointed at me and said, "Number 7 is one of the men who robbed us." I didn't hear what they said, but the cop standing with them sure did. He broadcast a direct message for me. "Number 7, go through the door in the back of the room on the left." Hear I go again, headed for the Tombs one more time.

Would I still be classified as a dope fiend and sent to the cattle floor, where all the drug addicts go? Dead right. My stomach turned over as soon as the elevator door opened, and I got hit with the acrid smell of urine and vomit. I immediately recognized fifteen or twenty people from the streets. Since I looked healthy — unlike most of them — they were eager to know where I'd been. Finally one guy asked, "Hey, Vinny, what are you in for this time?"

I laughed, because in the joint no one ever admits to guilt. "I got a real bum beef. Three counts of armed robbery and assault with a deadly weapon." Of course, no one believed I was innocent.

At about 8:30 that night, a hack came by for me: "Marino, pack it up. You got bail."

When I walked out into the fresh springtime air, I was startled to see my brothers standing there waiting. I walked right over and hugged them. "Hey, you guys! What are you doin' here?"

"We just put up your bail, brother," Frankie said. "And you want to know what we're doing here!"

I looked at him, puzzled. "You mean Phoenix wouldn't spring for it?"

Frankie shook his head. "No, hell no. Mitch Rosenthal gave me some cockamamy line about them being a nonprofit, so they couldn't get involved."

"No shit," I said. Mitch was probably afraid I might bolt on the bail, because I had left the place just a couple of months before.

I still didn't take the situation all that seriously. I was counting on that old line, "Justice will prevail."

The next night my attitude changed. My lawyer came over to grill me about the facts. I asked, "Why are you interested in all those details? They're not important. All you need to know is that I was asleep in the house at the time."

Cap looked at me intently. "Vinny, you may not think it's important, but we must tear that day apart backward and forward. The DA is looking for twenty-five years to life for you, so I would suggest it's time to get damned serious. Not only that, the victim and his wife are convinced it was you. That four-hour break came at the wrong time. It is *possible* for you to have done it, although it's not probable. I'd like to make the odds a little better in our favor, if we can." So during the next week, Cap questioned each person who had been in the marathon, plus the night man and anyone else who might have seen me moving around for any reason between five and eight o'clock on the fateful night of the crime.

A month later the grand jury indicted me based on the positive identification by the two victims. I was scared, and started to take the whole thing real seriously. I could end up behind bars maybe for the rest of my life. When the judge asked me, "How do you plead?" I said loud and clear, "Not guilty, Your Honor." For once in my life, I really meant it.

The trial was set for January 12, 1970, six months away.

BACK AT PHOENIX HOUSE the days passed into weeks, and then the months flew by until October when the leaves started to turn. All through the summer I kept my mouth shut and my nose flush to the grindstone so that nothing interfered with my progress and learning. I was mainly into self-discipline and lots of reading. I knew I was up against the wall. On the one hand, I had absorbed enough good from the programs I'd been in to know where I needed to grow; on the other hand, I didn't like any of them well enough to stay in when the blind impulse to run hit. I was, in fact, damn lucky to get this bum rap — the Phoenix House lawyers were standing between me and life imprisonment, and that kept me anchored. No way was I going to run, with that kind of stakes. Funny, huh? Hey, life is funny. Only you really need a sense of humor to appreciate the mess sometimes.

Because of my good attitude, Zinzarella called me in one day and told me I was being named chief expediter of the Eighty-fifth Street facility, effective immediately. I would be under nine coordinators. I thought about how I had predicted I'd be running the place in six months, and smiled.

My nine bosses were all happy I had been given the position since they knew I had the same job on Hart Island — plus I could run meetings, play a good encounter game, and still maintain my sense of humor. As they sat down around me at our first meeting, my primary interest was to get some motivation back into the house. They were all eager to know what changes I intended to make. I tried to avoid answering — I didn't want to sound arrogant. But after they continued to probe, I finally let them have it. "Okay, there are nine coordinators, and that's eight too many. We only need one."

They all started babbling incoherently just as I knew they would. But inside a couple of weeks eight of them got job changes and were rotated to facilities where they could get something positive accomplished instead of tripping over each other looking for make-work projects. By the time a month had gone by, Louie rotated my last boss and congratulated me for getting things buzzing again. Then he promoted me to the highest position a resident could hold at the facility, senior coordinator.

I had just officially assumed my new position and title when someone in the higher echelon got the bright idea that Phoenix

House should take advantage of its nonprofit status and begin to set up raffles, selling the tickets all over town. My turf was midtown, the theater district. I sat down with the crews at length and explained, "This is a very bad area. There's lots of drugs, lots of hookers, and lots of action. I'm sure, like me, that some of our people may run into dope fiends they knew before coming into Phoenix House." I didn't like selling raffles, anyway. To me, it was just another form of begging.

So six nights a week we loaded up the truck with tables, foghorns, raffle tickets, literature, and ex-junkies, driving down to Broadway where we sold chances for a dollar apiece. The nightly quotas meant we had to stay on the streets until early morning, and my premonition came true. By the end of the first two months, fourteen people had split and gone back to their prior lifestyle. Some incredible pressure came down on me out there, too. Numerous people stopped to offer me drugs. It took a tremendous amount of self-restraint to keep myself from slipping.

At the same time life was beginning to get very political at Phoenix, with six or seven directors from different parts of the city trying to force the central administrators to step down. As senior coordinator I was caught in the middle. Mitch and Natale had arranged for my lawyers; a new attorney would have been very costly, something like fifty grand. So I tried to stay clear by saying that my loyalty was to Phoenix House, no matter who was running it.

All the insurgents got fired a week after the hassle started. Phoenix House was grateful for the way I had handled myself and rewarded me with "graduation," which meant I would be earning a salary of $5,200 per year as the house manager.

The internal political flap at Phoenix had stirred the pot quite a bit, and suddenly a lot of new faces showed up with all kinds of new titles. Before I knew it I was reporting to a new area director, Jerry Brode. He called me in one day and laid out a clear directive: "Marino, I want you to personally lead the midtown crew. It made the most money for us, but I want the pace stepped up."

I said, "Jerry, you're my boss, and if you want me to go to mid-town and sell raffle tickets, I'll do it. But I am not taking any of the residents with me because too many have split and gone back to the streets. I don't think it's fair to them. Besides, if we're preaching self-help, we should start up some legitimate businesses and get out of the monkey business of begging people to buy a chance on something."

Brode stood up in anger. "Marino, I'm telling you to do what you're told, or you're fired."

Frank Natale agreed with me, but he couldn't change the raffle program, he said, because so many of the big guns were fascinated with the idea. What he could do was find me another job, but that meant a rotation — to Phalan Place House in the Bronx and a job in the financial office.

The next morning I moved to Phalan Place, and then went back downtown to the business office to meet my new boss. His name was Bernie, and he introduced me to my list of duties. Within ten minutes it was obvious I was going to be nothing but a glorified messenger boy. But what the hell, at least it was a change. I'd be making bank deposits and delivering invoices, things like that. Under the pressure of the upcoming trial, I didn't care, and just got behind the job and did what I was told.

But sometimes when I had nothing to do, I would look at the various houses' financial statements. I knew that any time residents were put on disciplinary action, they automatically had to give up either their WAM (walking-around money) or, if they were in the reentry phase, their stipend. That — with the profits from the vending machines at the facility — amounted to real money, which was not being returned to the financial department as it should have been. So most of the houses had extra slush funds, and the facility directors were keeping the money — not for themselves but for letting the residents go out at night, special food treats, stuff like that. Their intentions were good, but the money was an average of $50 per facility per month, and much more during the warmer months. About $10,000 a year — too much money — was falling between the cracks.

One month on the job and I had upgraded my position because I was saving the program so much money, and everybody in power knew it. With my own car and a personal driver, I now became the official troubleshooter for the financial department, and no longer did the bullshit clerical work. Instead, I was driven weekly to each of the sixteen Phoenix Houses, where I looked at their books.

People would erect all kinds of barriers to keep me at arm's length or try to get me to forget what I saw. I wanted to have a look at the foundation books, where the big money was found in public and private grants. The budget was $6 million in one fiscal year. An outsider was in charge of those records, and the closer I got, the more slippery he got. When I finally demanded an audit, I immediately got a job change to induction.

I was about to turn 31 and face the biggest drama of my life — the trial to decide where I'd spend the rest of it.

COURT TRIALS IN REAL LIFE are not as drama packed as in the TV show *Perry Mason*. Instead, they are tedious and drawn-out. My trial was twelve days of chain-rattling tedium. I will not bore you with the details. It was a lot of "he said, she said," and if it had not happened to be my life at stake, it would have put me to sleep. But please remember, it *was* my life at stake, and I had only just got myself back through the revolving door and finally graduated. If I went to prison for life, all my trying to get my act together would come to nothing. I know, as well as you, that many people might say, "So what? Marino's earned his prison time in a million other ways. So what if the rap they finally pin on him is bum? Isn't that justice too?" But it *was* my life, as I said, and I was running on some kind of hope that all my thrashing around wasn't in vain — that some more humane justice would recognize the good in me and the direction toward change I had taken. Innocent, I wasn't.

But innocent of *this* rap, I really was. And I was worth giving freedom to.

So for twelve days the arguments spun themselves out, the facts were presented, my witnesses were grilled and made to look dumb. Then the lawyers made their final appeals, the judge charged the jury with its obligations, and they filed out to deliberate. The rest of us settled down to wait.

I glanced around the room to see signs of encouragement. After half an hour, I felt my nerves coming unglued. What the hell could they be discussing for so long? Was I *in* Phoenix House or was I *out* of Phoenix on the night of the crime?

The first full sixty minutes with the jury deliberating ticked by on the clock. They had to be fighting — but over what? Suddenly a flash of emotion hit me in the gut and heart. It was a rush I had never experienced before. In a split second the feeling reached the tips of my fingers and toes, yet I was still sitting motionless, watching everything in total silence, like a hawk. The room appeared frozen for that one moment, and all the sounds were very distant, but I was still there, with everything in sharp focus, my mind racing.

Now, all my life I have been pretty much what I consider a stand-up guy. By that I mean that I always tried to do the right thing — if I am your friend, I will be to the end. On the streets I handled myself "right" or I would never have gotten away with what I did. I paid my bills and took care of business — that's "stand-up" on the streets. I always tried to help out my family and friends; money was secondary to that. As I was sitting in the courtroom waiting for the jury to come in, one thought filled my mind: "You say you're a stand-up character, Marino, but what are you standing *for*?"

I glanced at Mom and the rest of the family, who were waiting with me. Of course I stood for my family, but they had their own lives to lead, and I couldn't do that any better for them than they could for me. "What about starting a family and standing for that?" I felt I wasn't yet ready, even though I was 31 years old. "What about standing for a straight job and a career?" What kind of a job is there for a fourth-class former addict and ex-con like me? "Well, why not stay with an outfit like Phoenix House and make a name for yourself?" But the thought of hassling internal politics and peddling raffle tickets left me cold.

It dawned on me then that I could no longer stand up for anything to do with my former lifestyle. I had been at the edge of that pit for so long, I could never live there again. What I needed more than anything else in my life I had suddenly found — something to live for. I finally realized my purpose: to support life itself, wherever I find it, to support those who think enough of their individual lives to do something positive in the form of direct action.

People who wake up cold and alone in the gutter have a choice to make. The choice is between continuing on the trail that is destroying life or choosing a path that supports and allows a person to grow. Those are the only two choices you've got; your life is either going up or it is going down.

As I worked this out in my head, I was also terrified by the verdict and what it might hold. It seemed like forever but was actually just over three hours when the jury slowly filed back into the courtroom and took their seats. Before there had been smiles; none were now visible. The judge asked, "Has the jury reached a verdict?"

The foreman spoke: "We have, Your Honor."

The judge dictated, "The defendant will rise." I stood up with my hands frozen on the chair in front of me.

"We find the defendant not guilty, Your Honor, on all counts in the indictment."

I experienced a wave of tremendous relief. Mom came toward me, sobbing openly. I put my arms around her and knew right then that no matter what else might come in life, I could not put her through one more ordeal; it would certainly kill her. I cried with her and swore to myself, "From here on, my life is going to be positive!"

Vocational Training

I WAS A FREE MAN AGAIN. I knew I would have to leave Phoenix House for some better alternative, but nothing came to mind, at first, so I put it aside.

As things turned out, about six weeks after the trial, in March 1970, a Dr. Wiseman at Columbia Presbyterian Hospital in Manhattan had just called and said he wanted to discuss a drug prevention program. He had convinced the hospital administration they needed one, and he wanted to interview me for the position of director.

After I hung up the phone, I sat back and got hit with a heavy sensation of guilt about my past. I mentally ran through all the crimes I'd committed, the people I'd hurt, the racism and sexism and vices I'd harbored, the lives left behind me that were twisted beyond recognition, and the unbelievable number of people I knew who were dead or rotting in prison. I promised myself now I'd make as many positive contributions as I had negative.

Frank Natale could tell something was up as soon as I walked in. I told him how much I felt I owed Phoenix House. Then I told him about the job offer. Without blinking an eye he said, "If I were you, I'd take it. It sounds like a step up, and I wouldn't bet on things changing all that much around here."

I breathed a sigh of relief and held out my hand. "Frank, I love you for being who you are. This is not a goodbye. I'll give you as much time as you need to find a replacement, and I'll train him or her for you if you'd like."

TEN DAYS LATER AT COLUMBIA, I charged into the assignment like a bull hits the color red. Working eighteen hours a day, I scheduled drug seminars with all the hospital departments, spoke at outside meetings, let the emergency room know I would talk with any drug addict who came in and asked for help, and painted my office. I got the idea that it would be extremely useful for squares to know what to look for when a person starts using drugs. So I started talking to people about the telltale signs: a change in behavior, in habits, in dress and hygienic habits, those kinds of things. Before long I was being asked to come to schools, civic groups, and various churches to speak on the drug problem, which was increasing each day in New York. I always emphasized the importance of family communication and of stopping drug use before it starts or before it gets going full speed.

I'd been at Columbia only a few months when a surprise call came from Jimmy Selman, who had been the director of the Hart Island Phoenix facility. "Yo, Vinny!" he sang into the phone. "I had one helluva time tracking you down."

"Hey, Jimmy, what's happening?"

"A new program called RAP, in Washington, D.C. It stands for Regional Addiction Prevention, and Ron Clark is with me. We're right on the ground floor and could use someone like you, now."

"Well, I certainly owe it to you to at least check it out." We made plans for me to spend a weekend in Washington.

Selman enthusiastically described what they had going. I liked the general setup and the ideas he wanted to implement, but their funding was still uncertain. I told him my situation at Columbia was also up in the air because of money and asked what he wanted me to do in RAP. He smiled. "You'll have a free rein here. Start off as director of the treatment facility, and if we make it, the sky's the limit." I needed some time to think it over.

On the way back to New York Sunday night, my thoughts were jumping all over the place. I was already a director at Columbia, but the program really lacked teeth. We were basically referring people to other rehabilitation programs rather than doing anything ourselves. When I had asked if we couldn't open a detox ward, the hospital administration came back with a flat no. I headed into Wiseman's office the first thing Monday. He listened carefully and gave me the green light.

As things happened, by the time I moved to Washington I hadn't spoken to Selman for almost a week, and when I got there, he was gone. Ron Clark was now the executive director, and he wasn't at all like Selman. Not only that, he had no idea where Jimmy had gone. My only choice was to make the best of it.

So I went over to meet the people in the facility. About fifty kids were in residency — a nice bunch. I checked into my room and started working long hours to get the place in shape. But it soon became apparent that Ron and I were worlds apart when it came to basic philosophy and concepts.

Soon I heard about a hospital in Alexandria, Virginia, that was interested in setting up a drug rehab program. I sent them a résumé and they called me for an interview.

Then one day I overheard the girl at the front desk ask the caller to please spell a name again so she could take a message. The name was Rizzo. I flashed on Tony from Phoenix House and told the receptionist to transfer the call to my office. I shot up the stairs and eagerly lifted the receiver. "Hey, Tony! Vinny Marino here! How the hell are you?"

The woman at the other end was surprised. "Vinny? This isn't Tony. It's Imogene, his ex-wife. We're separated now. What's happening with Jimmy Selman?"

"Sorry to hear that. Jimmy was here until six weeks ago. Then he left, and we haven't seen him since."

"I know," she said. "He's here in Hawaii. I wanted to get as far away from the City as I could, after Tony, so I flew over here and started a new program, called Communiversity. Selman's here working as my director of induction, but I'm getting suspicious that he's back into drugs. Like, he disappears for days at a time. Vinny, I need someone reliable heading up induction, and I need that person now. This is a crucial time for the program."

"Could you use a guy like me?" I asked. "I'm looking to make a change anyway."

"Of course I'd be interested."

She explained that the salary would be $10,000 a year, plus room and board, and a car. Everything sounded good except the question of what would happen if we had major differences about the program philosophy and/or day-to-day policy matters. She said, "Look, Vinny. In the end, this is my baby. But if you don't like what's going on, this state is wide open. It's only been a state for eleven years and they need programs like this."

That did it for me. My spirit of adventure caught fire. "Ima, I'll take the job." I told her it would take me a couple of weeks. She wanted me sooner, but she agreed.

What on earth had I just talked myself into? What would Hawaii be like? Did the natives have a drug problem? How would I — a mean-streets New Yorker — fit in? Turning away from a wintery November day in Washington, I opened a newspaper and checked Hawaii's temperature. It was 78 degrees. That cinched it.

Clark seemed relieved and wished me well. I packed in less than an hour, said my goodbyes, and headed north to New York.

You should have seen the looks when I told everyone in the City what I had up my sleeve. Mom looked at me like I had lost my marbles. "My God, Vinny, you must be crazy. Hawaii isn't even civilized yet!"

Frankie was just as shocked. "You can't be serious. Six thousand miles? We'll never see you again."

Pop laughed. "You sure you're ready for those natives?"

When I left Frank at the gate and walked to the plane, it was starting to snow. It was a nonstop flight from Kennedy to Honolulu International. After about eight hours, I fell asleep. When I opened my eyes, the sun was coming up and the pilot announced, "Ladies and gentlemen, on the right side of the aircraft you can see the island of Oahu." The visual impact of the island below us was so astounding that I pulled back and took a deep breath to be certain I wasn't high or dreaming. I leaned forward and looked again to make sure. I had never seen so many different shades of green, and I was overwhelmed by Diamond Head crater. At that point I said to myself, "Dummy, if you don't like this lifestyle, you *belong* in a Manhattan gutter." If you've never been to Hawaii, you've got to understand that it's paradise — watching the sunrise wash dark blue and rose and flame-color over the turquoise breakers, while the waves break and slide silver back into the ocean. Seeing it for the first time really was like entering paradise.

WE HAD SIX WEEKS, START TO FINISH. Imogene didn't like my high-profile style, and the success I had in bringing in new residents didn't seem to help. At the request of Dr. Neal Winn, chairman of the board of Communiversity, I tried to work out our difficulties. He looked at me directly and asked, "Do you want to change jobs, or do you have a problem working with Imogene? If it's Imogene, are you going to run, or are you willing to stick around and see if we can't work it out?"

That last question brought the fighter in me to the surface. "Dr. Winn, I was once among the best runners in New York but no longer. If there's a way to work it out, I want to find it."

"All right then, I'll call a board meeting as soon as possible, and I'll invite you in so we can have some open dialogue."

The first board meeting didn't warm up relations with Imogene, but our respective work loads were separated. That was a beginning. But the night of the second board meeting didn't go too well. Imogene walked in flanked by two senior residents and looking extremely cold. Before she uttered a word, Ima tossed a sheaf of papers at each board member and at me: The board of directors and Vinny Marino had been fired.

Neal Winn's face went white. "This baffles me completely," he said stiffly.

I stood up, bowed, and said, "Well, I'm not at all baffled. I'm leaving. Good night, folks."

Walking back to the staff house to pack up, I explained what was happening to my girlfriend, Pat, who was waiting for me. Apparently during the week I was suspended, Ima had wired up the residents by telling them that I was attempting to take over her program. As a result, the residents were highly emotional and hostile toward me. In fact, Ima's boyfriend stood in my way at the door and said, "Don't go in the house. You're not welcome."

My first thought was to bounce him off the nearest wall, but instead I said, "Look, tough guy, my belongings are inside, and I intend to get them. So just stay where you are, and let's do this like gentlemen, because my patience could run out."

I took Pat by the hand and we went around him, heading straight for my room. Five minutes later, I was throwing things hurriedly in a bag when I heard some fierce knocking at my door. One of the residents was screaming incoherently out in the hall. I turned around: "Tell her I don't want to talk to anyone, please. I really don't want to get the residents involved, it's not fair to them."

Pat eased the door open and tried to calm the young girl, one of my new inductees, who was getting hysterical. Finally I agreed to let the kid in and I got her to slow down her crying. Through sobs she kept muttering, "Vinny, don't leave me here. You can't leave me here. You brought me here. Wherever you're going, I want to go along." Before I could tell her the truth (how the hell can I take you with me when I don't know where I'm going?), another resident popped in. Then another, and another, until six residents were standing in the room, threatening that if I didn't take them with me, they were all leaving for the streets, saying, "It's not fair, because you promised us that this was a good program, and we really believe in you, Vinny."

What could I say? I had in fact brought each of them into Communiversity, but I had no place to go and no idea what to do with six more people, even for one night. More important, I wondered, what were we going to do tomorrow?

As we were leaving, a young married couple named Bob and Rosie, graduates of the Mendocino Family Drug Program in California and also on Ima's staff, approached me. They asked if they could come along too. At first I was hesitant, because neither of them had ever backed me. But I figured two more couldn't make that much difference, and they might be helpful in handling the others. I was beginning to feel like the Pied Piper of Honolulu.

We all agreed our most immediate need was to find housing for the night. We decided our best bet would be to head into town to the Waikiki Drug Clinic and call some of the board members who had been fired that evening. Maybe they could help.

Within a couple of hours we were meeting with Neal Winn and a man named Mickey Hummer, who worked for the state of Hawaii. Both were men of intelligence, spirit, and integrity, and they carried a lot of weight in their community. I respected them, and their trust and encouragement meant a lot to me.

We hashed over the evening's events. The first order of business was to find a place to sleep. Neal suggested hotel rooms down in Waikiki.

"Neal," I protested, "I'd like to keep these kids all together, and I *don't* want them in Waikiki. That's where most of them got into trouble in the first place."

Mickey said, "Vinny, I own a small house in Kailua. It's empty, and would be a place to stay for a few days until we can sort out the situation at Communiversity."

"That's great, Mickey."

Our caravan had five cars, as we headed up into the mountains in a torrential tropical rainstorm. Rain fell on us in silver dollars as we inched up the steep slopes. Mickey led the way, and we followed over the Pali Highway.

I swore repeatedly and a couple of the girls giggled nervously as I eased the car around hairpin curves and down the steep windward side of the mountain. Just when I had about decided I had missed the turn and driven into the ocean, we reached level ground, and the rain let up. We found Mickey pulled over on the side of the road, waiting for us. He leaned out his car window to wave at us. "How do you like Hawaii now, Vinny?" I grinned. From the beginning, the outrageous beauty and power of Hawaii blew me away — even the high *pali* (cliffs), in a wild storm.

We followed Mickey through the quiet streets of the little town of Kailua. He pulled up in front of a small house. A light rain was still falling, and it dripped from tall trees onto the neat green lawn.

Mickey opened the door to the house and turned on the lights. One of them lit up the swimming pool in the backyard, and even in the rain it looked beautiful, like a blue jewel. We all followed Mickey into the house. It may have looked small to him, but to us it looked wonderful. There were two and a half bedrooms, a bath and a half, a kitchen, and a fair-sized living room. Except for a pool table, the house had no furniture, but most of us were tired enough to sleep standing up.

I took Pat's hands and led her into the kitchen. She looked so tired. I put my arms around her and pulled her close. I wished we had a place to be alone, but already several faces were peeking around the edge of the door. I started to jokingly yell at them, but Pat laughed as she moved out of my arms. After she told the others good night, I walked out to her car and kissed her.

"You are one fantastic lady," I told her as she pulled away. She waved, and I stood in the driveway watching her until I could no longer see her car.

I turned back to the house, breathing deeply of the cool, clean night air. Through the lighted windows, I watched the kids moving from room to room. For a minute I felt like turning my back and walking away into the night, but my own cocky self began to argue back right away. Okay, Vinny, it said cheerfully, here's your big chance. You've been telling all kinds of people what's wrong with their rehab programs. Now you can show them how you think it ought to be done.

I gave the girls one of the bedrooms. The guys crashed on the living room floor. I crashed in the other bedroom.

... Who Lived in a Shoe

I WAS AWAKENED IN THE MORNING by the excited voices of the kids. The sun was bright and hot. Since I hadn't gotten to sleep until about 4:30 A.M., I figured the day would be just as beautiful if it started a few hours later, and I'd be in better shape to appreciate it.

"How the hell can they be so cheerful so early?" I muttered.

But I struggled to my feet, stretched my muscles, and buttoned myself into the shirt I'd been using for a pillow. Through the open window I could see the kids laughing and playing around the swimming pool. I glared at them and stomped into the bathroom, where I shaved and showered quickly, annoyed that I had only one small towel.

Then I started to laugh. How could I get upset over a small towel? I had no sheets and no beds to put them on if I had them. I had no chairs, no tables — except for the pool table (which would prove useful as a bed) — no sofas, no rugs, no dishes. I had no food to put on the dishes I didn't have, either. And the small amount of money I had wouldn't last long with all the demands I was about to put on it.

I joined the kids in the yard. That was one thing I did have — plenty of kids, all needing things I didn't have. Nobody was complaining, though, and that made me feel good. I went out to get breakfast for everyone. Then I gathered everyone around me for a meeting. We talked about our situation and what we could do.

The kids were apprehensive and anxious, and I explained I honestly had no idea what I was going to do and that I didn't see how it would be possible for us to stay in the house much longer. They got really upset. As a matter of fact, a couple of the girls were crying.

Mickey returned, and then in walked Neal. Both brought bedding, towels, and enough food to get us through a day or two. Mickey showed the kids where the washer and dryer were. A little later Pat showed up with dishes, glasses, silverware, and a couple of brooms and mops. She even brought pots and pans, a coffee pot, some bread and peanut butter. She stayed and helped us make a pile of peanut butter sandwiches, and we all ate lunch together.

The kids were relaxed and content again, hoping everything was okay. But I was looking further down the road than tonight's dinner, and knew our problems were not over. If anything, they were getting worse because that afternoon four more kids left Communiversity to join us. I didn't know how they got the word so fast, but they did and within a week our population grew from six to sixteen. The only thing I really could feel when that sixteenth person walked through the door was fear.

I began to start talking to myself: Vinny, what the hell are you doing? There's very little money, a small house. What if a bunch more people want in? How are you going to house them? How are you going to feed them? And how on earth are you going to get a rehab program up and moving.

And I thought about the troops. What about Maria? She was the one who had gotten hysterical and convinced me to take her with me when I left Communiversity. She was only 16, her parents were divorced, and she was convinced she was unloved.

What about Alice and her brother Todd? They were 15 and 18. Again, it was a family thing, and he was into pot. He was also about to be drafted, and he told me he'd run away to Canada if he didn't have us.

What about Beverly, a local girl, 17 years old, who every time we gave her a "haircut" (criticism) cried big crocodile tears?

What about Kimo? He was the wildest of them all, the one who had the most trouble suppressing his urge for violence. I don't think there was a drug he hadn't used, and his personality had suffered — the more he used, the nastier he got, until nasty is all he thought he was.

Neal and Mickey tried to convince me things would work out. They wanted to establish a program in Kailua, called Windward Communiversity, and suggested that Bob and I could codirect. They asked me to meet with the rest of the directors from Communiversity. I agreed.

At the meeting they told me the board was bringing a lawsuit against Ima, who had withdrawn $50,000 of Communiversity's funds and put it into a cashier's check that she refused to return. The board hired a flamboyant attorney named David Schutter, and he and I felt an instant rapport. Unfortunately, ours was the first case David ever lost. He proved, however, to be a valuable friend and ally of Habilitat, as my new program ended up being called.

He called about a week later to tell me about one of his clients, Frank Cockett. His induction is a good example of how we recruit and initiate new residents. Frank was a Maui boy, young, married, with a kid. He was into barbiturates and alcohol, and when his wife threatened to leave him and take their son, he got a shotgun and threatened to kill her and her mother and father and to take the child. It ended with Frank driving his car into a tree and breaking his jaw, among other injuries. He was treated at a local hospital, arrested, and formally charged with attempted murder and kidnapping, and possession of a firearm. And he was sent to the state hospital on the island of Oahu.

I arranged with Frank's family to have him brought to me. I told them that if I did not, for whatever reasons, accept him into the program, my advice would be to have him sent back to the hospital so that he couldn't get into further trouble.

When Frank came over, we paired him up with four local guys — two from the island of Maui, the other two from Oahu — to take him on a tour of our facility while I sat down to talk with his parents. Frank was lazy, selfish, and self-centered. He didn't care about anybody in the world, had no knowledge of the word *respect,* wanted *what* he wanted *when* he wanted it, and abused his parents and his wife and her family. And of course things got worse as he became more and more involved with drugs and alcohol.

I ended the interview, sent for Frank, and asked the residents to show Mr. and Mrs. Cockett around. As I asked Frank to have a seat, it was easy for me to tell that I was face to face with an arrogant, cocky, young punk. I told him I had only two reasons for bothering with him. First, his parents reminded me of my parents, who had put up with a lot of shit from me. Second, Dave Schutter was a friend, and he had asked if we could be of some help because Frank had a serious drug problem and Dave didn't want to see him go to prison, where he would receive no help.

A lot of people still think jails rehabilitate. These are the same people who have no idea that one out of every 450 Americans is in jail. (At the time, only the Soviet Union and South Africa had a higher percentage of their citizens locked up.) How many of them, do you think, are improved by the experience? The truth is that all jails do today is punish and warehouse. I believed my program could become a real, workable alternative to prison, one that placed 100 percent of its effort into what the jails gave up on — the reconstruction of the individual. Whenever I hear somebody call a jail a "correctional facility," I have to laugh.

I told Frank he really had no choice. Either he entered the program or he would go to prison. I also explained that I could not guarantee I could get him probated to us from both Maui and the federal court here on Oahu. However, I emphasized that if this were possible, he would have to stay with us until he was clinically discharged. Otherwise he would be violating the court's stipulation.

I also explained that although Dave Schutter and his parents had brought him as far as my office, he couldn't become a resident unless he passed a rigid interview with me and some of his peers. Unless he could convince us he was willing to abide by our rules, he could leave and sort out his own problems.

He shrugged and said, "Well, I guess I have no choice. Let's go on with the interview." He didn't bother to say thank you, or even look alert.

I said, "Look, asshole, I don't know where you think you are or who the hell you think you're talking to, but I don't like your attitude. You've got all the ingredients to become one royal pain in the ass. I'm not your mother and I'm not your father, so I'm not going to put up with your bullshit. If you don't like that and your attitude doesn't change immediately, you might as well get the hell out of here now."

I could see the change in Frank's face immediately. I sent for the residents and told them to put Frank on the prospect chair (a chair used for inductees).

For the next five hours, Frank sat waiting for the interview to begin. Keeping a person waiting is an invaluable technique. It gives the potential resident a chance to observe what is going on. He or she is totally ignored by everyone, but he can't help noticing that everyone else is working, contributing something.

All around, Frank saw Maria, Kimo, and the others going about their daily chores — cleaning the bathrooms and woodwork and floors, checking in food shipments, making lunch, raking leaves on the lawn, and sweeping the pool area. They washed windows. They washed clothes. They washed the car. Frank could see this program was not some halfway house where a person can sit around and watch TV all day.

We were watching him, too. You can learn a lot about someone who has to sit and wait for an unreasonable amount of time. It's a small pressure, but it's pressure nonetheless, and Frank reacted predictably.

He was getting nervous as he sat. At first he was puzzled, and then, after several hours, he got bored and impatient. He was not permitted to go to sleep, however. He was told to stay alert but to keep quiet. He was not allowed to talk, either.

When he was finally called into my office, four of the residents and I immediately started bombarding him. First, we attacked his attitude and how he had walked onto the property thinking he was hot stuff. Second, we stressed that we didn't feel he actually realized the amount of trouble he was in because he figured David Schutter would get him out.

One of the Maui guys said, "You're really funny, Frank. You walk around like you're a tough guy, and yet your jaw is wired up — you're going to be sucking out of a straw for the next three or four months. You know what, sucker? If we decide not to accept you, you'll be running your Bruce Lee act in the state or the federal penitentiary, whichever one they send you to. You better knock it off and understand that this isn't Maui, and we're not the guys you were raised with. We're also here because if not, we'd be in jail. Now, let's get down to the nitty-gritty. What do you want from us?"

Frank didn't know how to act. He looked at me and asked, "What do *you* want?"

"Hey, Frank, I don't want anything. The one that's in trouble is you, not us."

In the ensuing conversation, we learned how long he had been using drugs and what type, how long he had been drinking and to what extent. We also learned that he really didn't want to work and was very lazy and was also flippant and sarcastic — altogether a swaggering Mr. Macho Man. He told us his nickname on Maui was "Oiler" — meaning someone who was slimy, slippery, and couldn't be trusted. We all started to ridicule him and make fun of the name Oiler, and I told him life was going to be totally different here. Frank started to get a little more serious. He asked again what we wanted.

I said, "Well, to begin with we're going to shave your head, but first you have to ask for our help."

He wanted to know why we were going to shave his head, and he was simply told, "That's the way it is. We don't give reasons around here and, frankly, it's none of your goddamned business. You don't have any choices, except to leave."

So he asked for help.

One kid, named Philly, said, "Louder."

Frank yelled louder.

Then another kid, Bobby, said, "Louder, I can't hear you." (It's hard enough to scream under those circumstances, much less with your jaws wired together.)

When we thought he had had enough, I said, "Frank, what do you really want?"

With tears in his eyes, he said, "I want some help! I don't *want* to go to prison. I'm sorry for what I did. I'm sorry I came over here acting like a wise guy. I'm not, really. I'm willing to do whatever you tell me, but please keep me out of prison."

Again I looked at him straight and said, "Okay, we'll accept you." We all hugged him and said, "Welcome."

Finally the day came to go to court. Frank was facing a federal charge in Honolulu and a state charge on Maui. I told the Maui judge that the federal judge on Oahu said he'd promised to give Frank a break.

The judge on Maui said, "Well, if the judge in Honolulu is giving him a break, I will, too."

THE NEXT CASE WAS NOT SO SUCCESSFUL. It shows what kind of cliff these kids live on all the time. A woman called me up about her daughter Linda, who was 16 years old. She asked for an appointment, and when she came, I had four females show Linda around and explain the program while I spoke to her mother.

The mother was very nervous, and stuttered constantly. It turned out that Linda was using drugs, the mother didn't really know what kind, and also drinking rather heavily. She had taken Linda to a few head shrinkers, who hadn't helped. She didn't know where to go or who to turn to, and someone at a local social service agency referred her to us.

She related that one afternoon when she came home unexpectedly, she found Linda in a stupor. She was on the bed, nude, with three young men, also nude. She screamed at the men to get dressed and chased them out of the house, and then she tried to help Linda, who was incoherent. She made coffee, gave Linda a bath, followed by a cool shower to wake her up.

Then she asked, "What's going on? Who are these people? Why are you in this kind of shape?"

Linda was dazed: "What people? What shape? I'm okay, Mom, I must have just had a little too much to drink."

From that time until the meeting with me she hadn't let Linda out of her sight. She didn't go to work, and if she had to go to the store, she took Linda with her. She told me that if this was what she had *seen* happen, imagine what was going on that she *didn't* see. Many nights Linda had come home real late, looking disheveled and obviously intoxicated.

When I spoke to Linda, she seemed very wired, fidgety, and couldn't look me in the eye. I explained what her mother had told me. She candidly said that although she didn't realize what had really happened that night, it was not the first time. I asked Linda if this made her happy.

"No," she said sullenly.

Then I asked her what drugs she was using.

"I use all kinds, but mainly barbiturates, and I drink a lot, mostly vodka."

"Well, it might be in your interest to enter our program and try to find out why you're trying to kill yourself." I explained that we had a long-range program and that the drugs and/or alcohol were not really the problem but only the symptoms, like a fever, a sign of how she felt about herself. Linda agreed.

So I sent for her mother and explained that it was best to say a quick goodbye, that our procedure was to cut off all family ties for two or three months. We would have Linda write her a letter within a week to let her know how she felt about the program. Then if the mother wanted to, she could call once or twice a month to find out Linda's progress, and after Linda earned the right to have a visit, that would be arranged.

But Linda started crying hysterically. She begged her mom, "Please take me home. I don't want to stay here. I don't want to have to be here for two years. I promise I'll be good, I won't use drugs anymore, I'll go back to school, I won't fool around with guys. I swear, Mom, I've learned my lesson. Please give me one last chance."

Her mother started crying. "Linda, I'm afraid next time I might not be around to help you."

But being as manipulative as most drug addicts are, Linda made her mother feel guilty: "I'm your *daughter!* How can you leave me and just turn your back on me! If you and Dad had gotten along, I would never have gotten into drugs. I swear, I've learned my lesson. Take me home, *please* give me one more chance!"

Linda's mom looked at me despairingly and said, "Vinny, I can't leave her. She obviously doesn't want to stay, and I really want to believe that she's learned her lesson and is going to do the right thing."

"Whatever you do is up to you," I said. "What we've got here is strictly self-help. But you should know that Linda needs a highly controlled, structured environment. Otherwise she's heading into serious trouble. If you let her manipulate you, I can't be of any help. I strongly recommend you get her into some place where she can be under strict supervision — and I wouldn't waste a lot of time doing it."

Three days later Linda was found on a bench in Kapiolani Park in Honolulu — dead from an overdose of a combination of barbiturates and alcohol.

THESE TWO EXAMPLES SHOW YOU what a drug rehab program is constantly working with — the danger of death and the need to provide a safe, highly structured environment for the addict to leave drugs and turn around in. That environment has to restrict the impulsive, manipulative personality while it breaks a physical and mental addiction and slowly turns the individual around to think and act positively. Act *as if* long enough and eventually you become.

Sitting on the Fence

I N THE NEXT FEW WEEKS, as the population in the house grew to twenty-two, I continued to meet with the Communiversity board. While I kept insisting I was still returning to the mainland, at the same time I was running all over town — to family court, circuit court, Halawa Jail, the state hospital, and the kids' detention home, actively recruiting more people, which made no sense at all.

I can't imagine how I functioned with two such contradictory goals. Maybe I was still playing out the role of the director of induction, or perhaps I had already decided to stay but hadn't admitted it to myself. Probably a combination of both. At any rate, during the day Bob and Rosie held down the fort at the facility while I kept busy promoting and pitching the program.

We were getting fantastic support from the Windward Coalition of Ministers. The only problem was that in order to get the food and supplies the organization furnished so generously, we also had to accept a lot of fellowship and well-meant sermonizing, which turned off most of our kids. I explained to the kids that if they couldn't handle the situation, they should come to me, and I would get them off the hook. And on the other side, I'm sure at times that some of our benefactors must have been shocked at the language they heard, especially from the newcomers. However, they hung in with us, and we made some good friends.

We were getting it together by now. We had printed signs designating the "Director's Office," "Kitchen," "Recreation Area," and so on. The place was spotless, we were eating fairly regularly, and we were making ourselves known and liked. We helped our neighbors with yard work and cleaned the streets and sidewalks, and did our best to be an asset to the area. In the early mornings we jogged through the streets singing, and soon nearly everyone in Kailua knew who we were.

After everything was cleaned at the house, the troops sometimes started in all over again. To some that might have looked like busywork, but it wasn't. The idea was to keep everyone occupied so they couldn't dwell on their desire for alcohol or drugs or being somewhere else. Addicts have that constant, crazy-making urge — those of you who've quit smoking or gone on a serious diet know what I'm talking about — and they absolutely have to stay busy. Preferably in physical motion, because the body as well as the mind needs constant attention.

In between jobs I ran encounter groups, and I gave talks on some of the ideas I wanted them to learn. A lot came from what I myself had learned at Synanon, Daytop, and Phoenix House. For example, I said that if you act *as if* long enough, you *become*. That was from Ralph Waldo Emerson. It works this way: You build your shell, your front, the way you want it to look, and then you grow inside to fit your shell. Meanwhile, the people outside are responding to the new you, so that helps reinforce your becoming what at first you only aspired to be.

From Thomas Edison I took another lesson: *If the mind of man can conceive and believe, he can achieve.* That's sort of the same as Emerson. If you can imagine something, with conviction, you make it real. If you can imagine your new life and believe in yourself, you will make it real.

Another of my favorites was Saul Alinsky, who believed the little guy could win, but only if he helped himself. This is gold, and it's the cornerstone of a forward-looking program. Like the old proverb "God helps those who help themselves," it was our rule for the program at Habilitat as well as for our kids: self-reliance beats relying on others every time.

I told them the four cardinal rules for the program, too: no alcohol or drugs, no violence or threat of violence, no sex, no stealing. These four rules allow people who are under great stress and have poor self-control to live together halfway peacefully. Of these, the no sex rule can be the hardest to understand, because having sex is not antisocial, like the other behaviors. But sex is the original dynamite social relationship, and it sinks ships unless people are ready to handle it right. Junkies coming into the program just aren't ready to do sexual relationships justice.

When I was in other rehabilitation programs, I also developed some of my own sayings — things that made a person think a little. Like "Yesterday, today was tomorrow. What happened? Tomorrow, today will be yesterday. What did you accomplish?" I'd ask the troops what that meant to them. It started them thinking about goals. Setting goals is the first step to getting somewhere without drifting.

From the beginning, I encouraged everyone to read. Some of these kids had never read even a newspaper, and I insisted they learn to do that. I used *Six Weeks to Words of Power* by Funk to encourage them to increase their vocabulary and use unfamiliar words. We set up a blackboard in a highly visible area, and every day we learned one new word. We called it "the word of the day." Everyone had to learn its meaning and how to spell it, and then use it at least ten times.

The response to the education efforts was amazing. It's probably true that our general population didn't include many who would become nuclear physicists or astronauts, but their positive reaction to a little mental stimulation was deeply gratifying. Many of our residents had never been exposed to much education before, and those who had been exposed had rejected it. I think the fact that they trusted and believed in me had a great deal to do with it. They knew I was for real and that I'd once walked in their shoes.

I also established a policy regarding the residents' personal belongings, which ensured that no problems would arise from one person having more material possessions than another. These rules still apply today. When residents come into the program, they are told to bring sneakers, socks, work clothes, underwear, and a couple of sets of dressier clothes. If the new resident arrives with more than this, he or she can send it home or donate it to the program.

The same rule applies to cash or personal property such as radios, electric razors, and so on. Later, when residents have been here for awhile and are doing well in the program, they are allowed to write or phone home and request some personal belongings. In this way, they learn that they must earn all privileges. They also learn there is no free lunch in life, and you get nothing for nothing — anything you get definitely must be earned. By the way, it's a good lesson for parents, too: If your kids never have to work to earn anything, they may balk at work when they grow up. So teach them while they are young.

DURING THAT PERIOD WE DID HAVE one unfortunate neighborhood experience. We lived next door to a family with several teenage kids. Their parents left for a long trip, and the kids threw a series of parties that lasted until morning and included booze and drugs. On a day after one of these parties, we found an almost empty bottle of vodka near the hedge on our side of the backyard. Of course, we allowed no alcohol on our property. I immediately questioned our people about it, and they all denied any knowledge of it. I guessed what had happened, but I had no proof. I figured that these kids next door deliberately put that bottle on our side to undermine our program.

The same thing happened the next time they had a party. On the third occasion, we actually saw the kids push a bottle through the hedge into our yard. Moreover, we were constantly rained with small stones thrown from their side of the fence over to ours. I became furious. I gathered several of my biggest, toughest, ugliest guys, and we paid a visit next door. I told the kids I knew what had happened and demanded an apology. One of them got abusive with me, and in the heat of the moment I told him if it happened again I'd rip his face off. Of course, we didn't actually touch anybody, but these people were trying to set us up, and I was really angry.

When we got back to our house, my guys decided we needed to sit down and talk. One said, "Hey, Vinny, you taught us that one of the cardinal rules is no violence or threat of violence. What's going on?"

I felt embarrassed, because they were absolutely right. I told them, "Okay, I blew it. I was wrong and I apologize, but I'm only human. However, if we had not caught these people, one or two of you guys might eventually have gotten blamed and thrown out. You might have wound up back in prison or in the streets shooting dope, possibly dying. I lost my head, but it's because I care. I can promise you, however, it will never happen again!"

The next day, the kids next door wrote a letter to the local newspaper saying they had been threatened by us, specifically me, for no reason. Sensing a lurid story, the newspaper prepared to play it up big. Fortunately, a friend of mine on the newspaper staff called me and I went down and met with the editor. I explained our version, the entire truth. In the meantime, the parents next door had returned home, and I also told them what happened. The story never appeared and the parents apologized.

I learned from this event that I had to lead by example instead of by sermon, and my people realized that I was human. I, too, am capable of making mistakes. Most importantly, the whole experience finally made me realize I was staying in Hawaii. I enjoyed the challenge. I enjoyed the trust the residents had in me, and I believed that I could succeed with my program.

I also knew there was a big reckoning ahead.

Bob and I continued to work as codirectors, but it was getting increasingly hard. Even though he and Rosie were good people, I doubted whether they could focus on teaching common sense, self-reliance, and responsibility. They tended to concentrate on lofty, philosophical ideas and goals that didn't make much sense to our teenage dropouts, who mostly spoke pidgin English.

One afternoon I returned from court to find Bob running a seminar on Erich Fromm's book, *The Art of Loving*. I listened to him for awhile, and watched the befuddled looks on the kids' faces. They obviously had no idea what he was talking about. I asked a couple of kids to explain his lecture, which confirmed my suspicions. Later I asked Bob to talk with me in private.

He yelled, "Vinny, stay out of it when I'm running a seminar! I'll take care of things in the house — you take care of things outside."

"Bob, you're pontificating and philosophizing to kids who just don't understand your language. They can't comprehend what you're saying. You're making them feel inferior, and they're going to split." That was the bottom line — the residents who get uncomfortable don't feel at home, so they get homesick for the streets. You've got to start from where the people *are,* not from where you are. That's basic to any rehab program, to any grassroots work.

We got into a full-blown argument. To settle it, I called an emergency meeting of the board of directors. I told them every ship has only one captain. I said, "Believe me, I don't want to leave, but he's turning off these kids, and I'm getting tired of patching it up."

The board asked Bob and me to each write a proposal on what we thought the program, the philosophy, and the goals should be. We were to submit the proposals in one week, and they would decide who would be the next executive director. Bob made it easy. At the end of the week, he submitted his resignation. He and Rosie would be gone within two days.

THAT NIGHT I DROVE to Kailua Beach. I could see the shining path of the moon on the water. I counted stars and listened to the surf. In my mind I hashed over the program I wanted to run. The four and a half years I'd spent in three of the country's largest and best-qualified therapeutic communities would let me make some well-informed decisions about what works and what doesn't work.

Sitting there on my rock, the water eddying and receding around me, I thought about what my own program would be like if I took it beyond its present, primitive state. I'd incorporate what I thought was valuable from the programs I'd been in and discard the garbage I didn't like. Plus I'd throw in some of my own ideas, which I had never been allowed to use before.

Still, the thought of accepting the responsibility for other people straightening out their lives was a little unnerving. What if I made mistakes — as I already had? What if, instead of helping somebody, I actually hurt them? I had quit using drugs, I had stopped my criminal activities and had learned to respect myself, but could I really teach these things to others? Did I realize what the responsibilities of a program director were?

The warm night wind rattled the fronds of the palm trees behind me. Down on the sand, the silver water pearled and fanned out with each wave. Off to the south horizon, a boat blinked red lights in the dark. One part of me was saying, "Hey, Vinny, the hell with all this responsibility and worry!" Another part was pumping adrenaline, eager to take on the challenge. Okay kid, I thought, moment of truth. This is where you prove you've got the guts to do the job.

I walked back to the car and drove home. Next morning I called everyone in and told them what I wanted to do. I told them all the things that had been running through my mind. I asked them to recommit themselves to new ideas, a new way of building new lives. They were excited and enthusiastic. We talked and talked. Finally I called Neal and told him about my plans. He was all for it. For the first time, I was on my way, captain of the ship.

Name That Baby!

THE NEXT DAY, I asked all the residents to help me come up with a new name for our program. One of the kids said, "Habitat." Then another one said, "How about Habilitat?"

The name Habilitat struck me just right, and I said, "Hey, I like that." Unfortunately, I was the only one who did. Everyone else was against it. A slight disagreement ensued, and I decided this was a good time to explain that Habilitat was not going to be a democracy. Democracy is for people who are mature. Drug addicts need a tighter ship, or they'll run it aground. I told them the new name was going to be Habilitat because it was unique, like us. Someday the name Habilitat would ring proudly throughout the state of Hawaii and eventually the entire United States.

With incorporation, I knew we could get our nonprofit status and apply for a number of grants that weren't available otherwise. We could also attract a lot of tax-deductible contributions from businesses and individuals. So within a short time, we were Habilitat, Inc., with the subtitle "Place of Change."

By now a sort of routine was in place at the Kailua house. After breakfast, we started with a morning meeting. We sang songs and performed spontaneous skits. For example, I'd have some of the troops pretend they were chickens laying eggs. Usually we did something that got a laugh, got the people in an up mood for the rest of the day. But it could also be a lesson in humility. At least once a week, everyone got to play the fool. The morning session was useful in more ways than one. For example, later in an encounter session, a guy might pull a macho number, but someone could destroy it by saying, "Hey, weren't you a chicken this morning?"

I strove endlessly to generate positive feelings and ideas to keep everyone motivated. I talked about my ideas, dreams, and aspirations — constantly painting the big picture. Eventually we'd have our own businesses, our own property, and we'd be recognized. We'd each and all together "be somebody."

Because I believed so deeply what I was telling them, they came to believe it too. I could feel that bunch of unrelated kids from widely diverse backgrounds and ethnic origins begin to pull together as family. From that time on, we've referred to ourselves as the Habilitat family. For some of the kids, it was the only family they'd ever known. For others, it was a temporary substitute for a family they loved but couldn't cope with.

One of Hawaii's ancient traditions is called *ohana,* the extended family. Years ago, when Hawaiians couldn't care for their own children for any reason — sickness, economy, the death of a spouse, whatever — they would farm their kids out to a family more able to provide for them. For all of us, the Habilitat Family was *ohana,* a loving and supportive group at a time when we needed it most.

Of course, it wasn't all sweetness and light. Sleeping bags and mattresses on hard floors get old fast, especially when someone in the corner needs to use the bathroom in the middle of the night and, in getting there, steps on a dozen sleeping bodies. And a bath and a half aren't enough for forty-four people, which is how many we had under one roof. Imagine what it was like when someone needed to relieve himself during the day and found himself thirteenth in line. (The seats were *always* warm!) Or imagine you wanted to take a shower and, guess what, you're number thirty-three. Keep in mind, too, that after the third shower in the morning, the water was always *cold.*

The board finally told me I had to do something. There was a potential fire hazard, to say the least. So with the help of a minister, Jim Ledgerwood, I obtained three large tents and two smaller ones. We erected them in the backyard and moved thirty of the residents into them. Of course, in Hawaii this is possible, even great. You couldn't do it in North Dakota!

At the same time, I was working on an idea to drain the pool and fill it with bunk beds that I would shield with an overhead canopy. I figured we could put about thirty more people in that big hole by using double-deck beds. But I hated the thought of losing the pool. When I came home tired and disgusted after something went wrong in court or when someone split, my attitude had an immediate effect on the kids. Within minutes, we would all be depressed and discouraged, feeding on each other's misery. That's when the pool offered an excellent release.

Maria was really coming around. She was a natural leader, and I counted on her to go along with anything I recommended to try to keep things in the house positive. When I'd come home in a slump, I'd ask Maria for a hug, then lift her onto my shoulder, rush out of the house, and toss her into the pool, clothes and all. Of course, within seconds, someone threw someone else in the pool, and it went on and on until we were all wet and laughing and had forgotten our problems.

Many times, I too was thrown in the pool fully clothed, wallet and all. When you have to teach by example instead of sermon, you have to go with the flow. Everybody would start laughing because Vinny had proved to be not only a leader but also a human being.

One such day a young man named Gary thought he was really slick. He locked himself in the half-bathroom so no one could dunk him, but his plan backfired on him. The guys quickly took the bathroom door off the hinges with screwdrivers, put Gary on the door, rushed him out, and heaved him into the pool. The funniest part of all was that Mickey Hummer chose to pay us a visit at that moment to see how we were getting along in *his* house. He sloshed through an inch of water in the kitchen and joined in the laughter. He didn't even threaten to evict us.

ALTHOUGH I FELT GOOD about the way we were all living and working together, my need for more staff members was well past the crisis stage. So I called a board meeting and asked the members to send me to New York, where I could round up some experienced people. I still wasn't getting paid myself, but some of the board members agreed to chip in to provide travel expenses. They would also take turns coming over to supervise the house while I was gone, and Pat agreed to lend a hand too. I took off for New York, explaining that I'd call two or three times a day to check on the facility.

In New York I headed for Phoenix House and looked up an old friend named Gerard DeLisio, who was about to graduate from that program. I told him I was looking for staff members for my new program and would like to have him join us. I told him honestly that we had no money, but we had a definite monetary commitment from a local foundation that would be coming in within a month to forty-five days. I also told him he could play a large part in developing the program and be in on the ground floor, and we could build it together.

Gerard came to a meeting at my mother's house and brought another old friend, Jerry Cousino, with him. Both had worked for me at Phoenix House. We all had a good sense of humor, but when it came down to the bottom line, we got things done. Jerry's long suit was public relations and fund-raising, and he had the glib tongue that goes along with such work.

Gerard agreed to come if Jerry would. He seemed worried about hot weather in Hawaii and wanted some assurance that I'd provide him with an air-conditioned room. I promised them that their quarters most certainly would be air-conditioned. I neglected to mention that they would be living in a tent.

They had not officially graduated from Phoenix House, so we had to break them out and take them to the airport for their departure to Hawaii. The driver of the car was a woman named Vickie Russo. Vickie was married to a childhood buddy of mine. He was also a resident at Phoenix House, trying to break his drug habit.

When we were safely airborne and there was no turning back, I told Gerard and Jerry a bit more about their air-conditioned rooms. I hastened to add that it was a *nice* tent, large and airy, and they would have it all to themselves. There was even a swimming pool beside it, and if they wanted to take a quick morning dip as a refresher, that was fine with me. When I stopped for a breath, there was only shocked silence. Then they began to laugh.

Within a few days, Gerard and Jerry felt right at home. Soon I made another trip to New York and returned with two more old friends, a Puerto Rican named Izmael Carrasquillo and a black kid, Mark Smith. Both were graduates of Phoenix House, and Izzy and I had grown up together.

I HAVE TO TELL A COUPLE of stories about that hard first period of growth. When I was living on the street, I survived by my wits and imagination -— any junkie does — because if you don't learn how to be clever, you don't survive. And now that I was building Habilitat, I had to be clever too.

Just before leaving on my first recruiting trip to New York, I lathered my body with a mixture of iodine and baby oil, which made me look like I had a movie star's tan. When people complimented me on it in New York, I said, "You got to be kidding. I only go out in the sun for an hour a week." They thought I must be living in paradise for sure. Of course, that was back in those days, when New Yorkers only sported tans if they were in the money and could get away. Tans meant success you could flaunt.

Back at the house, another trick brought us food. With forty-four bodies to feed, we were hurting in the supply department.

Although some of the local supermarkets were helping, soon we would have to find another source. I remembered that Synanon always held open houses for the general public, and we started doing the same.

When the visitors arrived, I explained the plans and goals of Habilitat and candidly answered any questions. The evening's finale was a tour of the facility, which ended in the kitchen — we would throw open the doors to our empty cupboards. It never failed. Every Sunday we were inundated with packages and bundles of food — canned goods, bacon, hams, chickens, furniture, blankets, linens, dishes, silverware.

Such scams assured our basic survival. Working through the less physical demons that inhabited the residents' heads took a different and more direct route, usually by playing "games."

Encounter Games

MARIA LYONS WAS AN ONLY CHILD, born on the Big Island but a product of California schools. When she was 14, her parents divorced, and she and her mother moved back to Hawaii, where Maria started smoking pot.

But that wasn't her problem. Her problem was that she was spoiled rotten and on top of that she didn't like herself. At least, that's what I saw right away. I knew something else was there, but that didn't come out until later.

Maria was like a lot of kids I see, maybe because of the divorce or the way her parents treated her. That probably made the situation worse anyway. Anything she wanted, she got. Her father was especially loose with his cash, probably out of guilt. You want a new bike? Okay, darling, you got it. You want a new outfit? Great, have one in every color.

Growing up like this, it's not surprising Maria figured the world owed her a living. They lose a tooth, the tooth fairy leaves a dollar, maybe *five* dollars, under the pillow. A birthday should be a celebration, but the way some parents run it, it's "What do you want for your birthday?" Go to a high school these days, and you can't find a parking place! Every 16-year-old kid has a car, and lots are fancier than the ones the teachers drive.

Anyway, I had met Maria at the Waikiki Drug Clinic, where she was hanging out with other pot smokers and runaways and — like all the others — was looking for real family, which she didn't have

190

at home. Her divorced mother worked for a downtown advertising agency, which left Maria alone all day and many evenings. We talked.

I asked her, "What do you want out of life?"

She shrugged.

I asked her, "What do you want to be?"

She said, "I don't know."

She was lonely, she felt inadequate and insecure, she didn't feel loved. Her story was typical.

After a month or two, she said she wanted to come into the program. Her mother agreed, reluctantly.

In the Kailua house, Maria felt like she belonged. She was articulate and very bright, yet she remained unsure of herself. She questioned why people liked her, because she didn't like herself. Because she was open to talking about such things, she took easily to the "games" we played.

In psychological language, a "game" is group therapy set up to handle behavioral problems. It's a powerful tool in teaching people to get in touch with their feelings, but because of the raw emotions involved, the game sessions must be carefully directed and monitored. I've always insisted that they be held only by me or another trained staff member. People need to get in touch with their feelings because otherwise they will be run by feelings they can't control. If you are run by your feelings, you tend to "act out." For example, you might hit someone rather than yell at them.

A new resident's first experience with an encounter session usually includes his or her own peer group and a staff member or me. These are called "house games" and are routinely held three evenings a week to discuss house business and to straighten out poor attitudes. It is here that residents like Maria first begin to understand what Habilitat is about.

I had been in Hawaii for some time before I heard the word *ho'oponopono,* an ancient Hawaiian process where members of a family get together whenever there's a beef and talk it out. The idea is to keep talking to each other until the conflict has been dissipated and a feeling of peace and harmony returns to the household. Our household games had the same goal. In such group situations, many individuals learn from others, just by sitting and listening.

The next step is participation in a "special game." These sessions are called by the facility director, staff members, or residents when the conduct of one or more individuals has become disruptive and damaging to the good of the facility. The object of the game is to get people to face up to their behavior and modify it to a point where it will be acceptable to their peers and the staff.

Most important, the process must do more than just open up the person — it must be skillfully handled so that he or she is also patched up at the end, so the effect of the game will be a valuable and positive learning experience and not a destructive one. When I use the words "patched up," I mean the equivalent of what a surgeon does. It is equally important to sew a person up psychologically by putting back all the right parts in the right places and restoring equilibrium.

The only hard and fast rule of a special game or any game is that no one can get up from his or her chair during the game except, with permission, to go to the bathroom. The purpose of this rule is to keep the person from running. (You've seen how often I ran — that's typical of a drug addict, avoiding the confrontation that might help the person recognize and handle his or her own responsibility in a situation.)

The chairs are placed in a circle facing inward so each participant can easily see everyone else. That way there's no front row, back row nonsense. The game begins when one person is "indicted" (chosen), either by the group leader or someone else in the circle.

From that point on, the person chosen cannot do or say anything to defend him- or herself until the game moves on to someone else. This prevents the game from being dominated by the loudest or most glib person. This was one of the modifications I made from what I had learned in prior programs. The person whom the game is focused on must sit quietly and absorb whatever verbal confrontation occurs. Everyone's feelings focus on this one individual, and the room resounds with shouted accusations, reproaches, and advice on how that person should change his or her behavior.

Sometimes someone who has a complaint about the way things are going in the house requests a special game, but often, to his or her chagrin, that person becomes the indicted one. When this happens, the person might hear more than he or she bargained for, but the process usually results in much emotional growth. It's a good way to teach people to stop whining about their problems and try handling them themselves. This experience is designed to force self-reflection. That's why I don't allow people to defend themselves against the accusations. A person who feels free to jump in with self-defense right away is using self-defense to fence out what might be useful to learn. And he or she can't hear with attention if he or she is just waiting to jump back with explanations and excuses.

After everyone has had their say, the group leader may allow the person under attack to explain his or her feelings; on the other hand, the leader may not. It's understood that while all feelings are valid, they are not always realistic or reasonable. Often people come to acknowledge that their feelings could stem from ignorance, perversity, or intolerance — racial or other.

The game may move on to several of the people in attendance. When it's finally over, all the "garbage" is left on the floor: Participants are encouraged to hold no grudges. Usually, afterward, everyone gathers for a cup of coffee or a snack, and they talk about what went on in the game.

At a later stage of the program, more sophisticated encounter groups deal with each person's "historical pain." Deep-rooted unaddressed problems are handled in extended encounter sessions or "marathons," lasting from twenty-four to forty-eight hours with only short breaks. One reason for the length is to exhaust and dissipate the participants' defenses so that they become more receptive to dealing with deeper issues. Incidents many years old may no longer seem to matter, but they still may be lodged deeply in a resident's psychological makeup. Often these old events are shaping and controlling a person's life. Here's an example.

Maria had been making steady progress in the first couple of months, but not until she experienced her first marathon did she take a big step forward. Typically, eighteen to twenty-five people participate in a marathon, including me and two or three other staff members who've been around long enough to understand and control the process. We're known as facilitators, and it's up to us to bring out the historical pain most people, like Maria, try so hard to conceal. Our goal is to help each participant face up to and address the crippling emotions that keep them from functioning productively.

Maria joined her fellow residents in the living room where the windows were covered to block outside light. Incense was burning, and the only illumination came from candles arranged in the center of the room. The point of this is to remove the participants from an everyday atmosphere, to invoke a feeling of serious inner reflection. It has no religious significance.

I was seated on one side of the room with a staff member opposite me. Maria and the others filled out the circle.

This was to be a one-way game. The game starts with a verbal comment to each participant concerning his or her behavior. Bits and pieces of that individual's behavior and attitudes are discussed so each person fully understands what part of their daily conduct is holding them back. They also learn what's preventing them from managing their lives with logic and common sense. When each staff member, starting with the most junior, has confronted each participant in turn, then I emphasize and extend what's been said, based on my own knowledge and what I've heard during the session. Before long, a great deal of sobbing and choked emotions tend to break out around the room. Remember, these are people who have a great deal in their lives to cry about — this is not indulging in cheap emotion. It is emotion that is felt by people who have come very close to killing themselves with their own behavior.

The first segment of a marathon usually takes six to eight hours. Then we have a pause, during which we play "message" music on the stereo while everyone listens in silence. This music is a good way to evoke emotion while sidestepping intellectual argument and defenses. Over the years, we've found that songs like "You've Got a Friend," "Mama," Daddy's Little Girl," and "He's Not Heavy, He's My Brother" have been effective.

About now, one or two residents usually begin to tap into feelings of sorrow, guilt, or fear, commonly having to do with some family member or friend. Most often these responses are tied in with strong feelings directed toward their parents or grandparents. Maybe they feel they let their families down in the past; maybe reverse. Sometimes they feel guilty for what they've put their families through, or they harbor bitter and hostile feelings because of what their families did to them.

These feelings can also relate to siblings or friends. The person might feel guilty about turning on a younger sister or brother to drugs. Or perhaps the resident let a friend die without trying to save him, or let a friend get arrested without warning him. He or she may have informed on a friend, who as a result went to prison. Or perhaps someone was betrayed by a friend, spouse, or lover. The list of possible situations is endless, and I think I've heard them all.

This time I noticed that when we played "Daddy's Little Girl," Maria began to cry. I asked her to please stand up. It was time to use a psychological tool called psychodrama or playacting. Standing up makes a person a little more vulnerable, a little more open than when sitting down.

I asked Maria if the song upset her. She nodded.

I asked, "Is it your father?" Again she nodded silently.

"Maria, look around the room and pick somebody who reminds you of your father."

Slowly, hesitantly, Maria looked at her friends. Finally, she went full circle and came back to me. Usually when people have trouble with their fathers, they pick me — it goes with the job.

I told Maria, "If I were really your father, what would you like to say to me?"

At first Maria said nothing.

"Come on, Maria. Tell me what's on your mind."

At this point, I didn't know what her beef was with her father. It could have been any number of things. I did know Maria, like any resident in her position, could be feeling guilt, hostility, ambivalence — any emotion.

Suddenly, she let me have it. For ten or fifteen minutes she did nothing but shit all over me verbally. She told me she hated me for what I did, for taking advantage of her, for using her.

Now I knew her father had abused her sexually.

I said, "What is it you want from me, honey?"

That set her off again. For another five minutes she shouted, cried, and shook, abusing me verbally for all the physical abuse she'd gotten when she was just entering puberty.

When she was finally quiet, I apologized. I said I was sorry, and I asked her how I could make it okay.

"What do you want from me, honey?" I said again.

In a little voice, she answered, "All I want is your love."

I said, "You have to forgive me first…"

I hadn't finished my sentence when she looked into my eyes, a mixture of hatred, confusion, and pleading. I went on: "… because if you can't forgive me, you can't love me. And I want your love, too. Can you forgive me?" From experience I knew that Maria might never have to forgive her real father and love him, but she *would* have to forgive and love that image of him inside her, because it was part of herself, before she would be able to forgive and love herself.

Maria was silent for a long time, then she wiped away her tears and said she thought she could. As we hugged, I knew she had begun to change.

The process of working on this historic pain can take a long time, but when it is finally accomplished, everybody in the group recognizes that he or she really does belong to the family. The residents find out they have friends who care deeply about them and will accept them exactly as they are. Everybody is rooting for everyone else in the room to successfully complete the program and take his or her rightful place as a useful, productive citizen.

At this point, we play inspirational music: "God Bless America," "A Place in the Sun," or "I've Got To Be Me." There's much hugging and kissing, as everyone basks in the profound feelings of warmth, affection, and goodwill that the session generates. The last four hours of the marathon are devoted to hearing feedback from the participants to find out what each one got from the session. Then the game culminates with motivational suggestions from the facilitators to the group. These reinforce the residents' strengths but also alert them to stay on top of their weaknesses.

At the end, we explain that as soon as we leave the room, both the hugging and kissing and the expression of historical feelings have ended. In everyday life, these residents must learn to function well, even when they experience strong feelings of love, anger, rejection, or guilt. Each of us has to learn that we must reserve these strong feelings for special times — perhaps for more sophisticated encounter sessions or private discussions. Then we all go for a walk on the beach.

WHAT HAS REALLY BEEN accomplished in a marathon is that people have aired their deep-rooted and profound historical pain. Then they have granted themselves or others forgiveness, and love and friendship has been established. After an experience like a marathon, it's very difficult for a resident to revert to playing an insensitive role. Participants know that someone will always be there to confront them and remind them of what took place during the marathon when they were hurting and vulnerable.

I believe that if a marathon is run very professionally, it is the closest thing to a natural high that a person can possibly feel — certainly the closest thing to feeling high on the heaviest drugs one has used. Many times, I will wait two or three weeks after a marathon, then call the same group back. We'll play a few of the same songs and ask what they have done to change their attitudes and behavior since the first group. Since residents know this backup session will probably occur, it reinforces their determination to improve their attitudes and behavior.

ALL THE VARIOUS GAMES can be powerful and effective instruments in teaching people to understand and deal with their emotions. Occasionally, however, for people who are seriously disturbed, the game experience can be dangerous.

For example, one incident shook all of us badly. A resident, a large black man who went by the name Wee Willie, was a Vietnam veteran. On completing his tour overseas, he had also done some prison time for a drug and assault charge.

One night, immediately after a marathon session, I was doing some paper work in my office. All of a sudden, I heard frightening screams and shrieks coming from the living room. I rushed out to find that Wee Willie had become agitated and tried to dive through a closed window. He was hanging halfway through, one arm shoved through one pane, the other arm through another, and his head sticking through the center pane. He couldn't move because he was suspended on the jagged shards of glass left in the frame, and was bleeding all over the wall, the floor, and on the grass outside.

The other residents were hysterical. We phoned for emergency help and tried to stop his bleeding and calm the other kids down. By now, even neighbors were arriving, responding to the noise and the siren, and the whole place was in chaos.

When Wee Willie had been cared for and taken to a hospital, I called a general meeting. I explained that Wee Willie's behavior had evidently been caused by two things, which had resulted in flashbacks. One was his experience in Vietnam, and the other was the fact that he had long used LSD. The flashback was triggered by one of the songs we had played on the stereo.

Willie survived this episode, was sent to a Veterans Administration hospital for further treatment, and later came back to visit us. But after his episode several of our kids went through their own terrifying episodes following his, wondering if something similar could happen to them. A few became so upset they decided to leave.

It was always demoralizing when one of the residents left. Because of the nature of the program, dealing with life, living on the brink of death and imprisonment, we were all close, so that no matter who left the others felt they'd lost a friend. And usually they didn't have so many friends that they could afford to lose one of us. Sometimes we were the first friends a newcomer had ever had. Some would get depressed, and they'd be tempted to do what they'd done so often already in their young lives — cut and run, split, get the hell out of this place — as if a geographical change would make a difference.

The kids would think one particular guy had a lot going for him, really had it made — and then he'd split. They'd think: if *he* can't make it, how can I? So when anybody came up missing, or openly took a hike, we all felt a sense of loss and maybe failure.

One time, though, someone splitting turned out to be funny. A boy left one day without telling anyone. As usual, the whole house turned out to search frantically for him. We scoured the neighborhood with no luck, and we were all feeling pretty low. Finally, we gave up and returned home — to find the kid sitting on the roof with a loaf of bread and a jar of peanut butter. We were so relieved we laughed and laughed. So did he, and the cloud blew over.

Making a House into a Home

WHEN WE WERE BUILDING Habilitat, the talents I used were the same ones that got me what I needed on the streets, turned inside out and bent toward good ends. Ever since I'd been a shoeshine boy I'd been a hustler and a learner, with an eye to the business opportunity.

The truth is, scamming was a part of my nature — something I did so naturally as not to be aware of doing it. Big corporate executives call it "problem solving." Well, me too. As soon as I found that it worked as well in my new, straight lifestyle as it had when I was on the street, I put my mind to our biggest problem: housing.

My idea was to create a situation that would attract media attention, in the hope that someone, somewhere, would come forward to help us find a larger facility. So I visited all our neighbors and asked them to begin complaining to the police department and say that we were making too much noise, then to call the department of health and say that too many people were living in a single-family dwelling, or call the Bishop Estate (owner of the Kailua land on which Mickey's house sat) and complain that too many people were living on a leasehold land facility. Maybe, I suggested, they should even call the fire department and tell them that it was definitely a fire hazard to have so many of us living together.

In Hawaii, much residential land is owned by large corporations and leased to individual house owners. In our case, Bishop Estate was our landlord's landlord, if you will, and because of the complaints the Estate soon wanted us off the premises. We were also in violation of the health regulations, so there was no way all the complaints could be ignored.

We received many citations and finally an eviction notice from the Bishop Estate. I now had the reason I needed to call my first press conference. First I found the man who could teach me how to approach the media effectively, Dave Braun, a person with a lot of newspaper and television experience. He acted as public relations man, promotions manager, advertising executive, and incidentally my secretary.

The news conference was a resounding success. Both Honolulu daily newspapers were there, along with the *Pali Press* and all three network television stations. Our need for a new home got plenty of exposure, and for the next week, carloads of food and supplies arrived, as well as some leads on property.

I was trying harder and harder to garner additional support from the square element ("square" meaning nonresidents of Habilitat). To do this we formed a group we called the Square Game Club. At our meetings, I would spend twenty minutes explaining what an encounter group was about. Then we'd actually launch an encounter group, to draw people into the process, wake up their understanding in a hands-on, feeling process. In the beginning this would be just a modified version of our games, which dealt with much rougher life problems. First I explained the process, then I answered whatever questions came up from any of the visitors.

We would all sit around in a circle and part of my explanation was "Okay, now you're not here to help Habilitat. You're not here to see what we do. You're here to find out if perhaps you have some problems — marital, business, personal, or whatever — that *we* can help *you* deal with." The groups weren't marshmallow stuff, though. We really got into some nitty gritty things. How to deal with each other in relationships, and how they could improve communication with their children by being more honest and open.

One night, a couple named Jerry and Joan Greenspan attended. When I asked about his job, he muttered he was an executive.

"What in the hell do you mean, 'an executive'?" I asked. Hemming and hawing, he said he was a CPA and worked for one of Hawaii's largest corporations in downtown Honolulu. When I heard "CPA," I'm sure my eyes lit up. I know bells rang in my head because I desperately needed a money person. Once again, just when I needed someone, it looked as if the right person had popped up.

Jerry Greenspan was witty, bright, and opinionated but also extremely honest. He had been through EST, transcendental meditation, and many other types of motivational groups. He said, "Vinny, I've experienced them all, and I really like where you're going. I'd like to be part of what's happening. How can I help?

So I asked Jerry and his wife to stay after the meeting, and over coffee I explained how desperately we needed the kind of knowledge he had. He agreed to take care of our financial records, and soon he was chairman of the board. He became one of the people I refer to as a "rabbi." This term has nothing to do with religious affiliation but is Italian slang for someone who is willing to generously share his or her valuable knowledge with others.

Finding Jerry Greenspan and Dave Braun eased some problems, but we still hadn't resolved our lack of space. I'd tried every possible avenue, and each dead end left me more frustrated in my search for suitable housing.

Then one of our board members heard about a beautiful old estate in Kaneohe, a town about four miles away. Included on the estate were a large, two-story house with a full basement, two smaller guest cottages, and three other buildings on an acre and a half of land right on Kaneohe Bay. It sounded too good to be true.

The owner, a widow named Mary Ann Bigelow, was looking for a tenant who would lease it and care for it properly. It had been neglected for many years; she had moved into a new house next to it. When I first telephoned and introduced myself, she told me very firmly that she was not interested.

After listening to her, I could hardly blame her. A year or so earlier, she had rented her place to a group whose leaders told her they intended to establish a drug rehabilitation program. They were, in fact, looking for an isolated spot where they could have sex parties and use drugs and alcohol. She had had a difficult time getting them out, and they seriously damaged some of the buildings and let the gardens deteriorate into a jungle.

I decided to try another approach. By lucky chance, Dave Braun's friend Eve Drolet was also a friend of Mary Ann Bigelow's. Eve interceded and explained that we were a reputable organization in desperate need of a place to live. Mary Ann agreed to meet us, and I brought her out to see our small facility. On the way over, I told her about our goals and ambitions and urged her to ask any questions she had.

When she arrived, she was impressed with the immaculate condition of the house and yard. She also fell in love with the kids, as they did with her. Of course, before bringing her over, I had long sessions with the residents and made sure they were well dressed. We also timed it so that at our arrival, they would be singing "Bringing in the Sheaves," a beautiful old harvest hymn. I explained to her that this session was part of one daily seminar.

Mrs. Bigelow gave me permission to look at her property. As I drove down the narrow road leading to it, I could see the location would be ideal. The main house sat on a point of land overlooking Kaneohe Bay, with a panoramic view of the Pacific Ocean. Steps led to the beach below, and a long pier extended into the water, with a covered boathouse at the end. The neighborhood was so quiet I could hear the small waves lapping at the shore. The beautiful blue-purple morning glory looped tendrils along the beach.

Mary Ann Bigelow's husband Lyman, a native of Massachusetts who had come to Hawaii in 1911, had discovered the secluded property while on some kind of a field trip in 1920, and during the next few years constructed his home, called Dreamwood. He cleaned out the dense undergrowth, leaving only the large trees, and he surrounded the buildings with spectacular gardens filled with hundreds of tropical plants he collected on his travels. The walks and driveways were paved with brick and laid out in symmetrical patterns. He had also built large ponds where he raised imported water plants, Japanese carp, and ducks. Colorful peacocks roamed the grounds in the daytime and nested in the huge monkeypod trees at night. Pigeons, pheasants, and chickens were housed in an aviary, and the greenhouses were filled with every type of exotic orchid, flower, and fern you could imagine.

After Lyman Bigelow died, Mary Ann no longer wanted to manage the large estate. Besides, too many memories there reminded her of losing Lyman. She decided to move into a smaller house next door, where she lived and from there kept an eye on the larger property.

On my first visit, I could only inspect the large house and get some idea of the extent of the grounds, but I knew I'd found the place I'd dreamed of as a home for Habilitat. Finally she agreed to talk to the board of directors, and after several meetings, she not only agreed to lease the property to us for $700 a month, but also gave us an option to buy.

When we took possession on August 1, 1971, we needed machetes to clear a path from the gate to the main house. And when we started to inspect the rest of the estate to prepare it for occupation, we realized that — as usual — we had a bigger job ahead of us than we had counted on.

First we found one of the guest houses apparently still occupied from time to time by some drug addicts. They would sneak in at night to sleep or shoot dope. The first time we went in there we found a set of drug paraphernalia, or "works," and I immediately had everything locked up. Then I put the building off limits to all but myself, my staff, and a few selected people who were assigned to clean it up. The guest house was filthy, infested with lice and other unwelcome animal life, and there was tremendous structural damage.

Other buildings needed work, too, and the gardens had been neglected for so long we had to hack our way through. For several weeks, all of us worked steadily to get the place to the point where we could move in.

The big house itself was in pretty good shape other than being over fifty years old and totally termite ridden. On the first floor was a small sitting room just inside the front door, and a large living room and dining room overlooking the bay. The library had a wood-burning fireplace that highlighted the glass display cabinets lining the walls. Originally, they had held Lyman Bigelow's collection from his travels. Also on the first floor were a large kitchen, a pantry, and a breakfast room whose windows framed views of the ocean and the small green islands of the bay. Everywhere you went, the windows said, "Hawaii! Paradise!"

Upstairs were two huge bedrooms with full bathrooms, another sitting room, and a small office. The house was built over a full basement with laundry facilities and a storage vault. We were almost overwhelmed with so much space and quickly realized we were going to need a lot of furniture. At the time, we only had a few bunk beds, a pile of mattresses, one dilapidated couch, a few chairs, and one old stove — for fifty of us!

On the day we moved into the new property, I called a press conference. When the reporters arrived to publicize our move, we showed them our odds and ends of furniture in our very large rented truck, which just dwarfed our stuff. The next day, the papers, TV, and radio described our plight. Donations streamed in.

We still lacked many necessities, though, so I approached a widely known local disc jockey named Hal Lewis, also known as

J. Akuhead Pupule (Crazy Tunahead) or Aku for short. Despite his name, Aku was a New Yorker from Brooklyn, so I felt sure he'd listen to my pitch. I was completely taken aback when he said, "Look, Vinny, I've seen every con artist who's come into this town for twenty years, and I've gotten pretty suspicious. You'll have to prove yourself first. *Then,* I'll help you. But first I have to believe in you."

Fair enough. In a short time, he became a consistent supporter of Habilitat as well as a close friend. He had a huge audience on all the islands, and he was responsible for the donation of most of our furniture, office equipment, bedding, linen, bunks, cookware, dishes, TVs, appliances, radios — you name it, he found someone to donate it to us. He even brought in a few used cars, which came in very handy.

A woman offered my staff and myself a house she owned on Kailua Beach, without charge. The place became our first staff house, and it was wonderful to have a place to go and relax away from the facility. The house was brand new and right on the beach. It had no furniture, but we were bachelors and didn't need much. We moved in a couple of beds and dressers, and that was it.

THE BIGELOW ESTATE WAS very peaceful. And we needed that, because our lives were full of drama. We never lacked for drama. Every one of us had a drama going on all the time. Where we'd come from was dramatic, and where we were was dramatic — sometimes *too* dramatic.

One night right after moving in, a call came in from Frank Cockett, who said he was in a nearby town, Salt Lake, not far from Pearl City. Frank said Kimo, who had dropped out of the Habilitat program, was threatening to shoot everybody in the house they were in. It was three in the morning and I tried to wake Gerard, my staff member, but I couldn't budge him.

I was hardly dressed before I was roaring through Kailua and over the Pali to Salt Lake. I double-parked the car in the middle of the street, and there's Frank. Now, Frank is Hawaiian and dark, but on this night, he was *white* and pointing to the backyard.

I tiptoed down the steps. I'd been around long enough to know when I heard the safety catch of a pistol click off. I said, "Kimo, it's me, Vinny. I've got to talk to you."

My eyes were getting adjusted to the dark, and finally I saw him. He had the gun cocked, pointed at his head. I didn't know what to say. If a guy's about to jump off a bridge, what are you going to tell him — the water's wet? Anything you say might turn him off. I said, "That's a really funny place to put a gun. You could get hurt like that."

He said, "It's too late for me. She broke up with me. She don't want to know me."

I said, "We can work that out later. Why don't you give me the gun, because you got neighbors around who might hear."

When he heard me say "neighbors," he turned the gun toward me. He asked, "What neighbors?" He was starting to panic.

I said, "Nobody's heard you yet. That's why I'm here. Give me the gun, and let me take you back to Habilitat before you wind up either dead or in serious trouble."

So he gave me the gun. Now, I'm a convicted felon, and I'm not supposed to carry a gun. So I took the bullets out, and I put them in my pocket and put the gun in the trunk of the car. We drove Kimo back to Habilitat and got him set up.

Then I went home, loaded the pistol, and walked into the room where Gerard was still sleeping. I stood right by his bed in front of an open window looking out onto the ocean and fired off three rounds into the wild blue yonder. Gerard jumped out of bed, pale as a ghost, too stunned to say anything. I said, "Next time, you son-of-a-bitch, when I say, 'Wake up, there's an emergency,' and you stay in bed, it's your ass." And I walked out.

THE NEXT DRAMA WAS entirely different. As we were settling into our new quarters, we turned the former library, a large room just inside the front door, into an office for Dave Braun and myself. Little did I know that by doing so I was kicking up a furor that would eventually threaten Habilitat's existence, change my status drastically, and completely reorganize the board of directors. It seemed like a simple move at the time, but it has since become known as The Infamous Throne Room Episode.

The Infamous Throne Room Episode

IT STARTED WHEN I RECEIVED a phone call from Bob Fisher, a Habilitat board member. He and Jerry Greenspan, who had become a board member, invited me to come over to Bob's house for a meeting. I couldn't for the life of me figure out what type of meeting they had in mind, nor did I know this meeting had been called at the urging of some other board members.

When I arrived at Bob's house, I said, "Okay, what's up?"

Jerry started by telling me he thought I had become a "fat cat" in my position as the founder and executive director of Habilitat. Furthermore, they said, my office was much too big and pretentious. They also mentioned the large, comfortable, recliner-type chair someone had donated, which I was using behind my desk. In all the programs I had been in, every director and assistant director had this type of chair. Aside from being comfortable, it was symbolic. It was the biggest chair in the room. Some people were intimidated by the chair, but everyone respected it, and that was the point.

My board of directors, however, had missed the point. They had begun referring to my office as the "Throne Room." They also insinuated that perhaps I might be losing my mind or, at the least, my sense of perspective.

I looked at Bob and Jerry and laughed. I thought they were crazy. I said I didn't understand their objections since the room was also used often for large meetings, encounter groups, and seminars as well as marathons. Also, it was positioned so I could easily keep my eye on what was happening in the house.

But no matter what I said, their minds were made up. They told me they had conferred with the other board members, and they had all reached the same conclusion: I had forgotten where I came from. As a result, they told me, they were putting me on probation.

I couldn't believe what I was hearing. Habilitat had been in operation for nine months, I was killing myself with work, and I was succeeding at something everyone had told me couldn't be done in Hawaii. Habilitat's population had climbed to over eighty, and now — for no logical reason — they were going to put me on probation?

Furious as I was, I managed to control my temper while I listened to them. Jerry and Bob were good friends, men I admired. They had also worked hard to help Habilitat succeed. Bob was a psychiatrist who had some experience working in and with therapeutic communities. That part really confused me, because I was sure he would understand the symbolic aspect of the director's office. Jerry's background was strictly business and finance, but at meetings held in Jerry's office, I had thought *it* was ostentatious. His company also had a sauna and a huge conference room. I was thinking, "How in the hell can this guy have the audacity to fault *me*?"

I thought about what they were saying, and then said, "Bullshit! You guys came on board to help give us credibility and to help open some doors. I also asked you to help me in the business area so I could develop as an executive director. I assumed the main reason to have board members was to help raise money, because we couldn't have gotten through certain doors without their credentials and their names on our letterhead and having them make calls ahead for us. But the board definitely wasn't to get involved in the clinical side. Really, guys, let's be honest, none of you has any idea what the day-to-day operation is like.

"Now you're giving me static over a completely insignificant matter that neither of you understands. I haven't done anything wrong. I simply chose a strategic place for my office. I also believe you're overlooking what's been accomplished here. Go home and think about it. I assure you, I'll be thinking, too."

At that time, I had ten staff people, including myself, all but two from Phoenix House. I called a meeting and explained what had happened. The consensus was that I should get rid of my board.

I explained that if I fired the board, I'd find myself in the same position that Communiversity did when Ima and her staff and residents shaved their heads and announced they were moving to the mainland to merge with Synanon. Communiversity became a laughing stock in Hawaii. Our track record was too short to get involved in a public battle with our board.

As I talked, I realized that *probation* was only a word, so I decided to go along with the board, but I didn't say anything at the time. Then I called a general meeting and explained to the residents what had happened. They also were mad, but I felt it was my responsibility to handle the situation calmly.

I said, "I brought you this far, and I'm not going to go off half-cocked and blow it. The same things I teach you must apply to myself. This is strictly business and not personal. The board members think they're doing the right thing. Let me figure out a logical way to handle it."

Early next morning, I phoned Frank Natale, then the codirector of Phoenix House, and asked him to come to Hawaii. I needed some outside help, which I felt Frank could give me. He arrived two days later, and I set up an emergency board meeting in my office for that evening. During the day, I told Frank what was happening.

When the board meeting convened, I introduced Frank and said I'd invited him to get the benefit of his long experience. The board then presented its complaints about my large office and the size of the chair I was using. Frank broke up laughing.

"You've got to be kidding," he said, "This man is working countless hours every day! I don't know how he wound up in Hawaii — I'd take him back in a minute and put him on my staff in a key position at Phoenix House if he was willing. I can't tell you how many phone calls and letters we've exchanged while he has been here, with him asking for advice and help. Instead of appreciation — and most of you probably don't even *know* what he has done — you're *hassling* him. What difference does the size of his office make? Vinny *needs* this office to hold staff meetings, other types of meetings with his troops, special groups — whatever. Right now we're having a board meeting in his office. Where would you like to hold board meetings? In the *kitchen?*"

Frank cracked up laughing again. The board members were squirming and nobody was making any eye contact. By the time the board meeting was over, I was given a raise in pay and elected chairman of the board.

This set Frank off again.

"You are literally making this man crazy," he said, grinning. "First you tell him his head and his chair are too big and you put him on probation because he has an office bigger than the toilet. Now you give him a raise and make him *your* boss? You're making *me* crazy, and I just got here."

Frank definitely made his point.

AFTER THE THRONE ROOM EPISODE, I realized I had made a giant step forward in my work, with Frank's help. I had learned that to lead, I really had to lead, and couldn't be afraid of using my brains and ability to build Habilitat's administration. At our next meeting, I explained to the board members that I wanted them to understand what I saw as their position. Technically they were not just there to wield power. I told them I was looking for people who would ask themselves, "What am I doing for Habilitat?" I didn't want a board that would only be active once a month, on board meeting nights. I wanted commitment. I also wanted a board that wasn't continually on my back. I needed board members who would go out and open doors, bring in some money or "in-kind" services, and help us keep our books straight. Their duty was to speak out for us in the community, and protect and strengthen the organization in every way they could. In other words, they were to function as they would on any board for a *profit*-making organization. If they did not agree, they should go someplace else. And I asked four board members for their resignations because they had done nothing to help Habilitat.

Next day one or more of these disgruntled ex-board members went to the press with the throne room story. The reporter, Mike Keller from *The Honolulu Advertiser,* called me and asked to come out. Frank Natale and I gave him a tour of Habilitat. In a day or so, a full-page article appeared, telling about Vinny Marino, Habilitat, and the "Throne Room." It was great publicity.

The truth is, part of the story was not so flattering. Frank told the reporter I had to take a lot of the rap for my recent problems: "He got himself in over his head. He's a damned fine clinician, but he's not a public relations man and he's not a fund-raiser.

"He also resents other people without his background or experience telling him how to run the program. That's a personality trait he will have to learn to overcome. In New York Vinny always had someone to turn to when he got in a jam. Here, he's on his own. He has to run a program which demands one type of personality of him. Then he has to be able to turn around and communicate what he's doing to the outside world, which takes another kind of personality.... He will grow into it with time. He has to, or he won't make it."

Life in the
Goldfish Bowl

IT MIGHT SEEM ODD, me sitting there letting my old friend put me down to the press. It isn't, really. If you're not honest with yourself, if you don't accept honest appraisals when they come your way, you aren't going to make it — just like Frank said. What he said made me sound human, that's all. I had a big mouth, and I could learn to control that. The important thing was, I had a good program, too.

In the end, the publicity worked for us, and in the weeks after the story appeared in the *Advertiser,* people came from all over the island to see the infamous throne room and my large chair. What had started out as a dismal experience eventually brought us many new volunteers, including a wonderful nurse who offered her services without charge. It also brought new board members, a tremendous surge of donations (again, thanks to my friend and Habilitat's friend, Aku), and offers of assistance from several doctors and attorneys.

As usual, we needed all the help we could get. We had ninety-two residents in the program at the time (age 13 to 51), nine of them in what we called "reentry." This was the last stage of the program, when residents are being polished to return to society. This is a stage in which residents can really contribute enormously to the program, both in terms of guiding newcomers and of helping the program become self-supporting — a crucial goal if you want to stay free of heavy restrictions and the paper avalanche required by government grants.

For example, Vic Modesto was one of the reentry candidates. He had come to Habilitat when we were in Kailua from the Navy base at Pearl Harbor, where he was stationed as an enlisted man aboard a nuclear destroyer. He was about 19, the son of a migrant Mexican farm worker in California. At home, Vic had experimented with a number of drugs. His favorite was LSD and he continued to take it on the weekends while in the Navy. When he began experiencing "flashbacks" on duty, his commanding officer had him arrested. As he was waiting for a court martial, one of his doctors called me to see if we could help.

I said we could try, so the Navy assigned Vic to eight hours of menial housekeeping chores on base during the day and to Habilitat at night and during the weekends. This was an unusual arrangement, but when I took Vic before the house in a general meeting, I expected my troops to go along.

I was wrong — very wrong. For almost eight hours, I listened to the residents tell me why I was wrong. They didn't want any part-timers in the program, because it gave him time to get loaded and come down before getting back.

My troops had a point. I had no control over most of Vic's day, and with the court martial coming up in two months, he could end up in the Navy brig and we'd have wasted our time. But I really liked Vic and finally I said, "Sorry, gang. He's coming in."

Once in, Vic roared through the first couple of months like a champ. This is when the resident lives in the equivalent of a goldfish bowl, when their behavior, attitudes, and habits are closely observed twenty-four hours a day. There is no privacy and there are no secrets. We have no private sleeping quarters here — only dormitories.

As the date for the court martial approached, Vic got very nervous. This was understandable, considering he might do time, but his doctor and commanding officer both spoke highly of him. Not one time in two months was he late to work or late getting back to Habilitat. The Navy even let me testify, and I said he showed a real willingness to change his life. I also mentioned that Vic had had a drug problem that the Navy should've detected a long time ago. In the end, the Navy gave Vic an honorable discharge and no time in the brig. He was a civilian again and free to do anything he wanted. He decided to stay in Habilitat.

We used the goldfish-bowl concept, by the way, for obvious reasons, but also because we can watch people like Vic carefully and learn what it was that brought them to us. At night, residents were assigned to make runs through the house every fifteen minutes to check the rest of the family, as well as look for fire, vandals, or any other problems.

If a resident can't sleep for any reason, he or she is free to wake up the person in the next bed and ask to talk. This information is relayed to the staff members via their night report. It is also brought to the front desk by the person being awakened so that whatever conversation ensued can be discussed.

Next day, a staff member will take that resident aside and ask, "What's happening? Why can't you sleep? What's on your mind? What are you experiencing?" In this way, small problems are solved before they become big. In addition, the resident realizes that his or her welfare concerns all of us.

It's a highly controlled, structured environment. For many new residents, this can involve extreme culture shock because there are so many "no's." Not even Vic's two years in the Navy prepared him for our long list of taboo activities — starting with no drugs, no alcohol, no sex, no stealing, no violence, and no threat of violence. Residents are also constantly being reminded to "do what you're told" or deal with the consequences.

For example, if someone used the last of the toilet paper and then left the bathroom without replacing it, there's going to be a consequence. Replacing toilet paper wasn't that simple a thing at

Habilitat then. To do it, a person had to go down to the guy in charge and get a key, go to the supply closet and take out a roll, lock the closet, return the key, and then go back to the toilet and put on the roll. It took time and effort, but if you didn't do that, it showed you were still a selfish creep and not thinking of others. And being considered a selfish creep is no small thing in a tightly knit family.

LET ME TELL YOU A FUNNY STORY about responsibility and another kind of goldfish pond. In these early days, several small fish ponds were on the property stocked with the expensive Japanese carp that look like huge goldfish but are called *koi*. Word got around that I loved those fish and the worst thing that could happen was to let one of the fish die.

But the pumps that regulated the pond water were as rotten as everything else and they'd stop at least once a week. Right away, you'd hear someone shout, "The pumps are down! The pumps are down!" And eighteen residents — one for each fish — would jump into the shallow ponds and bend over, grab a fish around the middle, and start walking the fish in circles around the pond — otherwise the fish would die from lack of oxygen. In fact, once when one fish seemed to be dying, a guy actually gave it mouth-to-mouth resuscitation.

Now I never even liked those fish, but it *was* funny to watch people who thought they were such hotshots, with their pantlegs rolled up, bent over at the waist, taking a fish for a walk. And in some strange way, it taught the troops responsibility as well as humility.

AS THE WEEKS PASSED, Vic had to prove he could responsibly handle a job. In the beginning, quite naturally, his jobs were very menial, much like those he had done waiting for his court martial: sweeping or mopping floors, dusting, cleaning bathrooms, simple landscaping, maintenance, or laundry duty. All Vic's jobs were overseen by senior treatment residents, who not only taught him the actual work but constantly reinforced the concepts that made Habilitat work. When Vic showed he was proficient at his new job and had a good attitude, he was moved to a more difficult and challenging position. This process was structured to build self-confidence, but also to keep Vic, and the others, a little off balance in the face of constant change.

After Vic had been around awhile, he was assigned to the kitchen, but we didn't just wave a magic wand and say, "Cook!" First, he was taught to wash pots, pans, and dishes, then to clean up the kitchen. Next he learned to serve meals, and finally he was assigned to help the breakfast crew. After that, he was made an assistant breakfast cook. If he had continued on up the line, he would have been an assistant dinner cook and then, the toughest job, dinner cook. Then he could become the "ramrod," which is assistant to the boss, and finally head of the kitchen.

Vic didn't go that route. He was shifted to another department, where he again started working his way up the ladder. It's a long, slow, careful process. If after being taught to do any of these jobs, Vic fouled up, he would hear about it in a game. The teaching was continuous, as was the challenge.

Part of Vic's challenge was Frank Cockett. Frank was headed for a good job somewhere down the line as a Habilitat staff member, and Vic Modesto apparently saw the same thing in his future. Before long a friendly competition developed between the two.

Both were ready for reentry now. Reentry normally lasted six to nine months and finished the eighteen-month to two-year program. Reentry today is very different from what it was in Habilitat's early years. Now we have a dozen well-established, successful businesses where the residents get hands-on vocational training. In those days, we didn't have much going for us in terms of business. But I was determined to build up Habilitat to fill what I consider a central need of drug rehabilitation programs — to teach the residents skills that can help them stay off the streets and out of trouble. They needed job skills and training to get jobs that would pay more than peanuts and would support families.

We started small. One of the first efforts was making sand candles and selling them in front of the Gem discount stores. I liked this project because it was very creative but didn't take the brains of a rocket scientist. The residents had a chance to express themselves and didn't have to strain. We did have some good artists, of course. We had some bad artists, too, and we had to melt down a lot of candles! Vic wasn't one of the best artists, but he could be trusted to take the troops outside the facility to the stores and return with them, as well as with the money they had earned.

That's the way it was at first. We sold watermelon slices and sesame bars at rock concerts. When Gem stores asked us to roast chestnuts for the Christmas season, we said we'd do that (although later we changed our minds). It was real nickel-and-dime stuff, but it helped. Besides, we had to start somewhere.

By now, in addition to private donations, we were getting welfare checks for some of the residents who qualified, and we received a grant from the Law Enforcement Assistance Agency (LEAA). Then, totally unsolicited, a Hawaii senator named Duke Kawasaki got us $25,000 from the state to upgrade our kitchen. I sent him a warm thank-you letter, little knowing that he and I would have much more to say to each other a few years down the line.

That was followed by money from the federal government: Title IV money, Title XVI money, then Title XX money, plus grants from the National Institute on Drug Abuse (NIDA). I was grateful for all of this, but I saw Habilitat getting sucked into the same dilemma I had objected to in other programs. The more government money we accepted, the more strings they wanted to put on our operation. As I saw it, running our own businesses would free us, at least partially, from government interference.

We headed into our first year-end holiday season with mixed feelings. The winter season has probably been hard on people since people began. Even in Hawaii there are people from places with depressing seasons, where life feels gray in winter. So people have celebrations to lighten up with — it's pretty much the same all over the world — Divali, Chanukah, Christmas, Kwanzaa — people sing, dance, light candles and fires and fireworks, eat, hang out together. For many of the kids, this would be their first Christmas away from home and family, and they would be feeling homesick. Some of them would feel homesick for a sense of family they had never actually had, a sense of brightness and promise and friendship that they knew about only from the outside — and that Habilitat could fulfill. Making the promise real is what habilitation is all about. So I was determined that this was going to be a holiday none of them would ever forget.

Our acquisitions department had been working for weeks, accumulating donations and gifts from parents and other family members, friends, and local and mainland merchants. These had all been carefully sorted and packaged so that the resident from the poorest family received the same number of gifts as the resident from the wealthiest family.

We also used some money to buy gifts for the patients in Children's Hospital in Honolulu. We hustled some buses so that we could deliver the gifts in person and sing Christmas carols to the kids there and to patients in other hospitals throughout Oahu as well. This was not only good PR, but it gave our people a chance to give, and to see that other people might be in need, too.

We trimmed several trees, and I established a pattern that we still follow at Habilitat every year: We had a traditional Italian celebration. On Christmas Eve, we prepared an elaborate antipasto, spaghetti with crab and tomato sauce, salad, shrimp scampi, baked clams, and homemade Italian bread. We finished with Italian pastries and Italian ice cream. The next day, on Christmas, we feasted on more antipasto, ravioli and lasagna with meatballs, Italian sausage, roast chicken, stuffed mushrooms and artichokes, followed by fruit, pastry, roasted chestnuts, tea, and Italian coffee.

Most of the food was donated from various Little Italys in the cities where relatives of residents and staff families lived. And we had music, and gifts, and dancing, and more music. Keep them busy, I thought, so they won't get depressed. And it worked!

New Year's Eve we celebrated Hawaiian style. Fireworks have long been an island tradition on that night. The practice stems from the Chinese belief that if you make enough noise, you can kick the old year in the ass and scare the New Year into being good to you. All of us agreed that we certainly needed a good New Year, and we staged a fantastic display with everything from aerial fireworks to firecrackers, again all donated by generous friends and merchants.

We fired the rockets and Roman candles from our beach over the bay, and the bright bursts of red and green and gold reflected in the water until it seemed like we were surrounded by lights. Noise from the thousands of firecrackers that we exploded nearly deafened us and the neighbors, and the smoke hung in the air like fog. All in all we felt we had given the old year a pretty good boot and the new one a hearty welcome.

We had made some major strides in one short year.

Ban or Bust

LIFE IN HABILITAT, as you have probably already guessed, is not all fireworks and dancing. Tensions can run pretty high sometimes, and once in a while there's a serious blowup. Our first summer at the Bigelow estate was one of the rockiest times for the program, and it was a tough time for me personally, too.

Shortly after I came to Hawaii, my old friend and fellow junkie Frank Russo split from Phoenix House and was back on drugs again within a short time. His wife Vickie — the woman who had driven the get-away car to the airport when I recruited my first staff members from Phoenix — threw him out of the house and told him that she was going to divorce him. Frank had a long history of drug abuse. He had first contacted me to ask for help while I was still at Phoenix House, and now he decided to give my new program a try. With Vickie's assistance, he made the trip to Hawaii and entered Habilitat.

At first Frank seemed to do well in the program, and he kept up the hope that he could eventually patch things up with Vickie. I, too, thought the marriage might be mended, so I encouraged Vickie to visit. At Christmas of that year, Frank was allowed to call Vickie, and he begged her to come for a short vacation, telling her that the Hawaiian sun and surf were just what she needed to get her through the grim New York winter. We all told her that a reconciliation might be possible if she could only see firsthand some of the changes in Frank. She finally agreed to the trip, arriving on

New Year's Day 1972. She left her 11-year-old daughter, Lila, with her mother in New York.

The visit went well. When Vickie returned to New York, she wrote to Frank, telling him that she would consider returning to Hawaii for the summer, when Lila had completed grade school, and that she was willing to give their marriage another try.

While this drama was playing itself out, I was having severe problems with my staff. They couldn't let go of Phoenix House routines, which dictated that residents in the program actually waited on staff members, serving them meals in bed and giving them all kinds of personal service. Although I didn't think that residents needed to be treated as equals — at least not at first — I didn't want them to be treated like servants or slaves, either. I wound up having to let most of the Phoenix staff go.

I was still trying desperately to get Habilitat off the ground. Izzy and Richie, with whom I'd grown up in Phoenix House, weren't really pulling enough weight. They were playing too hard, caught up in Hawaii's lifestyle of beaches, beautiful women, and tons of fun. That wouldn't have been a problem — if I had hired them just to have fun. In early March, I had had enough. I called them in and informed them that I was going to terminate them. "This is one of the hardest things I've ever done," I told them, "but your lifestyle isn't helping me to set up the program. Bottom line is I have to ask myself if I want to have friends around, or if I want fellow soldiers who're willing to help the program succeed." I had decided already, but I meant it when I said that it wasn't easy to see them go.

On top of all these difficulties, I started having trouble with a faulty disk in my back. It got so bad that I had to enter the hospital, and I left Gerard in charge of Habilitat. With the help of some of the older residents, he ran the program, though I stayed in close touch by phone and actually held a few meetings in my hospital room. I ultimately had to undergo surgery, and while I was in recovery from that I developed a hiatal hernia, and then phlebitis. In short, I was a mess, and it took me a while to get my body out of hock.

While the cat's away, the old saying goes, the mice will play. In my absence, Habilitat started to fall apart. In an effort to pull it back together, I convinced Vickie, Frank's wife, to come out with her daughter Lila to help run the women's side of the program. Gerard was still serving as acting director, but he didn't look forward to being second in command. On the day I got out of the hospital, he left the program. The residents had liked Gerard and were pretty upset at his departure, but when some of the seasoned reentry candidates stood up and pledged their support, the mood lifted, and for a little while it seemed that we were back on track.

By then, however, something was rotten in Habilitat. I could smell it, and see it, in the way people looked: shifty, uptight, and nervous. Vickie looked scared a lot of the time, and Frank often had a sarcastic look on his face. I began to focus on him, sensing that somehow he might be the source of trouble, but I couldn't figure out how to pin down my suspicions.

I put the house on a "ban." A ban is similar to a religious retreat, and it's a tool I use when things are not as they should be with the group. The facility itself might be getting too loose, or too many minor lapses in discipline might be occurring, or maybe an overall laxness in attitude starts taking over. When the troops have forgotten why they are here, we declare a ban.

Once the ban is set up, everything that is not essential to day-to-day operations comes to a stop. Except in cases of medical emergencies, no residents can leave the facility, and no visitors are allowed. There is no TV, no music, no radio; even smiling and unnecessary talking are prohibited. Work hours are extended from early morning until night and are interrupted only for seminars or games that stress Habilitat's values and philosophies. It's something like getting serious with a rowdy high school class — you tighten up discipline until everyone focuses on the job at hand.

Bans are often needed when a number of new residents enter the facility during a short period of time. Some are particularly hostile when they first come in. One might write, "Fuck Habilitat" or something like that on the bathroom wall, or someone will steal clothing from the laundry and leave a note: "The phantom strikes again!" During a ban, this hostility either gets worked out or the perpetrator splits, so that we no longer have a graffiti artist or a phantom.

The aim of the ban is to get the residents to realize why they're in Habilitat in the first place. During a ban, I remind them that in their initial induction interview they were warned that the program would be difficult. All of us at Habilitat work hard, play hard, and learn hard. The ban serves as a reminder of what we're trying to accomplish. If participants do not choose to stay and accept these conditions, they're free to leave. Often several do. It's like shaking the tree for dead branches or rotten fruit — we get rid of the people who don't really want to be here but who don't have the courage to leave. At the same time, those who think they want to leave, but really don't, are forced to get off the fence. In the end, the people who stay are more committed, because they remember why they are at Habilitat and what they have to do to stay.

Bans can last for days and sometimes for weeks. When the residents realize their priorities, I, in my role as program director, call an "amnesty." During this short period, usually forty-five minutes to an hour, anyone can confess to anything, with no repercussions. Residents who have broken rules in one way or another — stealing a cigarette or two (or maybe even a pack), borrowing someone else's clothes without asking, trying to get high on drugs, bad-rapping staff members or the program, harboring resentment, or anything along those lines — have a chance at forgiveness. If we sense, during the amnesty, that the atmosphere is still "dirty," we extend the session, and I call on different individuals whom I suspect are guilty of something. They usually stand up at this point and admit what they did, saying, "I stole extra food," or "Yeah, I tried to get high." If we still don't feel we've gotten the whole truth, I'll give the entire house a verbal reprimand, otherwise known as a "haircut." I tell them that I know they're still dirty and not being real.

Then I send them back to work, and in a couple of days we call another amnesty. By this time, the residents are usually pretty desperate and tired. They've been getting up early, working hard all day, and going to bed late and exhausted. In the interim periods, we hold many grueling encounter sessions and seminars. The more tired they get, the weaker their defenses become. During the second amnesty session, I tell them that the ban will continue for however long it takes until the house is clean again, even if it means staying on ban for months.

Sometimes we only need one or two amnesties, but sometimes we need as many as four to flush out the garbage and clear the air. Eventually, people either give up whatever they're holding on to or they split. As soon as we feel that the house is clean again — the trial period can last from two to six weeks — I remove the ban. Then, very gradually, the daily routine returns to normal.

During the ban I declared an amnesty after about two and a half weeks, and the usual minor infractions came to light. But I was certain I wasn't getting all the dirt. For instance, several items such as portable radios and electric razors were missing, and no one had fessed up to stealing them.

That weekend I finally found out what had been keeping me so edgy. It was very late when Toby, one of the night men, heard a vehicle pull up in a side street. He saw a young resident named Bruce get out of one of our vans and hide something at the side of the tool shed. When Bruce left the area, Toby checked the spot and discovered a set of works and a couple of bags of what looked like heroin. Toby awakened Vic, the reentry resident in charge of the house in my absence, and Frank Cockett, who by then was the house coordinator, and told them what had happened.

Bruce took off, after refusing to tell us who else in the house had been in on this little arrangement. He had been referred to us from court with the stipulation that if he left before completing the program, he would be violating the terms of his probation and would be returned to jail. As soon as he split, I called the Adult

Probation Department, and after flaking around for awhile, they finally put pressure on Bruce, who called me to try to make a deal. I told him, "Bruce, I don't make deals. Just tell me what you know, and then I'll decide what I'm going to do." So he admitted that he, Frank Russo, Claude, and Tommy had brought dope into the facility. They had also stolen the radios, the electric razors, and other things, which they had sold to get the drugs.

I told Bruce I'd give him a choice: I'd either take him back into the program and shave his head or turn him over to adult probation. He opted for the shaved head. After his, Claude's and Tommy's heads had been shaved, I brought them all into my office and sent for Frank Russo, Vickie, Frank Cockett, and Dave Braun. Two or three other reentry people were also present. When they arrived, I told Bruce to tell everyone what he had told me. Claude and Tommy backed him up, but Frank denied the charges and threatened Bruce. I pointed out to him that none of these people had anything to gain by accusing him. They had already had their heads shaved and they were going to have to work their way back into the family.

Even Vickie told Frank that she had been aware for some time that something had been going on. Every night he would leave their room with the excuse that he was going out for a smoke or a snack. According to the others, that was when they all met in the storeroom to shoot dope. I told Frank that he could stay at Habilitat under the same conditions as the others, and Vickie promised to stand by him if he'd admit his mistake.

Frank, however, chose to leave Habilitat. I still remember watching Lila follow him to the front gate. Big tears ran down her face as she pleaded, "Are you just going to leave us here like this? We came out here for you."

But he just kept walking.

Staying Alive

ALTHOUGH FRANK'S DEPARTURE was painful for us, coming as it did on the heels of Gerard's resignation and the radical restructuring of the staff, things were beginning to look up by the end of our first year on the Bigelow estate. Publicity was favorable, for the most part, and we were doing a good job of surviving, and even advancing, on our shoestring budget. Cec Heftel, who was later elected U.S. Congressman from Hawaii, then owned KGMB, a television station in Honolulu, and he became one of our biggest fans, producing a great minidocumentary about the program. Another supporter, Governor John Burns, attended our first anniversary luau with his wife Beatrice, despite a wild tropical storm.

Our on-site high school graduated its first eight students. We hustled graduation caps and gowns just like the ones "regular" graduates wear. As the "Grand March" from *Aida* filled the air, the eight walked slowly down the aisle between the rows of chairs set up outside the house. A light rain was falling, and the jacaranda trees were shedding those clear blue flowers onto the green lawn. When the names of the graduates were called to receive their diplomas, we could all feel their pride, because we were proud, too. We had all come a long way in a short time.

The next day, the newspapers were full of positive stories. It was beginning to look like the establishment loved us. This wasn't an accident — we courted the press and actively sought the support of the public. We knew that we had to have a squeaky-clean image in order to survive. Half our residents had been referred to us from the courts, and more than half had a history of serious drug abuse. So the generalizing labels "junkie," "thief," "ex-con" were hung on us regularly, regardless of the wide range of backgrounds and problems of the individual residents. This is a problem every organization like ours has to live with. People will say they approve of what we do — they just don't want us to do it in their neighborhood.

For this reason, we continued to hold regular open houses all through the first year and into the second, inviting not only neighborhood residents but also the public at large to come for a visit, tour the facility, and meet the troops. I also made lots of public appearances, and whenever we had a chance to take part in some do-good activity, we went for it, just as we had when we sang Christmas carols in hospitals during our first holiday season. Later, when the police department sponsored an island-wide highway cleanup campaign, our people picked up trash along twenty miles of Oahu roadside. Of course, we made sure the media knew about it.

We also made a big fuss over our first group of people to finish the program. On August 27, 1972, exactly nineteen months after our drive over the Pali in a torrential rainstorm to look for that house in Kailua, Habilitat had its first "graduates." We held a big luau, as we had on our one-year anniversary, inviting relatives and friends. More than eight hundred people watched as the roll of names was called. Each face glowed with pride, and plenty of cheers and tears welcomed the graduates as they came forward to be recognized. Of that group, Frank Cockett got the most attention in the papers, probably because his previous trouble with the law had gotten the most media attention, too. One headline read, "Former drug user praised in court." When Frank came up for final sentencing, the judge said, "If you had been sentenced nineteen months ago, the odds are very high I would've said, 'The public needs protection from you.' Now it appears you are making something worthwhile of yourself and working to make Hawaii a better place in which to live."

Frank, along with Dave Braun, Vic Modesto, Vickie, and one other member of the graduating class, joined the Habilitat staff. Two others went to work in a dress shop, another became a management trainee at a bank, and one went to work for a local radio station. I was very proud.

At every opportunity, I did whatever I could to keep Habilitat's name in the public eye so that people would hear and read about us and then, maybe, help us. By now our annual budget was way over $100,000, but even with that we were still far short of meeting our operating expenses. Besides, I had new goals. I wanted to buy the Bigelow property, renovate all the existing buildings, and construct some new ones. The buildings were badly run down; the walls were paper thin and infested with termites. I wasn't too worried about our safety in a fire, since I figured we could all just walk right through the walls if we needed to. We were, in fact, getting static from city and county inspectors and the fire department marshals, who said that we needed more bathrooms, which was certainly true, and that our walls were not structurally sound. We also needed another exit, as well as a fire escape. I recognized the need for these upgrades, but we had no money to pay for any of them. I couldn't use the operating money I was receiving for capital improvements.

I finally had a resident who was quite artistic paint a stairway and a door on the outside of the building. When the inspectors took a look at our new stairway and door, they were so impressed with this innovative lunacy that they left laughing, and let us get away with it. They knew that we were helping many local people, so they didn't want to hassle us unduly. They could see that we had cleaned up the place, and that everyone was busy all the time maintaining and improving the property. One day the governor's wife, who was confined to a wheelchair, came to visit us. Several of our larger guys just picked her up gently, wheelchair and all, and took her up the stairs. This seemed to prove — at least to me — that we didn't need wheelchair ramps. It was clear, however, that we weren't going to get away with it forever. We needed to make some serious money.

Fundraising continued, but we weren't able to break into the big time. At one point, we sent some reentry people to school to learn trades we couldn't teach: auto mechanics and hair styling, for example. We started our own auto shop, but when the beauty school students started trying out their newly acquired haircutting skills on the other residents, the results left something to be desired. Still, I think the guinea pigs generally preferred their crooked bangs to the other kind of "haircut" that we administered at Habilitat. The skills of our budding stylists improved with time, and the first resident to finished her course eventually went to work at a top salon in San Francisco.

Our first fundraising concert, held in January 1973 to celebrate our second anniversary, was more successful than the other initiatives. We held it in the Exhibition Hall of the Honolulu International Center, which seats 2500 people. We sold tickets for $10 each for a sit-down dinner and a fantastic show. For this concert Ethel Azama, Al Harrington, Danny Kaleikini, John Rowles, the Surfers, Zulu, Jimmy Borges, Rene Paulo, Iva Kinimaka, Melveen Leed, Nephi Hanneman, Kent Bowman, and many other island entertainers donated time and talent. We netted $16,000 — not bad, considering we didn't know what the hell we were doing.

At that time, we had seventy-one residents. Even with the big house on the beach and the cottages, it was beginning to feel as cramped as the old Kailua house. At night, so many bodies were spread out on the floor that we could have filmed one of those crowded hospital scenes in a war movie. We also had tents up again.

Because we couldn't afford to build on the property, we began scouting for a cheap second location, and on Valentine's Day, 1973, we found it. We moved some of our residents into an old building on the grounds of the Kaneohe State Hospital. The state had agreed to rent us the structure for a dollar a year. It wasn't in great shape, but it was large. I asked Beatrice Burns, the governor's wife, to help with the cutting of the traditional Hawaiian maile lei at the grand opening. I also asked a Catholic priest, a Protestant minister, a Buddhist monk, and a Jewish rabbi to bless the occasion. (I wanted to be on the safe side. God knows, we always needed help, and I wanted to make sure I had covered as many bases as possible.)

It didn't take long to get the Habilitat II facility bustling, and one day I went to see the administrator of the hospital to ask if we could also use a few acres of vacant land near our building. I said we wanted to plant a victory garden, which would provide a good learning experience for our residents and allow us to grow fresh vegetables for our own use. He seemed pleased with the idea and said, "Good, you can use the land on the right side of the road."

I asked, "What about the land on the left side of the road?"

And he said, "Okay, use that, too."

I then went to the commander of the Kaneohe Marine Corps Air Station and explained my plan. He offered to contribute the use of landscaping and earth-moving equipment as well as manpower. From there I went to the University of Hawaii and enlisted the help of several experts in agriculture. In less than two months we had a thirty-acre working farm, all planted and irrigated. Eventually, the farm not only supplied us with much of our food, but we were also able to sell the surplus to the hospital and to people in the community. Our residents learned about farming techniques, crop management, and product marketing, and we all enjoyed the fresh vegetables and fruit.

VICKIE HADN'T HEARD a word from Frank since the day he walked out of Habilitat. She had filed for divorce immediately and decided to make Hawaii her home.

One night during dinner I told her, "You know, I think I love you." She thought I was teasing her, but she soon realized that I

was serious. She couldn't give me a definite response right away
— she was still pretty shaken by her experience with Frank, and
she was worried about Lila's reaction, too. She needed some time
before she could make a serious commitment, so we occasionally
went out, and I made a great effort to establish a good relationship
with Lila. We played, went to the beach, talked a great deal, and I
even helped her with her homework. I thought she liked me, but I
knew how much she was still hurting because of Frank's caper.
Finally the three of us found a house and moved in together, and
on June 3, 1973, Vickie and I were married at Habilitat.

My entire family came out from New York for the ceremony, and
we did it up royally — limos, leis, singers, the works. Everybody in
the Habilitat family took part in the festivities. There's nothing like
a good wedding to fire up family feeling. We made a terrific team,
Vickie and I, and we've had some great adventures together.

ADVENTURES ARE FUN and exciting. They get the adrenaline flowing. In those early years at Habilitat, there was no shortage of adventures. Sharing adventures is not only a good way to build a
family; it also helps develop collective survival skills.

As I've already mentioned, one of my heroes is Saul Alinsky,
the twentieth-century community organizer. One of the messages
I got from Alinsky came to me through a story about his activities
in Harlem. One day Alinsky stopped a guy who was coming out of
a tenement and asked him how much the landlord paid him to live
there. The place was rat- and roach-infested and was painted with
cheap lead paint that was peeling. Kids were probably eating the
paint flakes, getting sick and sometimes even dying of lead poi-
soning. The guy said, "You kidding me, man? He doesn't pay me.
He charges me and I pay him!"

Alinsky said, "How can you pay to live in this piece of shit?"

"Because if I don't he'll evict me."

Alinsky then asked him how many families lived there, and the
guy told him there were forty. Alinsky said, "Well, what if every-

body decided not to pay? Can he possibly throw forty families out?" Through this one guy Alinsky organized all forty families, who refused to pay rent until the rats and roaches were exterminated and the place was repainted. The landlord went to court to get those people out, but he lost.

Like Alinsky, when I see something wrong, I want to change it. There's a lot that can go wrong in agencies that deal with drug abuse in the community, and in the early 1970s I began to get the sense that something was going seriously wrong with the Waikiki Drug Clinic.

The Waikiki Drug Clinic is a different organization from the walk-in induction center that Habilitat was operating in Waikiki under the Habilitat name. The Waikiki Drug Clinic was founded in 1967 by the United Council of Churches and the Waikiki Ministry. It operated out of a small cottage in the heart of Waikiki and served as a haven for runaways. People — mostly kids — who had experienced a bad drug trip or were living on the streets and had become sick could go there and receive free medical examinations, blood tests, and simple medication dispensed by competent volunteer physicians.

When I first found out about the place, I thought it was great. It seemed to be providing a much-needed community service; frightened runaways and sick kids could go there and feel safe. Even the police and ambulance crews brought in kids. After a while, though, the atmosphere at the clinic changed. A group of selfish and inept volunteers zeroed in on the clinic as a place to pick up young, inexperienced kids, both male and female, for sensitivity training, encounter sessions, and even massage groups. They were using the clinic as a front for their own needs. After observing these groups for a short while, I realized I didn't need a college degree to see that the volunteers were exploiting these kids. Group leaders would invite young participants to their homes to sleep or to get a bite to eat. The whole thing smelled bad.

I was determined to make some changes, but I knew it wouldn't be easy. I started by attending all the group meetings. Every evening during the week, I went to the clinic and sat in with a different group and listened to the nonsense. After I figured out the bullshit the leaders were trying to put over on the group, I would challenge them directly — a move that would stir up the dynamic of any group. The people who were running the clinic finally told me that they wanted me to stop coming because I was disrupting the whole place. I said that I wouldn't stop until they discontinued their questionable approaches to group work. Way too many sexual overtones and innuendoes came up in the group discussions, and the leaders were unqualified to perform any type of emotional therapy. "They might push some of the kids past the point of no return," I said. Besides, my gut feeling told me that these young people were actually being exploited sexually.

There was some attempt to exclude me from the meetings, but over the years I had built up some decent relationships with the clinic's staff and administration. Many of Habilitat's residents had been inducted from there. In the end, I wore them out. Encounter groups were suspended at the Waikiki Drug Clinic, and eventually the clinic itself closed down.

MY NEXT TARGET was the Department of Social Services and Housing (DSSH), which operated the entire state penal system, including Oahu Prison; the youth correctional facility, known as Koolau; Halawa Jail; Olinda, on Maui; the Kauai Community Correctional Center; the Kulani Honor Farm on the Big Island; and the Hawaii Detention Home for Adolescents.

At Oahu Prison (better known as OP), I had a good rapport with the inmates. I had been able to get many out on early parole so that they could enter Habilitat. The more time I spent talking to the inmates, the more injustice and inefficiency I discovered. The system needed a complete overhaul.

One of my ideas was to set up a labor union within the prison in conjunction with an established union on the outside. The outside union would supply the convicts with work from private industry: carpentry, cabinet making, metalwork — anything they could do inside the prison walls. My idea was that the convicts would get minimum pay, and half of what they made would go to the state to help defray the cost of maintaining them. The other half would go to their families, thus reducing the welfare and food-stamp monies that most families of convicts were forced to use in order to survive. It seemed like a good deal all around. The inmates would be doing productive work and learning a trade, and, in the process, would generate some needed cash to reduce prison costs.

In my plan, the government's only real obligation was to screen the material brought into the prison for the inmates to work on, which isn't such a hassle. At that time, we were doing similar projects at Habilitat. For example, we had a business packaging audio headsets for various airlines. We cleaned and sterilized them and sealed them into plastic bags, and we were paid a small amount for each headset. We also packaged the airlines' eating utensils. I figured the prison inmates could do similar work, and suggested that the prisoners, as union members, should have the right to stage a peaceful sit-down strike with the backing of the outside union. In addition, I argued that they should be granted conjugal visits.

In exchange for a minimum wage, the cons would perform their jobs, and would guarantee that there would be no drugs, no violence, no gambling, no liquor, and no forced homosexuality. If these guys were willing to go along with such conditions, it would make the administration's job much easier. The public would feel better, too, because taxpayer costs would be reduced. Even the conjugal visits were justified, because that would reduce, if not stop, the forced homosexual activity. By eliminating all the contraband materials and the unacceptable behavior, the inmates would help gain an earlier parole to Habilitat for those interested in the program, which in turn would ease the prison system's problems with overcrowding.

All this sounded reasonable to me, but the prison administrator didn't like my plan, and would no longer allow me or any member of my staff inside prison walls anywhere in the state. In February 1974, we bought a full-page advertisement in the Honolulu newspapers:

Who the Hell Does Habilitat Think They Are?

Compare us with Oahu Prison: Find out how many successfully rehabilitated persons have gone through that system on your tax money. Find out their recidivism rate. (Out of twenty-one persons who have successfully completed our program at Habilitat, all are gainfully employed, and none have been arrested or gotten into any trouble.)

Compare us with Koolau, which costs (with your tax dollars) four times as much as Habilitat to operate.

Compare us with methadone maintenance, and don't be misled by the low cost of methadone itself. Find out exactly the total cost for one person per month stabilizing on methadone.

And look at these figures, folks: Compare costs with using heroin addicts. An actual using heroin addict on the streets has to average stealing $300 a day to support a $100-a-day habit. If the twenty-nine court-affiliated people now in Habilitat who were on heroin were still in the community, committing burglaries, armed robberies, car thefts, muggings, etc., it would cost the community $8,700 a day, $60,900 a week, $264,625 a month, or $3,175,500 a year. In Habilitat, rehabilitation for the same twenty-nine people costs approximately $8 a day each.

Compare these monthly costs per resident:

State Honor Camps	$1,424
Oahu State Prison	$1,035
Koolau (HYCF)	$986
Detention Home	$735
Honolulu Jail	$549
Habilitat, Inc.	$250

The day after the ad ran, I called the press again, and this time I said that I was going to sue, claiming that Ray Belnap, the top prison administrator, was denying Habilitat equal rights under the law, since other rehabilitation groups were allowed inside the state's detention facilities. I said that he was being "arbitrary, whimsical, capricious, and spiteful." (Actually, our lawyers said that. What I say doesn't often get included in lawsuits, usually for reasons of "good taste.") Soon after that, when regular visits to the prison were resumed, I dropped the suit.

At about the same time, the morning newspaper published a story headlined "Heroin Problem Fades." Federal experts in Washington were saying that the heroin problem was over, now that government-administered methadone programs were in place. What bullshit. Methadone is a synthetic opiate more addictive than heroin and morphine put together. Addicts, many of them still teenagers, were swarming to the methadone clinics nationwide. I wrote an angry letter to the paper:

> I am truly disgusted at the apathetic, unrealistic approach to this problem that has ruthlessly destroyed so many of our young people for so many years. Can people in these United States be so unaware, so naive, so easily led — a second time? Many years ago, the experts claimed a high rate of cure in morphine addiction. Morphine usage, they reported, had reached a very low ebb. However, they failed to mention the soaring rise in the use of the drug that cured morphine addiction — heroin.

I went on to talk about the high cost of the program, and the social and physical side effects of the crippling methadone addiction (unemployment, constipation, water retention, weight gain). Eight of my troops also wrote statements about their own problems with methadone. One of the guys, then a facility director at Habilitat, had been a former methadone patient. He described withdrawal from methadone addiction as torture, more difficult than the withdrawal from heroin. (Methadone moves into the marrow of your bones, which makes it extremely painful.) Another said that he would rather be back on the street shooting heroin than using methadone again.

But all this was like trying to stop a river. The state and federal authorities just loved the idea of methadone. The government is a dinosaur — slow to think, slow to move, slow to change. Unfortunately, Habilitat's economic survival was becoming increasingly dependent on the so-called generosity of various government agencies. Our funding was coming from dozens of sources now, and too many of them were run by unimaginative, nit-picking, I'm-only-doing-my-job bureaucrats.

At Habilitat, I'd been talking about self-sufficiency for a long time. I knew that it made perfect sense to teach my troops that they had to be self-sufficient, and it made the same perfect sense for Habilitat. In fact, I felt that by not being financially independent, Habilitat was setting a bad example for its residents. The bottom line was, we had to try harder — a lot harder.

We had learned a great deal from that first benefit concert in January 1973. So I gave the go-ahead to have the tickets printed for a second one, and Dave Braun and I started the public relations work. In the evenings, I would go to Waikiki clubs and line up the entertainers to appear. No one turned us down. We were told, however, that we could not sell food anywhere in the International Center because the city and county had exclusive deals with their own vendors. That was okay with me, as my big gimmick was to give away free food and drinks that had been donated to us.

At the beginning of the event, the U.S. Marine Band was in place, ready to start playing the Hawaii state anthem and the national anthem, and our people were running around, passing out free food and drinks. All of a sudden the man in charge of the facility, Matt Esposito, came rushing up. He was shouting, "You can't do this! You can't give away food and soft drinks! My vendors are losing money!"

"Hey, Matt," I answered, "considering what we're paying you, that's your problem! I'm here to provide for our supporters."

As the man stood there spluttering, literally shaking with anger, the band started playing "Hawaii Pono I." I stood up, in proper respect.

We netted, after expenses, $26,510. I sent out a news release while the show was still fresh in the public's mind. In it, we disclosed the amount we had raised and announced that the money was going to be put toward buying our Kaneohe property, which would mean that Habilitat could have a permanent home of its own and could start a major building program. Then I revealed what all our expenses had been, including the 10 percent of our gross that went to the City and County of Honolulu for the arena, plus payments for security and lighting.

It happened that a local newspaper reporter who had a bone to pick with Frank Fasi, the mayor of Honolulu, latched onto the story and blew it out of proportion, turning it into a full feature article. During a meeting in my office, my staff said, "Vinny, you've got big trouble now. Don't tangle with Fasi." Just at that moment — I swear this is a true story — a large framed proclamation by Mayor Fasi that had been hanging on my office wall fell to the floor with a resounding crash. Shattered glass flew all over the place.

"Oh, shit," I said, "it looks like we are in trouble."

Sure enough, I soon got a call from Mayor Fasi, and Vickie and I went to his office.

As it turned out, the mayor was very reasonable. "I understand," he said. "You were used. The media doesn't like me, and you were the pawn."

"Hey, I know that now," I answered. "Look, Frank, you're Italian and I'm Italian."

"Wait a minute," he said. "I'm Sicilian!"

"Frank, that's even better," I retorted. "You're Sicilian and I'm Sicilian. You're a doer, you get things done for the little people. I'm a doer, I get things done, and I'm for the underdog, too. Why don't we form some kind of marriage where we can complement each other in the things we try to do?"

He grinned and said, "What! Married to you?" From that day on, we've been friends. One of the ways he supported Habilitat was by making one of his assistants available to help us draft grant proposals. Grant writing is an art, and many — if not most — long-term residential programs like ours were surviving on such grants at that time. That made for a lot of competition for the funds offered by private foundations.

We were still living hand-to-mouth, obviously, and it was long past the time to start some money-making businesses. Neither the beauty salon nor the service station had worked out too well, and several other operations under way had failed, too. We just didn't have the necessary capital to get started. All of our government grant money, plus the funds that came in from welfare and the courts, had to be allocated to daily operations. What we got from private sources — foundations, personal contributions, and fundraising events — disappeared like a magician's flash paper. What we didn't spend on the costly repairs to our aging facility was held aside in the desperate hope that we might accumulate enough to exercise our option to buy the Bigelow property.

We talked for hours, then for days, trying to decide what kind of business could best teach the troops a useful trade at the same time as it turned a decent profit. The real kicker was that the enterprise would have to require little or no initial financial investment. Our answer came from a soft-spoken recovering junkie named Bob, who had been the national sales manager for Synanon, heading up an ad specialty business there that had grossed $6 million a year. We hired him to show us how to get into sales.

Bob set up the suppliers, ordered samples, and started teaching twelve of our reentry people how to sell. For two weeks, eight hours a day, he held classes in one of the rooms in Hab II. I also arranged some meetings with local salespeople who volunteered to give our people the benefit of their experience. In the third week, the trainees practiced selling products to each other, and four weeks after Bob's arrival, our troops were on the street (in a productive way, this time), canvassing shops in Kaneohe and Kailua.

For people like our residents, selling isn't just a job. It also teaches them great survival skills, such as how to present themselves, how to meet and work with the public, and how to fit into the economic structure of society. At first, resistance to our group's efforts was fierce, and the rejection was very hard for my people to take. Every night, we'd have a feedback session to go over the day's experiences. We shared problems and devised strategies for working them out. There'd be another meeting each morning to build up the confidence and the positive attitudes of the sales teams before they started in again.

I'm proud to report that by Christmas of that year, our troops had taken orders totaling $900,000 gross — not bad for items like pens and pencils that were imprinted. While they generated needed funds, they were also learning sales techniques, how to handle rejection, and how to function as self-sufficient and self-confident individuals in the outside world.

Another fundraising project got underway in 1974: the *Friends of Habilitat Cookbook*. We made up a list of four hundred prominent island personalities and wrote them letters asking them to donate recipes for their favorite dishes. Responses came in from every category of celebrity: bank presidents, politicians, journalists, sports people, and top entertainers all got into the action. Governor and Mrs. John Burns sent a recipe for ono potato salad ("*ono*" is Hawaiian for "good" or "delicious"). A Polynesian performer, Tavana, told us how to steam fish Samoan-Tahitian style, and Don Ho offered a soup with pig's feet and ginger. Artist Jean Charlot sent in a recipe for a stew made with opihi (a local shellfish), singer Carole Kai came up with sweet-and-sour spareribs, and U.S. Senator Dan Inouye contributed the Vienna Waltz cheesecake. Other submissions came from Clare Booth Luce (a four-bean pickle salad), Jack and Marie Lord (watercress soup), University of Hawaii football coach Larry Price (Portuguese bean soup "Kaaawa style"), Mayor Frank Fasi (fried bell peppers), and championship surfer Fred Hemmings (ono fried rice).

The tide was slowly beginning to turn. In 1974 we passed the halfway mark on our road to self-sufficiency. In December of that year, our accountant Dudley Hoolhurst happily told me that 58 percent of our budget was now self-generated. We could boast of 54 graduates and another 123 people in residence. For the hundred we had on our waiting list, there was still no room at the inn.

THE NEXT THREE YEARS — 1975, 1976, and 1977 — were marked by rapid growth. Habilitat's population increased to 150, and our annual budget reached $1.5 million, which meant that we were desperately trying to come up with new ways to raise money. The handwriting was on the wall: It was clear that the day was coming when the "handouts" we were getting from the government and from certain charitable organizations would simply run out.

Some of the first symptoms of these new conditions showed up when the state dragged its bureaucratic feet while qualifying us to receive food stamps. We knew that our people were entitled to these benefits. Congress had expanded the food stamp program to include private, nonprofit institutions that were offering approved drug and alcohol treatment and rehabilitation, and Habilitat had been approved under those guidelines. According to Congress, the addicts and alcoholics at Habilitat were eligible, but we still had to go to court to get the state to take any action on the federal ruling.

In addition to this hassle, the Aloha United Fund (AUF) decided to get on our case. A local distributor of advertising novelties was kicking up a fuss. His company made a contribution to AUF each year, and he resented the fact that some of his money was going to support us while we were competing with him for business. Eventually we agreed that AUF would continue to fund us for another year, and then would take us off their rolls. The money came to only $16,000 at the time, which wasn't worth all the paperwork — or the strings attached — anyway.

In April 1975 we had our third concert, with a bigger lineup of stars than ever before. After expenses, our net was $42,000 — a nice piece of change. But we had the concert routine down pat by then. It just wasn't an adventure any more, and when it stopped being an adventure, it stopped being fun. So we didn't do concerts after that.

1975 was a year of growth in every way, marked most dramatically by the birth of our daughter on May 16. We named her Victoria, after her mother. Birth announcements went out to all members of the Habilitat family, who were by now spread around the world. "She is beautiful and healthy!" the message said. "Mom is doing fine! Dad is back to normal."

When we had found out that Vickie was pregnant, I had, of course, been happy and excited about the prospect of being a father. But I started wondering if all the drugs I had taken would cause some trouble for the baby. Sure, I had been clean for about eight years by then, but I still felt scared. I worried about my child in a way I never had worried about myself. When I heard she was a perfectly normal child, I let out a long breath in relief. It felt like I had been holding that breath for months.

Things were normal at Habilitat, too — that is, the drama never stopped, though at times, fortunately, the drama was comic. One of the residents, for example, discovered a unique way to get high. We called him the Aqua Velva thief because he'd move around from dorm to dorm, drinking a little out of each bottle of the aftershave we'd hustled from the manufacturer. He got away with it for a long time, until he started stealing from the residents' private stashes of cologne. He finally blew his cover on the day his breath smelled like Aramis.

Then there was Benny Harrington. He was from Boston and slurred his s's. We were on a house ban, and during an amnesty Benny got to his feet and told one of the longest copouts in

Habilitat's history. His guilt, he explained, stemmed from the time he had been asked to make a garbage run, which involves taking the trash from the kitchen to the bins outside. We'd been on the ban for nine and a half days, he went on, during which time he had been allowed no coffee and only one "shmoke" a day. He said, "I take the gahbage and I walk to the gahbage bin, and it's a long walk to the gahbage bin, and as I'm walking I'm thinking about a shmoke. When I get to the gahbage bin, I dump the gahbage, and I shpot a shigarette butt in the mashed potatoesh." By then, Benny had been talking for about seven or eight minutes.

"What?" Vickie asked impatiently. "Come on!"

Benny looked at Vickie and said, "I looked around to shee if anybody was watching, and I took that shigarette butt and I shmoked it, mashed potatoesh and all." Everyone cracked up.

One of the most memorable intake interviews was with an older guy named Joel. He was a dentist from Baltimore who had gotten into trouble by writing himself prescriptions for drugs. When I got to the point in the discussion where I told him that I was going to take his wig — meaning that he was going to get the standard haircut — he smiled, lifted off a convincing toupee, and handed it to me.

Though we did have our celebrations and our moments of comic relief, Habilitat's road through the mid-1970s was still mostly uphill. Increased enrollment in the program meant, at the most basic level, more bodies, and to take proper care of them we needed more money and more space. We did everything we could think of to bring in the cash: We sent our ad-specialties sales teams to Atlanta, Tulsa, Kansas City, and Denver, and we added custom-made wood plaques to our catalog. We reorganized our woodworking shop and started making tikis (carved Hawaiian figurines), benches, tables, and chairs.

After selling 15,0000 copies of the first cookbook, we started collecting recipes for a national version — a 300-page hard-cover book that eventually included contributions from Bill Cosby, Cher,

Carol Burnett, Hugh Hefner, Burt Reynolds, Steve Allen, Roy Rogers and Dale Evans, Barbara Walters, John Wayne, Phyllis Diller, Ann-Margret, Walter Cronkite, Jimmy Carter, Johnny Mathis, Olivia Newton-John, Bob Newhart, John Denver, Jeanne Dixon, Nancy Reagan, George Peppard, Lucille Ball, Betty Ford, Bing Crosby, and Bob Hope, among many others. It's probably not fair for me to pick a favorite recipe, but I will say that the last one in the book was George Burns's "Recipe for Happiness." In response to our request, he said, "I do not have a favorite recipe, and that is the truth. If the food is served stove hot, and there is a bottle of ketchup handy, I am a very happy man."

We also started a lawn-and-garden maintenance service and our own pool-cleaning service. We sold Christmas trees. We held a bowling tournament with the military, and a tennis tournament with local celebrities. We sponsored a benefit movie premiere in Waikiki. We put collection cans with the message "Why not leave your change for Habilitat — A Place of Change" next to cash registers all over the state. We cleaned a hundred miles of Oahu's highways in a trash-a-thon, getting local businesses to sponsor us at the rate of $2.50 a mile per resident. In our new T-shirt factory, we imprinted the names of these businesses, along with Habilitat's, on the shirts we wore, and collected hundreds of pounds of aluminum, which we sold for recycling. It all helped, and it kept us in the public eye.

The fundraiser that gave us the most visibility and money wasn't even our idea. When Jerry Greenspan and I met with Cec Heftel, who ran KGMB TV, Cec suggested a telethon and offered to pay the production costs and donate the air time.

I was a little skeptical. "What if the phones don't ring?" I asked.

"Vinny," he said, "even if you don't make money, you've got fifteen and a half hours of prime time. You can get your message about Habilitat across to the whole state of Hawaii, plus whatever tourists and visitors happen to catch the show. If you don't make money, I'll guarantee you $50,000. What can you lose?"

Jerry and I looked at each other, and we could both feel the adrenaline start to kick in.

I put Bob in charge of canvassing the business community to line up pledges in advance, just as they did for Jerry Lewis and the other national telethons. (You're nuts if you think that the head of McDonald's is sitting at home watching TV, decides on the spur of the moment to pledge $25,000, and shows up at the station half an hour later with a check.)

Almost every entertainer in town showed up to perform during our telethon, and many of them thanked us for what we'd done for friends they had in the program, and for what we were doing for Hawaii. Many of our residents and graduates told their stories. The phones rang constantly, and when it was over, our net was $122,000 — enough to make a big dream come true. Our lease with Mary Ann Bigelow was scheduled to expire in June 1976, only three months after the telethon. Just before the deadline, we exercised our option to buy the place.

When the papers were signed, I took them to the facility and called a general meeting — the most emotional and exhilarating GM in Habilitat's history. Vickie was by my side. "I have an announcement," I told the troops. I couldn't help grinning. I held the mortgage over my head and said, "The place is ours! We own it! Nobody can take it away."

The room erupted in cheers and applause. I don't think there was a dry eye as I went on: "The land we're sitting and standing on now belongs to Habilitat. We don't have to worry about getting evicted. We don't have to worry any more about the lease running out. And we did it as a family. A lot of people said we could never do it, and we did it. What the mind of man can conceive and believe, it can achieve."

NOW, I SAID TO MYSELF, all we have to do is conceive of what this place will look like when we get finished with it. I wanted to raze the existing buildings and put up several new ones. Yet, as always, more money was needed. And once again, an idea came to us, this time from an energetic disc jockey for KKUA, a man who talked so fast it was hard even for me, a fast-talking New Yorker, to keep up. Ron told me that he had seen our telethon. When he first tuned in, he said, he expected a piece of shit — all for a worthy cause, perhaps, but run by amateurs. What he saw had impressed him: It was clear that we had our act together and he had a proposition to make.

Ron told me that when he had done some programming at a station in San Diego, he had produced several Homegrown record albums — albums of original songs written by his listeners about their state. The albums were used as promotions for the station. Now that he was back in Hawaii, he said he was going to repeat the stunt, calling on the rich tradition of island music to produce the best Homegrown album yet. And, he said, he wanted Habilitat to get all the profits.

When I heard what Ron had in mind, and he told me how he would promote the album — and Habilitat — I naturally said yes, promising whatever help he needed. Every step of the way, it was a perfect promotion, and we learned a lot. Sales and entrepreneurship are the backbone of America, and this was a great way to get Habilitat and our residents into the mainstream.

Ron's morning show was one of the most popular rock and roll stations in the state. First Ron announced the contest, drumming up interest in it on his show whenever he got a chance. Songwriters and performers were asked to submit original songs about Hawaii. One by one, the members of the panel of celebrity judges, which included Don Ho, were revealed. When the entry deadline passed, the countdown began. The Homegrown contest was heavily promoted, not just on Ron's show, but on every show at the station. And every single time, Habilitat got a nice plug. Meanwhile, a second contest was underway to come up with the original cover art for the album. For this, local artists were encouraged to submit their designs.

Habilitat was handling the marketing, and we kept busy lining up stores to sell the album. Many shops already knew us from buying our advertising novelties and other products over the years. We were asking the store owners to buy the albums for $1.69 each — the call number of Ron's station — and to sell them for the same price. Some of the owners wondered why they shouldn't make a profit. We insisted that with all the promotion Ron was giving the project, the album would create tremendous foot traffic in the stores once it was available, and that traffic would increase overall sales. In some cases, this concept only got across after a lot of convincing — all good experience for the Habilitat sales department.

At last the judges chose the winners, and under a heavy veil of secrecy, the tapes were flown to the mainland where the records were to be pressed. Ron followed up by doing interviews with the people in the manufacturing plant, interviews with the people who were going to fly the finished product back to Hawaii, interviews with anybody he could think of.

In October 1976, the first shipment of albums arrived. When we pulled up with the albums that first morning to see lines of people outside the stores, we knew we were sitting on a gold mine. We decided right away to limit the number of albums we delivered to each store in order to create an even bigger demand.

I knew that the best deals were win-win deals in which both sides came away happy. This was my first win-win-win-win deal, though. KKUA got the audience ratings it wanted, making it the number-one rock station. The stores got free on-the-air promotion and astounding foot traffic. The singers and songwriters got their songs and their performances promoted, and many of them found jobs and made independent record contracts as a result of the album. And Habilitat got all that good exposure and netted nearly $53,000.

The following year, our fortunes continues to improve. We did the telethon again and produced another album. The money flowed in. We were on a roll. For me, part of the elation came from creatively (and not criminally) making money, and from passing on skills to kids who really hadn't had a clue about how to make a legit buck or how to support themselves for the long run.

Being independent feels really good. Independence is one of the most reinforcing rewards of going straight and learning job skills. Most of Habilitat's residents had had a good taste of what it feels like to be dependent on drugs and dependent on crime to get the drugs. That's what addiction is all about, after all. Achieving independence, becoming liberated in the best sense of that word, was the main plank in our rehabilitation program.

Leader of the Pack

WHEN YOU ARE not only out of the gutter but up and running, a funny thing happens: The same people who were urging you to get up, who cheered for you when you were down, wake up belatedly to the fact that you are no longer the underdog but have become the leader of the pack. And then they turn on you. It's part of the deal, I suppose. Their betrayal serves as a kind of badge of success.

For a few years, Habilitat was the underdog, fighting over scraps for survival. I continued to shoot off my mouth, ignoring the advice of not only my friend Frank Natale but practically everyone else around me. (I wasn't actually ignoring my friends — I just decided not to take their advice.) I knew that being controversial got me in hot water, but I also knew that it got Habilitat a lot of public attention. From the start, even in that little Kailua house, I firmly maintained that one day Habilitat would be a household word in Hawaii. Speaking my mind — and doing it loudly — was one of the ways I was going to make that happen.

The fact is that when you go on TV or radio, or when you hold a news conference, you wind up with thirty to sixty seconds to get your message across. If I say what a good thing Habilitat is, I come off sounding like a dull goodie-two-shoes and nobody's going to remember my point — that is, if I even get on the air. But if I call someone a moron, the guy who's sitting in front of the TV with his beer is going to remember me and my message.

The same is true of the print media. Whenever I talked to newspaper reporters or wrote a letter to the editor, I said exactly what I was thinking. Once, for example, I wrote a letter to the *Honolulu Star-Bulletin* commenting on the trial of a kid who had been beaten by fellow inmates at Koolau, the youth correctional facility:

> The despicable sloth found in Koolau, the stench of urine, the beating up of weaker youths, the mental agony that accompanies a person in Koolau ... all that is not new. I told you about Koolau long before this trial, and what did I get but a few mumbles and criticism for speaking out.
>
> Is there even a question about whether the state is responsible for the damage inflicted on one person who couldn't survive in that environment because he wasn't strong enough to fight back? You have the audacity to leave that responsibility up to the courts to decide?
>
> I can't believe the blindness in this state. Our elected senators and representatives take a tour through the facility and pass on public remarks that liken Koolau to a country club. Have they lost their minds? Would these same officials allow their sons or daughters to spend a summer at the state's youth "country club"?
>
> The truth about Koolau is so simple it deceives even our state officials.... Koolau turns out criminals!

I urged that the place be shut down. I said it was a tremendous haven for drug use, forced homosexuality, and violence. Taxpayers spent $1.2 million to house only 75 residents in Koolau for one year. At the time, Habilitat had 175 residents and our total operating budget was only $821,000. Koolau was paying its staff more than what our total costs were, and we had more than twice as many residents.

Furthermore, I recommended that Habilitat take over Koolau. The population of our main facility had risen to 95, and in Hab II we had 80 people in a complex designed for 25. These crowded conditions had forced me to declare a moratorium on accepting any more people. In my plan, Habilitat would not only be able to reduce the size of its waiting list, but would also accept all juveniles committed to the Department of Social Services and Housing, except those needing psychiatric hospitalization. These kids would first enter a maximum security building staffed by Habilitat graduates, where they would remain for thirty days before entering Habilitat. We would provide this service so long as we were granted complete autonomy with regard to program content and the use of Koolau buildings and land. I also wanted to dismiss all sixty-nine full-time state employees then working at Koolau, because they didn't know anything about how our program functioned.

The state officials reacted to this last condition with horror, explaining to me that these employees were civil servants and couldn't be fired. "What do we do with them?" they asked.

I said, "Give them big hats and horses and make them forest rangers. So what if we don't have any forests? These guys aren't doing anything anyway."

Expecting that the state might not be all that receptive to this idea, I had an alternate plan ready: We would take one out of every three juveniles committed by family court and use about half of Koolau's total land and buildings. I also presented a fall-back proposal that involved our using only one of the buildings, but still taking on one of every three committed juveniles.

As it turned out, the state didn't say yes or no. What happened is what usually happens when bureaucrats are confronted with a good idea: They asked to spend some of the taxpayers' money to do a study. And wouldn't you know it, they decided that they wanted back the building we were using for Habilitat II. They kept up the pressure on us until finally a doctor by the name of Dennis Mee Lee, the head of mental health, told me that if we didn't vacate the building, he would hold up our federal funding.

I looked him square in the eye and said, "Dennis, don't be a putz. How are you going to withhold federal money earmarked for

Habilitat because of a hassle over a building owned by the state of Hawaii? I'll see you in court."

Which I did — and we beat the bums again. As a matter of fact, every time we had to take them to court to get relief, we won. In this particular case, we got our money and we were also able to hang onto the building.

The rift between Habilitat and the so-called professionals in the mental health establishment in Hawaii actually went a lot deeper than a disagreement over a crummy building in Kaneohe. Habilitat was playing on their turf, and we were winning. Our methods, like those of similar therapeutic communities on the mainland, went against just about everything the "official" mental health practitioners believed. The chasm between philosophies ran all the way across North America.

By 1977 hundreds of therapeutic communities, or TC's, existed in the United States. According to the establishment, we were "the illegitimate child of the mental health movement." I disagreed. I was, in fact, becoming something of an expert on the subject. In the summer of 1977, just when the Department of Health in Hawaii started writing a new book of rules for live-in health programs like ours, I was asked to deliver the keynote speech in Montreal at the Second World Conference of Therapeutic Communities.

I stood up in front of the crowd of TC directors, psychologists, psychiatrists, and therapists and said what I truly felt: "If the TC can be called a bastard, what shall we call mental health, which prior to the TC movement literally squandered billions of dollars working with dope fiends? The TC is nobody's bastard. It is a legitimate response to a real need, created by ex-addicts who channeled their energies and intelligence to solve their problems by changing their self-destructive and socially disruptive behavior. Since the degreed and credentialed experts couldn't help them change, they had to do it themselves, using unconventional methods and techniques. And we are living proof that what we do works."

Our success had the so-called professionals worried because we were coming in off the streets, a bunch of thieving ex-cons with no formal education, and learning in two or three years what twenty years of schooling hadn't taught them. They wanted to soothe their pangs of envy and resentment by making up laws to regulate what we do and how we do it. The drug problem might have gotten completely out of their control but, by God, they were still going to control us.

Some of these professionals alleged that we are being cruel when we shave heads, put someone "in the dishpan," or hold "brutal" encounter sessions. But what about their methods? "First the professionals tranquilized their treatment populations so that no one would hurt themselves," I said. "Then came electroshock and insulin shock treatments. The real biggy was, of course, the frontal lobotomy, which reduced people to vegetable states." It's always amazed me that no one's come up with a rectal lobotomy.

Still, it was obvious that some people in the TC movement had swallowed the establishment hook, so that now they were running around in fancy suits and spouting psychobabble. If a guy came up and started talking about "differential opportunity structures," "inadequate socialization," "viable psychosocial communication systems," or "the pathology of schismogenetic patterning," would you know what the fuck he was talking about?

"The ex-dope fiend," I told the convention audience, "wants to parade around in a conservative three-piece suit and tie while the psychiatrists go the other way and wear groovy tie-dyed dungarees and talk hip to prove they're 'deep' human beings. Ex-dope fiends are not psychiatrists and should not act that way unless they, too, want to spend the time in classrooms earning their degrees. Nor will the professionals ever be able to equal our cunning, our ability to manipulate, our instinct for survival, and our knowledge of what makes the dope fiend tick, unless they, too, live our experience."

Now mind you, there were people representing many foreign countries in this amphitheater at McGill University, and I figure that they had to check their earplugs many a time. I would have really liked to find out how the word "asshole" got translated into French, German, Italian, Greek, etc., and I got a big kick out of telling them all that the conference, by and of itself, "sucked."

Not too surprisingly, Habilitat's high profile and my big mouth began to attract the interest of politicians back home in Hawaii. Most politicians will find a way to be photographed with anyone who draws the press like lightning is drawn to trees. They don't have to like the person — in fact, in order to ride the storm of publicity, attacking sometimes works just as well.

We did a lot to keep Habilitat in the spotlight, sometimes turning to impromptu — and characteristically theatrical — political commentary. I imagine that politics in the state of Hawaii is not too different from politics in any other state, but we do have one practice that I think is unique to the islands. Whenever someone decides to run for election, he or she gathers up all the family and friends, outfits them with garish signs emblazoned with the candidate's name and the position sought, and then the whole group collects in a spot by the side of a busy highway. They stand there for hours every day, rain or shine, waving their signs and calling to the people in the passing cars. Somehow I just can't believe that very many people vote for a politician just because they saw the person in the company of some cousins, or maybe a granddad, waving from the side of the road. And I'd be willing to bet that the distraction of the waving and shouting boosters has been the cause of more than one fender bender.

One year I got fed up with these wildly gesticulating gatherings on the highway, so we dressed up one of the staff members as a political candidate, complete with straw hat and sash, gave him a support group of seven or eight other people, and sent them out to stand on a busy corner, where they waved and called to the passing cars. The signs they carried said, "Hello — I'm Nobody, Running for Nothing — So Don't Vote for Me." We got lots of return waves and smiles, and we got a lot of media attention as we moved the show to different areas of the island.

On another occasion, we constructed a realistic jail cell, using exact specifications obtained from San Quentin, right down to the narrow bunk, toilet, tiny sink, and aluminum mirror. Three residents dressed up in hustled prison suits and a ball and chain made from papier-mâché, and climbed into the cell on the back of a flatbed truck. On all four sides we posted signs that read, "Build better people, not better prisons!" For an entire week, we drove the truck around town — to the Hilton Hawaiian Village and along Kalakaua Avenue to the prestigious Kahala Hilton Hotel, then into downtown Honolulu by the circuit court right next to the King Kamehameha statue and on out to Oahu Prison. Nowhere on the truck or cell was there any mention of Habilitat; I told my troops to say, if they were asked, only that they were "doing this for a good cause."

The media went wild, following the truck all week, running pictures in the paper, and putting film clips of the truck on the television news. Of course, they figured out that Habilitat was behind it, and naturally I didn't deny it when they asked. We were trying to make a point, and we knew by now that using humor was one of the best ways to do that.

But before long, like the proverbial lightning rod, I found myself drawing charges from local politicians in a much more serious confrontation. Back when Habilitat was surviving on peanut butter sandwiches, State Senator Duke Kawasaki had surprised us with a $25,000 legislative grant to build ourselves a new kitchen. Although we had never met, I always thought of him with gratitude, and of course I sent him a warm thank-you letter.

Then, in March 1978, right after our telethon, Kawasaki called for a full-scale investigation of Habilitat's financial operations. He actually stood up on the senate floor and publicly demanded the audit, when all he needed to do was to call the legislative auditor's office and request it. Such a simple act, of course, would not have attracted any media attention. Given my tendency to stir up controversy, any politician could virtually guarantee himself front-page newspaper coverage, and extensive radio and TV attention, just by mentioning my name. Kawasaki had made the right bet: The next day we were the lead story for both local newspapers, and we got lots of electronic media attention as well.

We were informed that along with the legislative audit there also would be an Internal Revenue Service audit and a food stamp audit. We were now dealing with both the state and the federal government. To add insult to injury, then Governor George Ariyoshi withdrew my name from his Advisory Commission on Drug Abuse and Controlled Substances, preventing me from serving another term in a position I had filled voluntarily and without pay.

Our contacts with the media informed me that earlier that week, at Kawasaki's request, Andy Chang, then head of the DSSH, had supplied a list indicating that 70 percent of our residents who were on welfare were from outside Hawaii. I pointed out that Habilitat received federal money, so we couldn't legally discriminate against out-of-staters any more than we could discriminate on the basis of race or gender. The charge that we were stuffing the welfare rolls with mainlanders was therefore absurdly illogical. If these people were in Habilitat and they qualified for welfare, they should receive the benefits to which they were entitled.

"Ever since we've gotten national exposure," I explained, "we have had people coming in here from all over the mainland and from foreign countries. It doesn't matter to me where these people come from, because they're human beings. If a person comes in here needing help, we don't turn them away. I can't be worrying about where they come from."

Chang stated that the DSSH was paying Habilitat more than $731,000 a year in welfare, rent, and counseling services. He also said that the Department of Health was paying Habilitat about $363,000 for drug abuse programs, all of which came from the federal government.

My answer was "So what?" If we qualified for state and federal help, we had evidently deserved it. At any rate, government money only filled a third of our budget; the other two-thirds came from fees charged to families of residents, private contributions, and our fund-raising and business activities. Our long-term goal was to become self-contained and fully self-supporting, and to be able to kiss federal and state funding — and all the compromises and frustrations that came with it — goodbye.

But at the moment, we were saddled with the legislative audit, which was clearly harassment because it was clearly superfluous. In compliance with state and federal requirements, Habilitat was privately audited every year by an independent firm, and we also submitted a yearly financial report to the Department of Social Services and Housing and to the Department of Health.

"Go learn how to run your state hospital," I told the DOH, "before you criticize me. The same goes for the DSSH and their prison system, which sucks. Nobody in state government really has any knowledge about Habilitat and what we are accomplishing. Nor do I think anyone really cares."

The next morning, Habilitat was once again the subject of the *Honolulu Advertiser*'s lead story. My friend Aku did his damnedest to defend me. All the local TV stations carried the story, too. Knowing that I had nothing to worry about, I really didn't care about the audit, and my troops were excited by the drama of the whole affair. However, as we had feared, the collection of telethon pledges fell to 60 percent of our forecast.

The audit took almost eight months to complete. By law, we were supposed to receive a copy of it and to have a chance to respond before any information was released to the media. You can imagine my astonishment when I got a phone call one evening from a local newspaper reporter, who told me that he had a copy of the audit and of the state's allegations. Did I have any comment?

Several months earlier, Vickie and I had been watching TV one evening, and someone — I don't remember who — was being pestered by reporters and kept saying, "No comment, no comment," in answer to whatever they asked. At the time, I said to Vickie, "One of these days I would love to do that."

She just laughed and answered, "You could never do that."

Now my chance had come, and I got a lot of satisfaction out of repeating the phrase "no comment" to all the reporters' questions. They had expected my usual explosion and were dumbfounded when they couldn't lure me into any kind of discussion. Far from dampening the media's interest in our story, my refusal to comment seemed to fuel their fire. On the following morning, while I was driving to work, I passed a newsboy on a street corner. He held up his papers, and across the front page, I read, in huge red letters, "Habilitat's License Being Pulled." Even in my anger and despair, I had to chuckle: Habilitat had never had a license.

By that point it was fully apparent that the state had declared war, and for the next thirteen days and nights, my staff and I pored over the reports, ripping the state's charges to shreds. Then we carefully explained the truth and returned the corrected copy to the auditor's office.

My board of directors was naturally unhappy about the unsupported charges. They were cautious people, however, and most of them believed that our best approach would be to murmur some apologies and try to make peace. I explained to the board that out in the streets, where I had received my education, I was taught that (1) you never defend, (2) you always attack, (3) you never attack on your own turf, (4) you always attack on their turf, and (5) you always take out more of them than they take out of you.

Then I called a news conference. As soon as I stepped up to the podium, I opened fire. I charged the DSSH with rampant incompetence, I attacked the Department of Health for its miserable operation of the state hospital, and I called the people who ran the state prison system a bunch of idiots. The whole time I was mouthing off, one of the local TV reporters kept waving a piece of paper at me, but I was too wound up to pay attention. Finally, Vickie came up and whispered, "Vinny, listen to him. He's on our side." So I turned back to the reporter, who handed me a document from the U.S. Food and Drug Administration which was scathingly critical of the DSSH, accusing the state agency of gross negligence for not having been on Habilitat's property for almost three years. I read the letter aloud.

When the press conference broke up, my board members were in a state of shock, having realized that we had no reason to apologize to anyone. We were a reputable organization, and the state of Hawaii had not only been unfair and abusive, it had also been negligent in its own duties.

I went home with Vickie and our daughters Victoria and Lila, whom I had adopted. Later that day, we turned on the TV to find out what approach the media would take. We were amazed to find that in the coverage on every station, the tide had turned. All the media now were staunchly supporting us. Tears ran down my cheeks, and when I looked at Vickie, she was crying, too. Seeing our faces, little Victoria, who was only 4, got scared, and she began to cry, along with Lila. I took them in my arms and said, "Don't be upset, my sweethearts — these are good tears. We won! We beat the rats!"

Our War
of Independence

ALTHOUGH WE WERE cleared of any wrongdoing by the IRS and the United States Department of Agriculture, we didn't get completely out of the line of fire. For a while, though, things cooled off slightly. In fact, Habilitat was starting to receive some unsolicited praise, and much of it was coming from the mainland. The first accolades came in a story Steve Allen wrote for the *Los Angeles Times.* Steve had been one of Synanon's early supporters; now, twenty-five years later, in an article about drug rehabilitation centers, he described Habilitat as one of the best. From the *New York Post,* columnist James Wechsler, chimed in:

> This is a time when the word rehabilitation is in wide disrepute, consigned by the tough-minded to the vocabulary of obsolete sentimentalities. But those who have refused to concede the debate is over should find sustenance in the story of Vincent Marino's remarkable journey from the depths of hell.
>
> It has been a rough pilgrimage from New York's "Little Italy" for Vincent Marino, who once awakened from a heroin binge to find a "dead-on-arrival" tag tied to his big toe and who had last rites administered to him on too many occasions and so narrowly evaded a long-term sentence in 1970. By every current standard of rage, he might have been easily branded socially incurable. Now —

and for all these years — he has been rescuing and rehabilitating others. Mission impossible?

About three weeks after these articles appeared, Frank Fasi gave a talk at Habilitat. His son, Carl, who had a long history of drug use, was facing forgery and burglary charges and had gone to court that week. Carl was being held in jail and Frank refused to bail him out. Frank believed in the policy of "tough love," which states that you have to take away the safety net and let the individual in trouble really hit bottom before you can expect any change. With a shaking voice, Frank told our residents, "I only wish my son were sitting here tonight among you."

Frank Natale of Phoenix House in New York, the late John Mahar of San Francisco's Delancey Street, and Frederick B. Glaser, head of psychiatry at Toronto's Addiction Research Foundation, all evaluated Habilitat for the press and gave the program high marks. We were getting other visitors, too — our first nationally recognized celebrities. Local celebrities had supported us all along, attending luaus and graduations, performing at concerts and telethons, contributing recipes for our cookbook. We valued these friends tremendously, but national stars ultimately put us on the map. The first to visit, in May 1978, was Shaun Cassidy, the singer and star of the TV show "The Hardy Boys." When Shaun was 15 and 16 and growing up spoiled, the son of two famous movie stars — Shirley Jones and Jack Cassidy — he had problems, too. And after listening to some of the residents tell their stories, he realized that their problems weren't all that different from his own. The problems are universal and they aren't always expressed with drugs.

Before the year was out, former heavyweight world champion Joe Frazier visited us, and in 1980 Bob Newhart and Don Rickles came. Newhart and Rickles had heard about us from Danny Kaleikini, a local singer. Pretty soon, we were being asked to present Habilitat's story with a seminar in Hollywood.

I'd been conducting seminars in Hawaii since 1971. In 1978 I teamed up with Dr. Judianne Densen-Gerber of Odyssey House to do a workshop on family survival techniques called, "Is the Family Unit an Endangered Species?" Odyssey House was one of the country's better-known rehabilitation centers, and Judy and I shared a concern about what was happening to the family unit.

My mother always told me children were borrowed, but most people in this country believe that they own their children. This attitude is wrong-headed and dangerous. Parents don't own their kids; they owe them: They have a responsibility to them. The truth is, kids should have more rights, and their rights should be better protected than they are these days. Many years ago, a child was born into a larger family or community situation. The churches greeted the new child, and villages rejoiced at the addition of another life. Each child was part of an extended family, which in Hawaii is called the *ohana*.

The concept of *ohana* influenced every aspect of Hawaiian life. When one family didn't have enough to eat, others shared food. No one went without. It was a loving, caring community — a big family. This is what Habilitat is, and has been since its beginnings. In the spirit of another ancient Hawaiian practice — *hanai,* what we would probably think of as "adoption" — we took in the "strays," and gave them love and nurturing.

Kids today are often born into social isolation. They experience constant uprooting and an absence of grandparents, aunts and uncles, and cousins. More and more parents are abusing their kids — psychologically, physically, emotionally, and sexually. At the same time, parents are compounding the problems in family life with drugs and other destructive habits. They are becoming poor role models and, not surprisingly, the kids are mimicking them. Who else is going to teach them how to behave? A lot of people who came to Habilitat as teenagers are second-generation drug and alcohol abusers. In way too many families, substance abuse is an ugly, awful merry-go-round.

In spite of the strong emphasis on family that still persists in the complex culture of Hawaii, the response to our seminars in Hawaii was miserable. We advertised in the papers. We put up posters, distributed flyers, and got publicity from all the local media, but the people did not come out. I could only hope that in California the response would be more enthusiastic.

When I arrived Ginnie, Bob Newhart's wife, greeted me with a long face. "We only have about fifty acceptances," she said, "which means we might have a hundred attending. I think that's terrifying. The feedback I'm getting is that a lot of parents don't want to show up at a thing like this. They're afraid people will think their kids are on drugs. And some of the parents I talk to say, 'Oh well, these are very socially acceptable drugs.' They're talking about everything from grass to coke to Quaaludes. What're we going to do?"

Not everyone in Hollywood was unable to play the hear-no-evil, see-no-evil game. Carol Burnett had recently revealed that one of her children was having serious problems with drugs. The night before the seminar, Richard Pryor had accidentally set himself on fire while allegedly freebasing cocaine, and this event brought us a lot of media focus.

Celebrity visits to Habilitat worked for us in several ways. They were a real boost for the residents; it made them feel good that well-known people cared enough about their situations to take time from their busy schedules to stop by. The visits and the resulting photo opportunities also gave Habilitat broader recognition and credibility. Naturally, we reprinted the stories with the pictures of the celebrities and included them with publicity mailings. With the attention came more money, which we plowed right back into Habilitat, and into the residents' lives.

BIT BY BIT, THE MONEY did come in. Our building project finally got under way in May 1980, when First Hawaiian Bank approved a $600,000 loan. It was hard to believe: There I was, a longtime junkie, a thief, and an ex-con, now straight and responsible enough to get a bank to lend us more than half a million dollars!

The building endeavor itself turned up an unlikely source of funds. As I watched a bulldozer cruise toward one of the old brick walls to knock it down and make room for the new building, an idea flashed into my mind and I hollered for the operator to stop. I went over to the guy and said, "Don't knock it down. Take it down one brick at a time. We're going to sell those bricks."

Frank Cockett was nearby and he shouted, "Vinny, let him knock it down. We're only getting twelve cents a brick."

"No, Frank," I said. "That's what we were offered. I've decided we're going to sell them for a minimum of $25 each."

"Each?"

I grinned. "That's right, Frank. We're going to sell them for a minimum of $25, and a maximum of $1000."

Vickie's only comment on the idea was "I think the old man has finally gone off the deep end." But we did sell those bricks. We washed and dried them, laminated them, then put a felt backing on the bottom and a brass plate on top. For a contribution of $25 or more, we'd engrave the donor's name and any other brief sentiment on the plaque. The donor also got a brief history of the Bigelow estate and a "stock certificate" showing "ownership" of Habilitat.

In fact, we offered two kinds of stock. On one certificate we played it straight, writing that the donor "has made a worthwhile contribution toward the fulfillment of human potential representing but a minute portion of the infinite worth of a human life." The second type of stock certificate turned out to be more popular. It entitled the purchaser to "full protection against and exemption from involvement in future audits of Habilitat, waking up in the morning to find Habilitat has moved in next door during the night, Habilitat's picketing your place of business or camping out on your front lawn, or being called a 'moron' by Habilitat's executive director." We took in $44,000 — not bad for a pile of funky bricks.

Around this same time the Department of Health — without recognizing the irony of its gesture, I'm sure — finally issued us a license to operate, apparently the same license that we had never had before and that the newspapers had claimed was being revoked. What can I say? With government agencies, that sort of meaningless rigmarole is par for the course.

I'd also been working with some writers on my autobiography. Playboy Productions took an option on the movie rights, but the option ran out due to a writers' strike, and the movie was never made. I would soon have to worry about a much bigger "option" on my life story: In January 1981, I had a heart attack.

While meeting with a board member, I began to feel some pain in my chest and left arm, so I headed for the doctor's office. I was still wired up to the EKG monitor when the doctor told me that I was having a heart attack. I looked at him blankly. "You've got to be kidding," I said.

"No, I'm not kidding." His voice actually sounded pretty grave. "We have to get you into a hospital right away."

"I can't do that," I argued. "I'm going to Los Angeles in two days to do 'The Mike Douglas Show.' Why don't you just give me a gross of nitroglycerin pills? I'll go do the show, come back on a red-eye flight, and go right into the hospital."

The doctor frowned and said, "You can't do that. They don't let people who're having heart attacks get on planes."

"You think I'm going to wear a sign that says, 'My name is Vinny Marino and I'm having a heart attack'? Give me a break, Doc!

He insisted, and I went home. Vickie rushed to the house. I kept telling her I was okay, but in fact I was in heavy denial, just like before: "Who, me? A junkie? No way." Only now it was, "Who, me? Having a heart attack? Absolutely not." Finally I agreed to go to the hospital, but only after eating some fried eggs and bacon. I can't believe I did that. I even buttered the toast and salted the eggs. Plus I drank a large glass of milk, which I'm pretty sure was not skim.

I was hospitalized for six weeks, during which time the doctor suggested that I might think about having surgery to remove a blockage in one artery. I decided to postpone the operation. The truth is, I was scared. I found a doctor who said if I drank herb teas and ate properly, I could reverse the damage without surgery. In time, my fear went away, and I got on with life — a good thing, too, since there was so much to get back to, though not all of it, sad to say, was pleasant.

WHILE I WAS IN the hospital, DSSH told us that we were losing one of our biggest money sources, Title XX funds. For several years, DSSH had received $10 million in federal Title XX funds to purchase services the department was unable to provide. Of this allocation, $2 million went to private treatment facilities such as Habilitat. In the fiscal year starting July 1, 1981, however, DSSH received only $510,000 to spend on services from private treatment facilities. I had known that cutbacks like this were coming, but even so, I wouldn't have minded having a little more notice.

Duke Kawasaki was continuing his attack on Habilitat, and I went down to the state capitol with a bunch of my troops to stage a demonstration. When the dust finally settled, in late April, the $100,000 we'd been promised by the House had been whittled to $50,000. By then, we'd been duking it out with Duke for nearly four months, and I decided that I had better things to do with my time and energy.

One of these things was handling the day-to-day business of getting people to manage their lives and of keeping Habilitat's doors open so that their recovery would be possible. After all the struggles of the past months, I felt that it was time for a little lightheartedness, so our latest fund-raising initiative was a fashion show for dogs. In the first week of June we staged Habilitat's first — and last — annual "Canine Fashion Show" in a downtown Honolulu park. It didn't raise much money, but it did get us a lot of favorable publicity and, perhaps most important, it helped to raise the troops' spirits.

At the fashion show we sold cookies we had baked ourselves using a recipe devised at Habilitat's kitchen one day when the cooks ran out of both butter and margarine and substituted peanut butter. We sold every single cookie and decided that we were going to give Famous Amos some competition. We transformed our kitchen into a cookie factory, and within a year we were producing and selling between forty and fifty thousand cookies a month. Wally Amos became a good friend, helping us out with marketing and even making his ovens available to us when we needed them.

Our fund-raising work had developed a broad range. In 1982 we took over the Honolulu Club — a private social and athletic club downtown where Tom Selleck worked out regularly — for a "Las Vegas Extravaganza." This was a black-tie benefit at which people could use funny money to play poker, blackjack, and craps while listening to entertainment by Dick Jensen, Loyal Garner, Jan Brenner, Vic Leon, and others. Our total take at the end of the evening: $100,000; our net, $80,000.

Our construction business was just getting off the ground, and our Christmas tree sales were well ahead of the previous two years. But as the holiday season approached, we didn't have much reason to celebrate. The state was late in making $150,000 in payments for treating residents sent to us by the courts. Christmas of 1982 looked like it was going to be a bleak one for Habilitat.

I spent the next few days in meetings with members of my key staff, trying to come up with ideas that would bail us out. We talked about giving workshops to people from other TC's, teaching them how to be less dependent on government funding. Even with all the government handouts we had received — and even though we suddenly weren't getting any more — we were already approaching the 70 percent mark in self-reliance. I thought that if we shared our secrets, showed other communities how to raise money through telethons, landscaping, Christmas trees, cookies, and other fund-raisers, we'd have another real money-maker. If we signed up six hundred or so people at $1,000 a head, we'd clear an easy half million after expenses.

I also sent letters to the commissioners of the National Football League, the National Basketball Association, and the National Baseball League, offering to lead seminars on drug abuse for any team of the commissioner's choice, and at no cost:

> I will explain why people use drugs and what drugs can really do to athletes. I will dismiss the myth of recreational drug use and lay out in a clear and concise manner how anyone can avoid getting involved with drugs, no matter how socially acceptable drugs seem to be in any peer group.
>
> All of this will be done in a way that will not demean the players or give them the impression that they are being lectured. They will enjoy the workshop, and they will thank you for introducing them to it. If you like what I do, then we will sit down and negotiate, at a nominal fee, my doing the same workshop with all the other teams. If you don't like what I do, of course, we shake hands and say aloha.

Whatever value these and many other ideas had, none of them produced any immediate cash. (It's a shame the professional sports idea didn't go. Later events indicated that they could have used the help. They should've listened.) Habilitat's money worries were becoming more and more burdensome. The construction crews were operating at a small profit, but the cookie business was barely breaking even. The only real money-maker was the Christmas tree operation, which we expected to net $100,000. The only trouble was that most of the orders for trees were prepaid, and the money had been spent long ago.

The National Institute on Drug Abuse (NIDA), one of the leading federal agencies funding educational and treatment programs, announced that it was cutting all its funding to Habilitat as well as to all other centers locally and nationally. NIDA had been giving us nearly $300,000 a year. All told, in a year's time we had lost more than $600,000. The effect of this shortfall on the daily operations of Habilitat was devastating. I bit the bullet and let nearly half of my staff go. I spoke with each person privately and explained that my decision had nothing to do with performance, but that it was simply a matter of keeping the doors open. I made sure they understood that if the situation changed, I would rehire as many of them as I possibly could.

The hell of it was, this retrenchment didn't seem to change anything. I called another staff meeting. "I'll be honest," I said. "If something miraculous doesn't happen fast, we won't be able to make the January bills. If we don't come up with $268,000 by January 15 —"

I didn't have to finish the sentence. I don't think I had ever sounded so negative.

Vickie and Frank Cockett reminded me of a guy on the East Coast whose best friend's son had just entered the program. The man had promised that if we got the kid off drugs, he'd give us $100,000.

"Why not ask him for the money now?" Vickie asked. "Just ask him for $268,000 instead."

"I've never met this guy," I complained. "His friend's kid has been here only a few weeks. How am I supposed to —"

Vickie ran out of the room and came back a few minutes later with an additional proposal asking for another $200,000.

"Hey, wait a minute," I said. "I just asked how I was going to close for $268,000, and you give me a proposal for $200,000 more? You want me to ask him for $468,000? What are you — a comedian?"

"Why not go for the whole enchilada?" she asked.

I looked at Vickie as if this time she were the one who was a few bricks shy. She was grinning. Frank started to smile, too. In a couple of minutes, we were all laughing.

"What the fuck," I said, "let's go for it!"

When I got the guy on the phone, I said, "This is Vinny Marino at Habilitat. I'm going to be on the East Coast in a couple of weeks,

at the end of November, and I wondered if we might get together."
He was available on December 5. I said that I could juggle my calendar. I hung up and turned back to Vickie and Frank.

"What the fuck," I said. And we all started laughing again.

NOW, $468,000 IS NOT chump change. Although I felt that rush of adrenaline that comes with the start of every new adventure, I was nervous, too. To ask someone you've never met for almost half a million dollars when the guy doesn't even know why you've requested a meeting with him was quite a prospect, even for an old scammer like me. An awful lot was riding on this gig — a lot of hard work, a lot of hope, and the futures of a lot of people — and I didn't want to blow it.

When I got to Washington, D.C., a combination of the time change, the cold and damp December weather, and the jitters kept me from sleeping. My mind raced all night, and by dinnertime the next day, I was wiped out.

It was hard to eat dinner, and hard to make small talk. Over espresso, I made my pitch. This was the greatest role of my career, and I got very emotional. I told him about the political skullduggery. I told him about all the bullshit with funding and how much of my life was now caught up in Habilitat. I told him about the troops and how much Habilitat needed to be independent so we could get on with helping people.

"Okay, how much do you need?" he asked.

All of a sudden, I felt as if I had half the sand in Hawaii in my mouth. I cleared my throat and said, "$468,000." I actually saw the numbers move in front of my eyes as I said them, as if the figure $468,000 were floating across the room in neon lights.

He didn't even blink.

I had brought the two proposals that Vickie had written up, and he asked to see them. I told him that one was for $268,000, and that the other for $200,000 was for the new cookie factory. He nodded and ordered another cup of coffee. He would've made a great poker player — I couldn't read him at all. We talked small talk, and then he said that he had to go meet his business partners, and that he would drop me at my hotel on the way.

I knew this didn't mean that we were home free yet; we wouldn't be until the check — if he gave us one — had cleared the bank, but I thanked him like I've never thanked anyone in my life. I thanked him for the youngest to the oldest resident at Habilitat. I thanked him for the newest to the oldest staff member. I thanked him for the board of directors. I thanked him on behalf of the state of Hawaii and of Guam and was about to extend to him the gratitude of Tahiti and Bora Bora when he interrupted me.

"I'll give you an answer at noon tomorrow," he said.

Noon came without a phone call, then two o'clock, then three. Four o'clock came, and still no phone call. Finally, at four-thirty, he called me up and said, "How you doing?"

I laughed. "Hey, what's the bottom line? Can you help us?"

"I can give you $400,000."

I had to sit down. "Thank you," I said. "You can't know how much I thank you."

We will never be able to repay this guy. If it weren't for him, Habilitat could in no way, shape, or form be in the kind of position we're in now.

The contrast between this man's generous spirit and the narrow-mindedness of government drones came particularly clear to me a month later. Ken Kiyabu, the chairman of the House finance committee, along with six members of his committee, paid a surprise visit to Hab II. One of my staff members told them that the visit had not been cleared by me and that they would have to leave.

"Are you saying that state legislators can't come on state property to look at a state facility?" Kiyabu asked.

"Yes, that's right," my assistant director replied.

Kiyabu looked at his pals and said, "Well, we'll see you down the road when the session starts, and you guys come and ask for money."

The next day I told the media that the legislators had, in fact, been trespassing. They weren't visiting a state facility; they were making a surprise visit on a private, nonprofit institution that happened to be occupying a building owned by the state. It's a significant difference. Tenants have a right to be told in advance when the "landlord" is coming to look around. I told the press that legislators were welcome at Habilitat any time, but that we expected them to be courteous enough to call first. I also told them that if Ken Kiyabu ever offered me any money, I would tell him to stick it up his nose.

A legislative hearing on budgets for all social services in Hawaii was going to be held two days later, and I said that I was going to be there. "I'm coming out of a tree," I warned the press, "and you should be there to catch my act!" The hearing fell on a Saturday, which is generally a slow news day, and the newspaper and TV reporters knew that good old Vinny was always ripe for a headline, so they all showed up.

The committee chairman asked the assembly of representatives from the various funding recipients to give their names, their positions, and the organizations they represented. As I sat there listening, I thought, there are enough titles around here to rule the goddamned world. Finally I stood up and said, "If it pleases the chairman, I'd like to have the floor." The TV cameramen jumped to their feet, and the spotlights came on.

"These people should go out and earn their own money, or at least match government money dollar for dollar. The legislature should audit them, the same as you did us. I find it strange that Habilitat was the only program in the history of Hawaii to be audited. Don't you care where the money is going?

"How much is going for salaries? How much for food? How much for utilities? How much for vehicles? This is the taxpayers' money. If it were coming out of your pocket, you'd want to know."

I paused, and Senator Ben Cayetano said, "Vinny, is it true you told Ken Kiyabu to shove his money up his ass?"

That got a very big laugh, and I grinned. "No, sir, I said 'nose.' You know me, Ben. I would never talk like that."

The crowd roared with laughter.

In the end, the legislature offered us $67,000, and I turned it down. I told them Habilitat had declared its independence.

AS I'VE SAID BEFORE, independence is what Habilitat is all about. The kind of financial independence Habilitat is still working hard to establish is the foundation on which our residents can forge another kind of independence — their freedom from addiction and from the grief and destruction it has brought into their lives. At Habilitat, we're always waging a double "war of independence." Those of us who are constantly out there drumming up financial, political, and moral support for the program are trying to clear the ground for the troops who must fight even more difficult battles. Every day, our residents go into battle with themselves, with patterns of thinking and behavior that sometimes hold them in an iron grip, with lives that have disappointed them, with a system that has given them too little, and with the dark demon of hopelessness. Those of us who have gone through our own wars now commit ourselves to helping others get through theirs. These are wars of faith, wars of liberation, struggles to the death. Communities like Habilitat do what they do because they believe that victory is a real possibility. And they fight for keeps, because they know that our society can't afford the price of defeat.

Tomorrow,
Today Will Be Yesterday

LOOKING BACK, I REALIZE that if I had arrived in Hawaii in the 1990s instead of the 1970s, with the same energy, insight, talent, and instinct, I would never have been allowed to open a program like Habilitat. Our professional associations, especially the psychiatrists and psychologists, have seen to that. In the past two decades, they have managed to install enough roadblocks to dampen the efforts of any Vinny Marino who might try to start a recovery program. Drastic and callous cuts in government funding, along with sheer obstructionism on the part of the legislatures and government agencies, continue to make the road rougher for programs such as Habilitat and for the people who need them. As if their road wasn't rough enough already. In the mid-1990s, maybe more than ever before, Saul Alinsky's wisdom applies: Little guys who want to win have to help themselves.

As a wily shoeshine boy from Mulberry Street in Little Italy, I never would have imagined that I'd wind up where I am today, but I did know that if I was going to get anywhere, I'd have to rely on my own wits. It's been tough going for me — all those drug highs and lows, overdoses, crimes, the prison time, the grief I caused the people I love. It seems a century since Turk filled that first eyedropper with junk and I gained those untrustworthy "wings." But I *have* flown, in spite of everything. No thanks to the drugs, but thanks to what I've gained from going through those years of hell. My job now is to make sure that people who are trying to get out of their own hells get the chance to learn something from their experience. I want them to build up *real* wings: the strength, confidence, and self-respect that will keep them from turning back to drugs. Like the shoe-shine boy I used to be, I guess I'm still offering a service to people, but the scuffs on these folks' lives take a lot more polishing.

Habilitat has now passed the quarter-century mark. After all our struggles, we've made it. From our first six kids and our borrowed cottage, Habilitat has put down strong roots. As long as drugs continue to rip people apart, and as long as people need a place to go to put themselves back together, Habilitat will offer its help — with or without government support. The relationship between governmental funding sources and organizations like Habilitat has always been rife with problems. It's definitely no easier to go it alone, but more and more it seems as if that's what we have to do. The fact that various agencies that supported Habilitat in the past have cut or eliminated their contributions is a reflection of how our government continues to turn a blind eye to the gravity of the drug problem and the amount of work — and money — it takes to get one junkie clean for good.

Drugs are still devastating this nation, and the government is still screwing up. At the beginning of 1996, the media is touting the success of law-enforcement agencies in their "war on crime." What doesn't get mentioned in all the self-congratulatory talk about crackdowns and convictions is the long-term suffering and desperation that lies behind the crime rate in this country, much of which stems from drug addiction. Official discussions of "the drug problem," though they're saturated with good intentions, are almost always ridiculously naive. Good intentions are not enough, not when whatever money gets allocated to drug treatment has to wind its way through the bureaucracy. Not when public servants who never took a drug in their lives proceed to tell us how to straighten out substance abusers. It's like those poor old nuns back in my elementary school giving us lectures on sex. My own experience as a user and my experience in organizing Habilitat has taught me that unless you can face head-on what a big problem drug addiction is — for yourself or for the person you're trying to help — you'll get nowhere fast. I'll say it again: You've got to start from where people are, not from where you are.

You, I, and all the rest of the taxpayers have paid billions of dollars while our politicians have pussy-footed around. For drug dealers, it's still business as usual, and new users are getting hooked every day. And while our prisons are filled to the bursting point, with conditions for inmates getting worse all the time, drug offenders just keep getting jammed in together, spit out after a few months or years, only to be shoved in again when (as so often happens) they tangle with the law again. Some success story, I'd love to see how our finance experts crunch the numbers when they go looking for a return on the American taxpayers' investment.

Government policies are like fashions — they keep changing style. In the 1980s, the fad in drug treatment was short-term programs — really short-term, generally no more than twenty-eight days. What a joke! To encourage the insurance companies to go along with this scheme, the American Medical Association and the American Psychiatric Association lobbied Congress to declare that alcoholics and drug addicts are "diseased." That way, insurance companies can make "third-party payments." This philosophy gave further impetus to the craze of the twelve-step programs and all their silly variations.

I am not talking about Alcoholics Anonymous, Narcotics Anonymous or Cocaine Anonymous as being crazy. I actually like those support groups and I think they are valuable. What I am really furious about is that all these Band-Aid programs opened up in hospitals, where the fee is anywhere from $10,000 on up to $50,000 for twenty-eight days of "treatment," and all the hospital does is merely teach the Twelve Step concept. When the twenty-eight days are up, the suckers are referred to a meeting nearest their home.

What bothers me is that if the "patients" enrolled in these hospital programs were really ready to straighten out, they wouldn't
need to go into a Band-Aid program and pay that kind of money.
They could have gone to AA, NA, or CA and gotten their head
straightened out for free. This to me is a major scam by the medical profession. I think the founders of Alcoholics Anonymous
would turn over in their graves if they knew how these Band-Aid
programs are turning the free Twelve Step meetings into a multi-
billion dollar business.

And what did this Band-Aid approach accomplish? It's not all
that clear to me, except that the medical profession crammed a
few more bucks into its already full pockets. When the insurance
companies got hip to this game, they set a ceiling on how much
could be billed for an addict or an alcoholic to be "treated" or
"cured." Finally, we realized that none of this worked, and many of
the programs shut down, leaving us with a lesson in what *not* to do.

Many of us had already learned this lesson — the hard way.
Anyone with a serious drug problem (and if it's a drug problem, it's
already serious) won't get a whole lot out of the routine parade of
psychologists, psychiatrists, social workers, and lawyers. You
can't set arbitrary limits on how long it takes to turn someone's life
around 180 degrees. One thing is certain: It takes more than
twenty-eight days. And it takes more than six months, the limit the
government usually sets. What a waste of money to start helping
desperate people and then to drop them before they're ready to
make it on their own. In the computer age, we might call this
approach "garbage in, garbage out," except that it's not the drug
users who are garbage, it's the inadequate and even cynical system
that will not commit to extensive, long-range interventions into the
lives of deeply troubled people.

It seems that our country, for all its strengths, comes up with
too many short-sighted answers to its chronic problems. Like the
users, we're stuck on the immediate fix. Anyone who, like myself,
has been intimately connected with the drug problem knows that
it takes about two years before a person is ready to rejoin society.

If it could really be done in twenty-eight days, the success rates of all those drive-through treatment programs would have been a lot higher, and the drug problem in this country would be considerably less urgent. In the official version of the drug problem, the numbers almost always seem to be way too low. In Hawaii it's estimated that one year of housing for an inmate costs $28,000. Okay, that's part of the truth — $28,000 covers operations. But what about capital costs? Let's get real here — we're looking at more like ten times that amount.

Drug programs around the nation are in a real tight spot. They've gotten hooked on government money. A lot of them have become totally dependent on public funding. That means they have to dance to whatever tune the bureaucrats are currently playing. When word comes down from on high that twenty-eight days is "in" as a time span for treatment, these programs overhaul their services and their methods to conform to this lunacy. Although they're staffed with well-meaning people, maybe even some street-wise former addicts who really know the score, there's not much that programs can do if all their money comes from one pot. Unless they diversify their funding sources, they have to toe the government line, which means that in spite of their efforts, a lot of the people they're trying to help are going to slip back into drug use when they are released prematurely.

Through all these budget crises and whimsical shifts in rehabilitation philosophy, Habilitat has maintained its standards and its commitment to full-on, long-term, no-bullshit drug treatment. We've always gone for the whole enchilada. To help people with drug problems, and to help them turn their lives around for good, you've got to do the whole job: Straighten out their thinking, help them mature emotionally, teach them what's important and ethical in their lives and in society, insist on their integrity and honesty, and provide them with marketable working skills. This last element — working skills that can really help them get a job — is essential if they are to become responsible adults. If a program doesn't accomplish all of this, the individual will, sooner or later, revert to old ways of behaving.

Drug addiction is not a fun topic. It's not something that people like to chat about at cocktail parties or on the golf course. But it's a major problem in American culture, hitting the poorest of us the hardest, but not sparing even those in the uppermost echelons of society. Stories about people undergoing treatment and recovering their dignity and control over their lives are not always heartwarming. I've recounted some pretty terrifying events that have happened in the course of our work at Habilitat. It's hard, harder than most people who've never had a drug problem or cared for someone with one can imagine. And that's part of the problem: Before you can create an environment in which addicts can really recover, and before you can understand what a huge financial commitment each individual participant in a recovery program requires, you have to be able to *imagine* (if you haven't been there yourself) how much of an ordeal it is. At Habilitat when we seek financial support (which is always), we like to bring potential benefactors in to see how the program actually works. It's best if people can actually watch some of the process, not only to see that we're getting results but also to see just how difficult the process is.

And we do get results. It doesn't always happen, but it happens enough to keep me and a lot of other people committed to keeping Habilitat going. Remember Hooks? He was my buddy who got hooked on heroin with me when we were kids. Hooks was a true friend. He stuck by me through all the crazy stuff until we both got completely wasted. Years later, Hooks came out to Habilitat. He went through a painful detox from methadone, but did great after that. He's married to a woman on our staff and now lives in Honolulu.

That's what Habilitat is here for. The story I've told in this book is not just about me. It's about Hooks, too, and people like Frank Cockett, Maria, Griffin O'Neal. It's about the pain they and their families endured. It's about Habilitat. There are thousands of stories like ours, about people who were falling into a black hole or over a cliff but caught themselves, very often in the nick of time. Many of them — like me, Hooks, and the staff at Habilitat — have made up for our pasts. We're putting back what we stole from life.

Yesterday, today was tomorrow. Those of us who've had trouble with drugs have to ask ourselves about what happened yesterday. We have to face it, understand it, in order to change our lives. *Tomorrow, today will be yesterday.* All of us have to keep this in mind. Working at Habilitat, we are always asking ourselves, what did we accomplish? And we have to answer honestly. As citizens of a country in the grip of a terrible crisis that destroys lives every minute of every day, we need to examine our approaches to drug treatment and ask ourselves the same question. If you want tomorrow to be a better day for yourself or someone you care about, start now to do what you have to do. I hope this book has helped you imagine what you can accomplish.

Habilitat is simply an unconventional, unorthodox, nonmedical, highly successful program. Most important, Habilitat embodies common sense and logic along with our philosophy and program elements. We track residents after they have completed the program for a period of five to ten years. This helps us measure our success.

Habilitat can work for anybody but doesn't work for everybody. Babe Ruth didn't always hit a home run and Mohammed Ali didn't win every fight. I am reminded of when Vickie and I took Victoria to college on the mainland. Sometimes you have to say "Good-bye" now to say "Hello" later...

Appendix:
Habilitat's Solution

HABILITAT HAS PROVEN its success for over a quarter of a century. This section summarizes the program elements that have made Habilitat so effective.

Prevention

Public awareness, information, and education are three of the most effective deterrents against substance abuse. Habilitat reaches out to the public through its information and referral services. Habilitat's National Drug Abuse Prevention Campaign has become one of the most effective, far-reaching, and sophisticated of all internally funded information and referral services in the United States.

Habilitat's hotline is staffed 24 hours a day by recovering substance abusers (senior residents) as well as seasoned staff, to ensure that first-hand experience and qualified information is available to every caller. Referrals are given, upon request, to almost every known program or support group in the United States, based on the specifications of the inquiry. The hotline number is (800) USA-2525.

Induction

Many situations prompt the seeking of admission into the Habilitat program. In the majority of cases, previous attempts at rehabilitation have either failed or the treatment ultimately proved to be insufficient. In other instances, the judicial system decrees that an individual commit to treatment, henceforth presenting a second chance at a meaningful life. The inability to manage one's life is a common denominator among those that have sought the help we have to offer.

All applications and inquiries pertaining to admission are routed through our Induction Department, which constitutes the initial contact for potential residents or their representatives. Because few substance abusers actually decide to seek help on their own, Habilitat's Induction Team is usually first contacted by distressed parents, spouses, or friends. In some cases, lawyers, judges, parole and probation officers, or social workers make the referrals.

Our Induction Team is composed of highly experienced individuals who are more than familiar with the idiosyncrasies associated with the addictive personality. Being more than ready to be of assistance, they qualify and evaluate all applications and proceed to facilitate the admission of the candidate, based on certain prerequisites.

As we are based in Hawaii, local applicants are screened through appointments. Speaking engagements and seminars are conducted by our staff in schools, clubs, and various correctional facilities upon request. Nationally, requests for admission particulars are received and entertained through our toll-free number. These pertain to mainland inquiries accumulated through referrals made by various agencies, psychiatrists, physicians, and outreach programs, as well as requests emanating from literature on the Habilitat program.

Three standard procedures are taken prior to actual acceptance into the Habilitat program. The pre-admission screening starts with preliminary testing to detect the presence of communicable diseases. The second step is a comprehensive psychiatric evaluation conducted by our consultant psychiatrist, to rule out mental illness and a complete physical examination. Finally, to determine the sincerity of an applicant's desire to change, a personal interview is held at our facility by clinical staff members and hand-picked (senior) residents.

The Induction Team eases the transition process by providing initial orientation. They ensure that every new resident who is taking the first step toward change gets started on the right foot.

Treatment

Treatment is a highly controlled and structured phase during which residents are closely supervised. The early part of this phase comprises the most vital evaluation period where most of an individual's inclinations, strengths, and weaknesses are established. Residents are initially assigned to the Orientation Crew to help familiarize them with the rules and guidelines of the program, as well as the basic concepts taught.

During this transition period, the residents are encouraged to meet and become familiar with other residents. The various therapeutic tools are introduced, as are the basic mechanics of the program.

Immediately after the orientation period, residents are assigned to various menial working crews and responsibilities are awarded on an earned basis. During the day, aside from the time consumed by regular job functions, time is allocated for academics at Habilitat's on-site high school, and for seminars and encounter groups, leaving no time for fruitless endeavors.

There are three basic tools in the treatment phase through which residents learn how to express their feelings, thoughts, and creativity: morning meetings, seminars, and encounter groups.

The first tool, the morning meeting, is composed of forty-five minutes of singing, skit playing, laughter, and "lunacy." Designed to encourage interaction, it serves to encourage expression and allow residents to sublimate with positive energy.

The second tool, the seminar, is incorporated into the curriculum to assist in broadening the scope of the resident's thinking and ideals. Guest speakers are scheduled, as are pro and con debates (on current and relevant issues), audio visual material, and recreational activities.

The third tool, the encounter group, also known as "the game," is the program's most effective and essential tool. It is the venue where peer pressure is best exerted and normal frustrations and hostilities are released. Based on opinions expressed by their own peers, individuals are given an idea of what is seen of them — hence, a notion of what they have to work on. At one point during the group, the residents are given an opportunity to openly discuss their fears and insecurities, giving their peers a glimpse of their more personal side. Personal direction and guidance is given by the group and its leader to those who are involved in the encounter group — constituting an objective viewpoint for a variety of situations.

In the treatment phase, residents are taught a new way to compromise with emotional immaturity, to cope with common pressures, anxieties, and disappointments without relying on intoxicating substances. After a couple of months, residents are encouraged to reestablish communication with their families, initially through written correspondence and phone calls, and eventually during visits. Recreational activities such as beach trips, picnics, fishing trips, outdoor sporting activities, and movie outings are granted on an earned bases, under the auspices of staff members, older residents, and graduates of the program.

At Habilitat residents work hard, learn hard, and play hard. The treatment phase provides the foundation for a new lifestyle, one focused on responsibility, self-reliance, self-awareness, confidence, and a commitment to change.

Reentry

The resident is advanced to the reentry phase after approximately six months. At this stage, much of the structure found in the treatment phase has been reduced and the individual is compelled to make the gradual adjustments required from the highly controlled environment (and its imposed discipline) to a period of self-initiative, overseen by staff.

Greater demands are placed on an individual, starting with vocational training. Emphasis is placed on responsibility and accountability. At this point, the resident is expected to cope with a normal work day agenda, something most of us take for granted, such as using their own alarm clock to get themselves out of bed and to work on time.

From this point of the program, residents are obliged to learn a practical and marketable skill. They earn a nominal stipend with which they are taught to formulate a budget, as they would normally do in the real world. Actual contact with people and elements outside of the program becomes mandatory, thereby providing the exposure needed while gradually reentering society.

The game or encounter group is still part of the program. Played two evenings a week, it keeps individuals in tune with why they came to Habilitat and what they hope to accomplish. After the normal work day, reentry residents assume various responsibilities that include the filtering-down of information to newer residents. Constituting the longest phase of the program, it is during reentry that an individual develops consistency and good work habits.

After seven to ten months in reentry, an individual is elevated to a phase known as post reentry. In this phase controls are decreased and individuals are given more opportunity to make decisions regarding education, occupation and future goals. The scope of responsibilities is increased, thereby encouraging self-direction and independence.

At this point residents are encouraged to become more directly involved with the outside community and in the process avail themselves of external support groups such as Alcoholics Anonymous, Narcotics Anonymous, and Cocaine Anonymous. If the individual's desire is to further pursue formal academic endeavors, this option is made available.

The final phase of the program is referred to as the senior post reentry phase. Resembling the post reentry stage in many ways, it presents more opportunities to prepare an individual for conventional life. The teaching is now geared toward realistic goals and the ensuring preparation. More emphasis is focused on employment and guiding an individual's actual reentry into mainstream society.

Education

One of the most important aspects of the Habilitat program is the emphasis placed on academics. We have found that people involved with substance abuse have either seriously interrupted or completely disregarded their formal education. Everyone without a high school diploma is required to attend classes five days a week. Adolescents receive instruction in various academic subjects while residents over eighteen attend only math and English classes.

The teaching staff consists of state-certified teachers who are based at Habilitat. The average class ranges in size from between four to seven students per teacher. This student-teacher ratio allows the instructor to work very closely with individual students, allowing accurately designed academic programs to meet the students' varying requirements. Furthermore, this affords the teachers an opportunity to know the students on a personal level. To offer material that may not otherwise be covered, all classes meet together in a large group on Fridays for a special lesson prepared on a revolving schedule by one of the teachers.

In addition to the fundamental goals of any educational program (to improve basic skills and to promote academic growth), there are several specific goals upheld for our students. A condition for graduation from Habilitat is that all residents over eighteen earn a high school diploma. Another goal is to enable adolescents to return comfortably to a normal school environment. A final goal is to instill the desire and motivation for a post-secondary education. Many of our graduates pursue college degrees.

Vocational Training

We firmly believe that the task of molding and reorienting an individual demands that practical skills and sound work habits be developed and instilled. The objective is to extensively prepare an individual for post-habilitation life by establishing a strong vocational foundation.

In its over quarter century of experience, Habilitat has developed a diverse and commercially viable vocational training program. Incorporated are business operations in the fields of construction, marketing and event promotions, landscaping, painting, automotive repair, computer operations, and office administration. All in-house meal requirements of the residents are satisfied by the Food Service Department, which trains residents in food preparation and kitchen management. We also have a 24-foot salt water deep sea fishing boat. We use this boat to teach commercial fishing and at the same time enjoy the benefits of our catch in feeding the family here at Habilitat.

With the exception of the Clinical Department, practically all of Habilitat's businesses and departments are run by residents, under the supervision of staff members with years of experience in their respective fields. The result is a highly practical and effective instructional format that exposes the individual to actual, on-the-job training. These various vocational training options assist in subsidizing a small percentage of the program's substantial operational costs, not to mention promoting a true sense of pride, proprietorship, and respect for hard work.

Health Services

The Health Services Department of Habilitat focuses on the medical needs of the residents. Extending from the pre-admission stage through to the completion of the program, the medical services provided protect the health of an individual, as well as that of the collective population. Prior to entering the program, the prospective resident, along with the induction representative, completes a medical history survey which makes the health services staff aware of special medical needs. When prospective residents arrive, they are subjected to a comprehensive series of tests to rule out the presence of any dangerous communicable diseases, thereby allowing their admission into the program.

After successfully completing the interview, each resident receives a complete physical examination by our physician, including additional laboratory work and a psychiatric evaluation by a licensed psychiatrist. At the time of the physical, the resident also receives immunizations for mumps, measles, rubella, tetanus, and (when applicable) hepatitis.

By the time a person is in the program for one week, we have a complete medical history on file. For the duration of their stay, residents are each seen periodically by a group of select physicians who work in conjunction with our staff. On a case by case basis, the services of a dentist are made available, as needed.

The physical well-being of our residents is of paramount importance. No efforts are spared to ensure that the best medical care and facilities are readily accessible, should the need arise.

Nutrition and Dietary Care

In remaining consistent with our policy of health maintenance, Habilitat has incorporated into its Food Service Department a nutritional consultation program. Nutritional counseling for weight management, hyper cholesterolemia, and other dietary concerns is made available through our registered dietician who, working with the Health Service Department, ensures that all dietary needs are observed. All meals, including vegetarian, are carefully planned and portioned to provide balanced quantities of essential nutrients. Habilitat recognizes that a balanced diet and regular exercise pave the way to developing a healthy lifestyle.

Physical Fitness

Last but not least is our sophisticated physical fitness program. We have on our property a gym, complete with jacuzzi, a state-of-the-art aerobics room, a steam room, and a basketball court. We also are involved with softball, baseball, volleyball, and walking and jogging for fitness. We truly believe that straightening out someone's emotional state and helping them intellectually and mentally is not complete without a physical regime to keep their bodies toned and fit.

Praise for Habilitat

Many people have endorsed Habilitat over the years. Here are a few excerpts:

"By most normal standards,... Vinny Marino should either be dead or incarcerated. But this very unusual man saved himself from death and jail! He's also found a unique way to help others save themselves. Like Vinny Marino, his 'school of survival,' Habilitat, is one of a kind."
— Dick Clark

"Habilitat is the work of a master craftsman. I have a very high regard for this program. Each of its parts articulates smoothly with other relevant parts. There is a sense of continuity extending from the first contact to the period of time following graduation in which many graduates have contact and support from other graduates. There are few programs in my experience with this high degree of organization. The quality of care is superior. The program is highly structured and tightly coordinated. It integrates treatment, vocational, and educational components very well. This is no small achievement. The program succeeds in creating a feeling of 'family.' The health and vigor of this program is evident and all due to the teachings of Vincent Marino, a master craftsman."
— Edward C. Senay, M.D., Professor of Psychiatry University of Chicago

"I do hereby proclaim January 27, 1994, as Habilitat Day in the City and County of Honolulu in appreciation of the dedication of Vinny Marino and the Habilitat staff toward helping others...."
— Frank F. Fasi, Former Mayor of Honolulu

"With your visionary leadership, you realized that the treat-met and rehabilitation of the substance abuser is just as important as the law enforcement efforts on our war against drugs and alcohol. Those who have successfully gone through your programs have much to be grateful for. You have given them back their lives; you have given them a second chance. This is a great achievement."
— John Waihee, Governor of Hawaii (former)

"Following his own rehabilitation, Vinny decided to dedicate his life to helping others, and in the last two and a half decades the organization he created has touched and helped thousands of people and their families....The Senate whole-heartedly wishes Vinny Marino and his Habilitat continuing remarkable success."
— Senate of the State of Hawaii, 1994

"The success of Habilitat's drug treatment program reflects your strong commitment to those you serve. You have wit-nessed it all, a front line soldier in the battle against drugs; you have seen the anguish, the suffering, the self-destructive behavior that torment those who live with drug dependency. From these experiences, Habilitat came to be, offering hope and renewal — a second chance."
— Daniel K. Akaka, United States Senator (Hawaii)

"For a quarter of a century, Habilitat has instilled confidence and resurrected 'new life' in scores of men and women in Hawaii. Habilitat serves as one of Hawaii's immeasurable resources and will continue to be one far into the future."
— Patsy T. Mink, Member
United States Congress